Timewatch

Hay House Titles of Related Interest

YOU CAN HEAL YOUR LIFE, the movie,
starring Louise Hay & Friends
(available as a 1-DVD program, an expanded 2-DVD set,
and an online streaming video)
Learn more at **www.hayhouse.com/louise-movie**

THE SHIFT, the movie,
starring Dr. Wayne W. Dyer
(available as a 1-DVD program, an expanded 2-DVD set,
and an online streaming video)
Learn more at **www.hayhouse.com/the-shift-movie**

THE DALAI LAMA'S CAT, by David Michie

THE LAST LAUGH, by Arjuna Ardagh

LINDEN'S LAST LIFE: The Point of No Return Is Just the Beginning,
by Alan Cohen

THE MAN WHO RISKED IT ALL, by Laurent Gounelle

PUSHING UPWARD, by Andrea Adler

All of the above are available at your local
bookstore, or may be ordered by visiting:

Hay House USA: www.hayhouse.com®
Hay House Australia: www.hayhouse.com.au
Hay House UK: www.hayhouse.co.uk
Hay House India: www.hayhouse.co.in

Linda Grant

VISIONS

HAY HOUSE, INC.
Carlsbad, California • New York City
London • Sydney • New Delhi

Published in the United States by: Hay House, Inc.: www.hayhouse.com®
Published in Australia by: Hay House Australia Pty., Ltd.: www.hayhouse.com.au
Published in the United Kingdom by: Hay House UK, Ltd.: www.hayhouse.co.uk
Published in India by: Hay House Publishers India: www.hayhouse.co.in

Cover design: Gaelyn Larrick • *Interior design:* Tricia Breidenthal

Library of Congress Cataloging-in-Publication Data

Grant, Linda.
 Timewatch / Linda Grant. -- First edition.
   pages ; cm
 ISBN 978-1-4019-4323-3 (softcover)
 1. Families--Fiction. 2. Time travel--Fiction. I. Title.
 PR6057.R316T56 2014
 823'.914--dc23
                              2014028832

Tradepaper ISBN: 978-1-4019-4323-3

1st edition, December 2014

Printed in the United States of America

To my father, Lawrence B. Grant. Some of my earliest and fondest memories were of my father reading to me the Uncle Wiggily stories about the adventures of a certain gentleman rabbit.

And to my aunt, Aline Grant, and my "honorary aunt," Dorothy B. Hughes, who fostered my love of reading by sending me books on my birthdays and at Christmas.

PROLOGUE

Swathed in a blanket against the chill of the early morning air, Max Hauptman sat on his veranda in an ornate mahogany chair carved by some long-dead Portuguese. On a table beside him stood a scarcely touched plate of *caldeirada,* his favorite fish stew, and an almost empty cup of *cafezinho.* A brightly feathered *papagaio* (a birthday gift from Carlo) moped on its perch in a brass birdcage.

Death would claim him very soon, the old man knew, but he felt no fear, only a kind of impatience to get it over with and move on to the next stage. In preparation for the great event, his senses were beginning to shut down. The triumphal dawn chorus of the birds that had awakened him for years was only a faint squawk now, and even with his new hearing aid he could barely decipher what people were saying. The rows of coffee trees digging their roots into the red soil of the hillsides, the outbuildings containing the equipment to work the *fazenda,* and the stable housing his purebred horses were little more than a blur. But sharp and terrible still was the inner vision, which had revealed to him a new way of accomplishing his destiny.

He had been fortunate. Like so many others who had lost everything during World War II, he had fled to Brazil. Believing that his plans would be expedited if he belonged to the *parentela* or extended family of one of the elite, Max had ingratiated himself with an influential landowner, Dominic Bartoli. His alliance with Bartoli was cemented by his marriage to the man's daughter, Luisa, who, upon inheriting everything after her father's death, had turned it all over to her husband. Never had Luisa denied him anything.

Wealth was power. He sniggered at two-bit dictators like Saddam Hussein, lacking the wit to see the necessity of adapting one's methods to the times. Through religion, the early popes in the Dark Ages and medieval period had controlled kings and their people just as some desert princes were able to do even now.

Today the fight for supremacy was being fought on a different front. Economic power had become the primary means of achieving one's ends. Slowly, Max had gathered the threads of power into his own hands, adding textiles, chemicals, and steel to his late father-in-law's coffee plantation—his factories in São Paulo turning out goods for export all over the world. And now the chance that he knew would come was here.

Tires crunched on the gravel as a car drove up. A car door slammed. Even before his dim eyes saw the figure dressed in a tan trench coat over a navy blazer and tan trousers, he smelled the musky odor of his son's cologne.

"Papa, you look better today."

A lie. He was worse and they both knew it, but they had to play this little game of make-believe.

"Carlo," he said, waving a feeble hand to the chair beside him.

His son, his body muscular and fit from years of horseback riding and other sports, sat down deferentially beside him. Luisa had given him two other sons, but this, the youngest, was the only one who mattered now. It was important that Carlo see beyond the pitiful wreck of what his father had become to the man he had once been.

"You have everything you need?"

"Yes, Papa."

Those eyes, dark like his mother's but filled with a steady flame of awareness that she had never possessed, looked at him with respect. Carlo was one of the very few people he had ever loved—certainly more than Luisa, whose adoration had dwindled eventually into a submissive adherence to his wishes. She'd been dead for years. He never missed her.

"When do you leave?"

Carlo glanced at the Rolex on his wrist and replied, "In a few minutes."

A vague unease crept over Max; he brushed away the feeling. With all his failing strength, he gripped Carlo's arm and said, "This will be the most important thing you ever do in this life. These next three days are our last chance to complete the Plan. Do not fail me!"

With an oddly feminine gesture that reminded Max of Luisa when she was nervous, Carlo patted the thick black hair springing back in waves from his low forehead. "I won't fail you, Papa."

"Call me when you've completed your task."

"I will."

He was only vaguely aware of Carlo's departure. Already in Max's imagination Carlo was driving down the dirt road leading to the highway twisting over the hills to São Paulo and the airport, where a pilot would be waiting to fly his son in the company jet.

San Francisco would be pleasant this time of year, everything in full bloom. He'd never dared go there himself: too many people might have recognized him. Perhaps in another life he'd visit. He'd sucked the last drop of vitality from this one. But he had to hang on, at least until Carlo called. The window of opportunity would not be open long.

CHAPTER 1

Carlo Hauptman   San Francisco, June 17, 1992

The plush leather seat of the Gulfstream and a hot breakfast of eggs and steak washed down with cups of steaming hot cafezinho along with reading *The New York Times* had made the plane ride go pleasantly fast.

The customs official, who greeted him at the door of Papa's private jet, had taken only a cursory look around the inside of the jet and then left. And, as usual, the official had never found—and had never even looked for—what was hidden in the cleverly concealed compartment. The formalities over and the official gone, Carlo retrieved his briefcase from the compartment. Carlo's driver, Juan, had been waiting for him.

After a few pleasantries and the drive through the heavy traffic of San Francisco, they drew up to the stately entrance of the grand dame of Union Square, the St. Francis hotel, where many presidents and celebrities had stayed since its opening in 1904. It was also Carlo's favorite place to stay when he came to the city on Papa's business.

Juan brought the Lincoln to a smooth stop, got out, and took Carlo's bag out of the trunk. "When will you be needing me again, sir?" he asked as he opened the car door for Carlo.

"Not until Monday at eight o'clock when we leave for the airport."

A broad smile creasing his lined face after accepting Carlo's generous tip, Juan said, "Very good, sir. I'll be waiting here for you."

At the bottom of the broad flight of steps leading into the hotel, a uniformed doorman was waiting to escort him into the lobby. A new man, Carlo observed. He nodded at the doorman and waved him away impatiently.

Striding into the wood-paneled lobby that gave the feel of a men's club, Carlo barely noticed the display of photographs, vintage keys, and other memorabilia hanging on the walls. He briefly noted the time—11:45 A.M.—on the distinctive master clock hanging over a circular seating area. Time to eat, but first he would check in.

The lobby host at one of the front-desk stations recognized him and greeted him with a wide smile. "Mr. Hauptman. Welcome. How was your flight?"

"Fine, Miguel, fine."

"We have your usual suite ready—reserved from yesterday until Monday—in the Landmark wing."

Carlo nodded, signed the register, and gave his one bag to the bellhop hovering nearby. His briefcase he would carry himself.

After tipping the bellhop, who had shown him to his suite, Carlo walked into the adjoining bedroom and threw his trench coat and briefcase onto the king-size bed. He quickly opened the combination locks and then lifted out the hard-sided case that held the Czech-made Skorpion. Molded compartments held a holster and two curved magazines holding .32 caliber bullets, as well as a pouch for the magazines. While the stock was just over 10 inches long, it could be extended to 20.4 inches. A gun permit made out to him lay on top of the stock.

"Only for an emergency," Papa had said.

Carlo devoutly hoped that no such emergency would occur. Even though Papa had made him practice with the gun until he could hit a target, he didn't feel comfortable using it. He was good at hunting animals, but he had never killed anyone. Murder was what hired assassins did. And that reminded him that after he had conducted some business here in San Francisco for Papa, he would have to call the men Papa had hired.

Sighing heavily, Carlo picked up the gun and put it in the safe. No point leaving it around for some nosy maid to discover. This trip would definitely not be as fun as his previous ones, but as Papa had emphasized many times, his Plan *must* prevail.

CHAPTER 2

Caleb Morgan   San Francisco, May 17, 1992

Caleb Morgan found himself walking through a forest of towering oaks. Looking up at their spreading branches, some of which were thicker than the width of a man, he had an uneasy feeling that they were possessed by a kind of awareness. Pagans like the Druids, with their ideas of wood nymphs and gods and goddesses, used to believe that.

His feet dragging on a wet, leaf-strewn path, the realization hit him that he didn't want to go any farther. He wanted to go home. It was quiet, too quiet for his liking, and too dim. The shadows played tricks on you, made you see things that couldn't possibly be there—like the faces he glimpsed peeping out at him from behind the bushes, faces that didn't look human. They had eyes and noses and mouths in the usual places, but something about their features was very different from those of your normal, everyday humans.

A light fog rising from the ground and swirling about him made it hard to see. It was just like one of those old movies where the vampire suddenly leaps out at you. Whoever staged this might have been more original.

It was effective, though. He could feel his nerves twitching and his heart speeding up.

Ahead in a clearing stood a man of vigorous middle-age, wrapped in a heavy rust-colored cloak reaching just below the tops of his well-worn black boots, his brown hair drawn back in a 17th-century-style queue. He was leaning on a gnarled oak staff. The man from his vision of two nights ago, the man who called himself Jeremy Morgan, his ancestor, born in 1631, or so he had said. Waiting for him.

Reluctantly, Caleb found himself walking into the clearing. Didn't seem to have any control over his damn feet; they just kept walking him right on over to the man looking at him with intense green eyes.

"Greetings, kinsman."

"It's you again!"

When the man threw back his head and laughed, did the gloom lighten for just a moment? Irritated, Caleb asked, "What's so funny?"

"I beg your pardon, Caleb, but you are a gentleman of uncommon stubbornness."

"You aren't real! Get lost!" Caleb shouted.

"It does not advance matters for you to be uncivil and disobliging, kinsman. I am not a phantom of your overheated brain. I existed in the seventeenth century and still do. Do you not remember what happened yesterday with the elevator?"

"You did that?"

Jeremy nodded.

The incident was still fresh in Caleb's mind. He had stepped into the elevator in his new building—so new you could still smell the paint—and the elevator had abruptly begun zooming upward. Whoever had heard of an elevator roaring out of control *upward?* After coming to a halt at the 12th floor, the lights had gone out and then the elevator had plunged downward. With his heart hammering in his chest, he had gripped the metal railing as he'd shouted, "Stop, just stop!"

He'd thought he had heard a ghostly laugh; then the elevator had shuddered and stopped gently at the main floor.

"So what do you want, Jeremy?"

"As I said before, I desire you to undertake a task of no small importance. Call your closest blood relatives together immediately."

"Why should I?"

Jeremy drew his cloak more closely around him. "If you do not heed my words, a cruel oppressor will arise and you will die—all of you Morgans—along with many others. And worse."

"So let me get this straight: you want me to invite a bunch of strangers to my home, just on your say-so because something terrible will happen if I don't?"

"The present timeline is unstable."

"And that means?"

"That the present will shift into something altogether different—and nasty—in which none of you Morgans will have been born."

"Even if I believed your far-fetched story, what can I—we—do about that?"

"On June 21 a window of opportunity opens when you Morgans can fix the present timeline in place."

Caleb gritted his teeth. Jeremy was worse than that guy who had tried to stall him over a land deal. "So how do we do that?"

"When you and your relatives are gathered together, I shall enlighten you further."

"Wait!" cried Caleb as fog began wreathing Jeremy from his head to his boots.

As Caleb's hand connected with something, he came out of his vision to find himself sitting in his chair in his library, a glass of wine, which he had just knocked off the table beside him, spilling onto the Chinese rug.

Though the fire in the grate cast a welcome heat, he felt a chill go through him. His hands shaking, Caleb rang for his butler, Cummings, and told him to clean up the mess on the carpet.

Bearing a roll of paper towels and a bottle, Cummings walked with his usual soft tread into the library and silently set to work blotting up the spilled wine.

Abruptly, Caleb asked, "Cummings, do you believe in visions?"

His bald spot gleaming in the soft lamplight, Cummings looked up and said, "I believe there is some biblical precedent for these things, sir, not to mention doctors Freud and Jung, who analyzed dreams and suchlike for the benefit of their patients."

"Yes, yes, but I'm talking about the sort of thing where you're told to do something."

Something suspiciously like a smile touched Cummings's mouth fleetingly. "A spirit guide, sir?" Cummings asked, pouring a little white wine on the red stain.

"Not exactly. Cummings, how long have you been with me, fifteen years?"

"Sixteen and a half, sir."

"Long enough. Would you say I am a man given to strange fancies?"

"No, sir, I would not. You have always appeared to be an eminently sensible, practical man."

"Thank you, Cummings. Now, I'm going to tell you something in confidence. Will you swear never to tell this to another soul?"

"Very well. I swear it."

"I've just had another vision of an ancestor of mine, Jeremy Morgan."

Encouraged by Cummings's sympathetic nod, Caleb went on. "He insists that I call my Morgan relatives together."

"Why, sir?"

"Because if I don't, a 'cruel oppressor' will appear and my relatives and I will die along with a lot of others—whatever that means."

"Do you know who these relatives are, sir?"

"Not offhand, but I can find out. Last year I hired a firm to look up my family tree. The information should be somewhere here in my library along with a memoir written by this same Jeremy Morgan."

"Perhaps you might want to contact your relatives and tell them that you wish to hold a family reunion. I daresay they would be most eager to visit an elderly, rich relative."

"No doubt. But what is this all about? I resent some spirit dictating to me. I won't have it!"

"Would it not be best, sir, to ask your relatives to visit you as Jeremy has suggested twice, so he won't plague you with even more visions? You would lose nothing, but might have some interesting experiences."

Caleb shifted restlessly in his wing chair. "Perhaps. I'll think about it."

CHAPTER 3

Caleb Morgan   San Francisco, May 18, 1992

The next morning Caleb paused in front of his office building to admire the glass-and-steel structure. He had done well as a developer, and this was his crowning achievement. The doorman greeted him and opened the door. Caleb walked over to the elevator and stepped into it.

The door closed. Caleb waited in some trepidation, but nothing untoward happened. After moving sedately up to the 12th floor, the elevator came to an almost soundless stop.

Feeling profoundly relieved, he walked into his outer office where Gloria Stanchon, his secretary, was wearing her usual funeral outfit, a dark suit of a severe cut and a discreet strand of pearls around her neck. She stopped typing long enough to flash him a quick smile, which revealed a set of brilliant white teeth. Then, jerking her head in the general direction of a bundle of letters already neatly sorted and opened for him, she said, "Mail," and went back to bludgeoning the keyboard.

He had thought briefly about replacing her with some agreeable young thing with a more colorful taste in dress, but he knew he never would because Gloria was too efficient, too altogether necessary to him. She knew exactly what he needed, even before he needed it.

When he'd hired her 20 years ago, he'd been impressed by her blonde, blue-eyed good looks, innocent of makeup, except for a dash of lipstick, and short, neatly cut fingernails with only clear polish on them. The woman was still very attractive, even though at 42 her hair was now showing touches of gray.

She was an enduring sort of woman who would have made some man a fine wife. Why had she never married? She probably scared men off—too strong for most of them. It was their loss, his gain.

Shaking his head, he walked briskly into his office, where he relished the thought of looking over the plans for the new condominiums he was building in Oakland.

Collapsing into his brass-studded, leather chair, he began thinking about the events of the night before. One thing was clear: the trouble lay with Jeremy and not with the elevator. Maybe Cummings was right, that the sensible thing was to do what Jeremy asked. Being stubborn about the matter might bring more trouble.

And there was another reason. Up to now, his work had consumed him. A family would have taken time and energy, so he hadn't bothered to marry. Women were always available to tend to his physical needs.

Once, though, he had met a woman who had really intrigued him—his cousin, Elizabeth Morgan from Winnipeg—some city in central Canada about which he remembered vaguely hearing that the winters there could be brutal. He'd never met anyone like Elizabeth. She was, well, different.

They'd gone into an antique shop where she'd picked up what looked like a folding knife with a worn wooden handle into which were carved the initials *R.G.* She gave a small cry, and her pale complexion went even whiter against her red hair curling in luxuriant waves around her shoulders.

Without thinking, he put an arm around her. "What's the matter?"

With a faraway look on her face she said, "I see a man wearing old-fashioned clothes, standing on the deck of a small ship being fired on. I think he's the captain. He's looking down at a boy lying on the deck."

He believed her; he didn't know why. Maybe it was a sort of knowingness that infused her words.

The owner had noticed Elizabeth's distress and hustled over to them. A young guy with a neatly trimmed beard and barely concealed admiration in his eyes—no doubt he had been ogling Elizabeth from the time they had arrived—asked, "Is there something I could tell you about this knife, miss?"

Elizabeth gave him a sweet smile—the kind that made you want to take care of her.

"It looks so old."

"Archaeologists have found pocketknives with bone handles dating back twenty-five hundred years to the Bronze Age."

"Where did this knife come from?"

"Colonial America. The knife was called a gully, often used by sailors for eating and for cutting things like the tangled rigging of sails."

"Whom did it belong to?"

"A Captain Roger Golding. He was instrumental in rescuing some militiamen from Indians back in the seventeenth century."

Caleb picked up the knife and ran his thumb over the crudely carved initials. He opened the blade, tarnished now, and then snapped it back into the handle, which curved slightly at one end. The knife felt comfortable, familiar even, in his hand. He had to have it.

"How much?"

"Two hundred dollars."

"A little pricey."

"It's part of American history, but I could give it to you for 175 dollars."

"Done."

Caleb paid for the knife. With mischief dancing in those eyes of hers—an unusual color, brown with flecks of gold—Elizabeth said, "I'm glad you found something that appeals to you, Caleb."

And all he could think of to say was, "Me, too. Let's go get some lunch now."

That was the last time he'd seen Elizabeth. Work and more work had filled his life. Until lately, he had seldom thought of her. She'd be an old lady now, probably with grandkids, but it would be interesting to see how the years had treated her. Yes, he would invite Elizabeth and the rest of his relatives and see what happened.

For several months now, his lawyer had been even more insistent than usual that he make a will. What was the point of that when he still wasn't sure who should get his fortune? A charity? A relative he'd never met? He'd toyed with the idea of meeting some of his relatives but hadn't done anything about it. Maybe this was the time. Couldn't hurt, and maybe he'd get Jeremy—whoever he was—off his back.

Pressing the intercom button, he said, "Gloria, come in here. I need you to send out some letters. I want them to go out as soon as possible."

CHAPTER 4

Jason "J.J." Kramer Kenora, Canada, May 28, 1992

Spring had come suddenly, as usual, to Kenora. Mingled with the smells of damp earth were gas and oil fumes from the semis bound for Thunder Bay and Toronto. Peering through the window, with *Stevens Antiques* picked out in gothic lettering, J.J. could see a strip of newly green grass and the sidewalk separating a row of shops from the parking lot. Beyond all that was the boardwalk, where he planned to walk during his break and check out the boats lying at anchor in the harbor.

Wearing his usual outfit of dark slacks, button-down shirt, sweater, and bow tie—this one with polka dots—Mr. Stevens was stretching and taking a deep breath as he always did before he went out on his daily walk.

"I'll be back in about half an hour, Jason," Mr. Stevens said. "And if anyone wants to buy the Rolex, don't sell it for under a thousand," he joked as he walked out the door of his shop.

"Sure, Mr. Stevens."

Mr. Stevens was a great boss. He never questioned Jason about dumb things that parents wanted to know, like how he did on the latest test. His marks were always good—better than good—high enough to get him into just about any university. At 16, he still had time to make up his mind where to go.

Pulling open a drawer, he took out his favorite catalog and sat down.

The sound of the bell jangling made him jump up and smooth down his red hair. Customers. But when he looked up, he saw that it was Davis, a big grin on his face. He was wearing his usual summer uniform of shorts and T-shirt. The girl with him wasn't anyone you'd notice right away. She was kind of skinny, with short brown hair lying flat behind her ears. She had a way of moving, all graceful and flowing, like she didn't have any bones—sure of herself, too.

"J.J.!" said Davis. "Thought you might be here. How long you staying in Kenora?"

"Only a week, just to open the cottage. Then we're going back to Winnipeg. Near the end of June, we'll come back for the summer. How's it going?"

"Okay. Hey, J.J., this is Crystal. Her parents just bought a cottage around here."

The girl nodded, her cool stare making him feel uncomfortable. She flicked a glance around the shop, her gaze lingering on a heavily engraved Victorian tea set as she said, "You're lucky to work here."

"Yeah, but today I'm just helping my boss take inventory. I don't have regular hours until later in June."

Davis broke the awkward silence by saying, "That catalog looks familiar."

J.J. held it up so they could see the cover.

"Eftonscience! Do you remember last summer when we ordered one of those Fresnel lenses?"

"Yeah. I got into *so* much trouble."

Crystal edged closer to the counter. "What's a . . . that lens?" she asked. The warmth in her eyes made her seem prettier somehow.

"Well, the lens focuses sunlight so you can cook stuff, if you want to."

"That's the small lens," interrupted Davis. "Tell her what the big one does."

"The ad said the big one could melt asphalt, so this guy here wanted to try it, of course."

"Figures," said Crystal, giving Davis a sidelong look composed of equal parts amusement and affection.

"But we could only afford a little one. I thought it wouldn't work because you can't get as much heat from it as from the big one. Anyway, Davis was in the city that weekend, so he stayed with me. We went outside Saturday morning and put the lens in the sun on my driveway."

"And forgot about it," said Davis.

"Until my dad went to get his car out of the garage. Was he mad when he found out that a piece of his driveway had melted!"

"I told you it would work. What are you going to order this time?"

After opening the catalog, J.J. riffled through the pages until he found the one he wanted. "How about this one?" he asked, pointing to the picture of an aluminum ball connected to a base of the same metal by a plastic insulating column. "But it's kind of expensive."

"A two hundred thousand volt Van de Graaff generator," read Davis in awe. "No way! Imagine what we could do with this!"

"Let me see," said Crystal.

As Crystal bent over to read the ad, J.J. had an almost uncontrollable urge to touch her hair, which looked as soft and silky as a baby's.

"What's so great about 'demonstrating lightning and Saint Elmo's fire,' whatever that is?" she asked, looking at him now with a friendly interest that was causing a warm flush he could feel making its way up his chest and face. That was the curse of the redhead, the pale skin that reacted to your every emotion.

J.J. was horrified to hear his voice coming out in a hoarse croak as he answered, "I think it's 'the repulsion of like charges' they're talking about that's interesting."

"So?" she asked with a challenging look.

"I told you—you should have taken physics," said Davis, giving her a friendly push. "With that thing we could really make people's hair stand on end—or your cat's, J.J."

"Uh, you should see the lasers in here."

Crystal probably thought he was a real geek. Not that he was out to impress her, but why was it that he could yak his head off with the girls at school but with this girl he seemed to be screwing things up in a big way?

Davis shoved his hands into the pockets of his shorts. "Last week my dad took me down an old trail not many people know about and showed me some pictographs that could have been made by my ancestors. When you come down in the summer, maybe we could go exploring."

"Yeah, I'd really like that."

"What are pictographs?" asked Crystal.

"Paintings on rocks. The natives who lived around here made them about eight or nine hundred years ago," explained Davis. "If you want, you can come with us."

"Sure."

"I can see your boss coming back, J.J., so we'd better go."

"Okay. Nice meeting you, Crystal. See you in July, Davis."

As Davis walked out the door, Crystal turned and waved. J.J. felt a massive burden roll off him. Maybe she didn't think he was such a geek after all.

On their way out, Crystal and Davis almost ran into Mr. Stevens, who smiled at them in his old-fashioned, polite way. Coming over to the counter, he said, "I think it's time for a snack."

As Mr. Stevens led the way to the back of the shop, J.J. remembered his first day of work there, two years ago, how impressed he'd been by the sheer amount of stuff, some of it really old. A rolltop desk, a curvy-legged writing table in some dark wood, and a fire screen embroidered with roses stood in no particular order next to musical instruments and tables holding tea sets and antique china. But his all-time favorites were the antique pocket watches.

His boss had begun right then teaching him how to tell the difference between "good" stuff and just plain junk. Not that his boss handled out-and-out trash, but "one man's junk was another man's treasure" as he used to say. That's why an expensive Martin guitar, for example, sat next to a cheap imitation.

And just last week Mr. S. had asked him to do something really weird—hold some pieces of jewelry for a minute or two in his hand.

"Just to see what you might pick up," he'd said. "Most good antique dealers develop a sense about objects. They can tell intuitively if a thing's a fake or not. If you're really good, you might be able to tell something of its history, too."

Then he'd gone on to tell him about a truck driver, George McMullen, tested in 1973 by a Professor Norman Emerson of the University of Toronto. After handling something dug up from an archaeological dig, George could spout all sorts of interesting stuff about the object. Then the professor would take George out to potential sites and let him nose around. George would describe in detail the people who had lived there so that at a later date the professor could come back and excavate the site.

Getting impressions like that from touching objects sounded more than a little weird. Even though he kept trying, J.J. wasn't very good at it. It had been a big waste of time, until one day he had picked up a pewter candlestick and felt a strong vibe and heat in his palms.

Into his mind flashed the picture of an old lady, dressed in a long, black dress with a big white collar, her hair tucked into a white cap with long ties coming down to her shoulders. She was sitting erect—not slouching like people did these days—at one end of a highly polished table. She was frowning and clutching a candlestick. It looked as if she was getting ready to throw it at the young guy sitting at the other end of the table. He didn't look too happy, either, his shoulders hunched over and his hands clenched as though he wanted to hit her but didn't dare. There was a gloomy, hateful atmosphere about the whole place.

The thud of the candlestick hitting the floor had jerked him back to the present. He was sweating buckets, and his hands were icy as he rubbed them on his jeans.

Mr. S. had babbled on about his "amazing ability." Just great! Why couldn't he learn to do something he could really use, like knowing how to act cool with a girl?

"Try one of these tarts, Jason," said Mr. S.

The tart didn't taste anything like his mom's; it was too sickly sweet and had a gummy texture that tasted yucky.

"Some coffee, Jason?"

"Uh, no thanks."

Mr. S. poured a stream of the bitter-tasting stuff into a porcelain cup decorated with blue flowers and gold leaf. "Jason, would you hold this pin I just bought and see what impressions you might pick up from it?"

He handed him a bronze pin with a solid head, about as long as his middle finger. It was a little weird, this psychometry stuff, but one quick try to satisfy his boss, and that would be it.

"Take your time, Jason. From what the dealer who sold it to me said, this pin has been around for a long time. It's going to outlast both of us."

Reluctantly, J.J. picked up the pin. It was about three inches long and felt cool to his touch at first until a tingling began in the center of his palm. At the same time, a pressure began building in his forehead.

"Take it easy, Jason," he could hear Mr. S. saying.

Realizing how tense his muscles were, he began to relax, and then the pictures started coming.

"It's kind of misty. I seem to be in a place with a lot of trees and a woman in a long blue-and-beige-checked dress with what looks like a thin rope tied around her waist. She's kneeling in front of something. I can't see . . . Oh, it looks like a kind of well or pool of water with tall grasses and some little bushes around it. She's holding the pin and muttering something. Now she's throwing the pin into the water."

"Can you understand what she's saying?"

"Not the words, but I'm getting the general idea. She's praying to the goddess of the pool to give her a son."

"Any idea of the place or time period?"

"Not really."

Without warning, he felt himself being caught and whirled high in the air. At the same time, he could feel Mr. S.'s arm steadying him.

Now he was being sucked up higher and higher until he began to make out the outline of an island. It looked like . . . Britain.

Trembling at the end of what felt like a giant string, he sensed himself being slowly lowered until he was hovering over houses of clay and others of timber, some painted in bright colors. Smoke began rising from the center of town, where a fierce-looking woman with hip-length red hair streaming behind her was driving a chariot and urging on her warriors with harsh cries. Big, blond, bare-chested guys with long moustaches, their skin tattooed in blue swirls, dashed back and forth, slashing with their axes, swords, and spears at anything that moved. Women warriors wielded swords right beside the men and helped set fire to anything that would burn. Soon the thatched roofs of the houses were blazing.

Pandemonium broke out. People were running out into the streets, where the invaders thrust these people back into their burning homes. J.J. could see their faces distorted in screams of agony as they kicked and fought their attackers. Then everything went blank.

"Jason, lad, come sit down over here. You're white as one of my Pop-Tarts. What happened?"

For a moment he couldn't speak; it was all too real.

Then Mr. S. was guiding him to a chair and thrusting into his hands a cup of coffee. "You've had a shock. Here—drink this."

But he didn't want one of those awful-tasting imports that gave you a jolt worse than a cola drink.

"Would you like to tell me what you saw?"

"There was this woman throwing the pin into a pool and then this burning town . . ."

When he'd finished, his insides were all knotted up and his shirt was stuck to his back with sweat. J.J. shuddered as the memory of the burning town washed over him again.

Mr. S. was looking reverentially at the pin. "The provenance of this pin—where it came from—was Roman Britain. You must have had a look into that era, Jason."

He was waving his hands around in the way he did when he got excited, saying, "I think you may have had a glimpse of the eastern tribes, led by Boudica, queen of the Iceni tribe, wreaking revenge on her Roman overlords by setting fire to Londinium in A.D. 60 or 61."

"Why would Boudica kill everyone—even kids—in the town?"

Mr. S. crossed his legs and took a long sip of coffee. "Probably because she was angry with the Romans, who had treated her family so badly that she wanted revenge on anyone who had cooperated with the enemy."

"What did the Romans do to her?"

"Well you see, after her husband King Prasutagus died, the Romans stole his estate. When Boudica objected, they whipped her and raped her two daughters."

"But what connection does the pin have with that?"

"The pin might have been manufactured in Londinium or belonged to someone living there." Mr. S. peered at him and then said, "Why don't you go home a little early, Jason? Your mother's invited me to dinner. I'll see you then."

Glad to escape his visions of the past, J.J. wheeled his bike out of the storeroom and into the sunshine. He needed to spend some time in his favorite place near the lake.

CHAPTER 5

Jason Kramer   Kenora, May 28, 1992

Pedaling furiously on his bike, J.J. barely slowed at the curve where the dirt road ran past the dump. While watching the boats on the lake, he had lost track of time, his mind a jumble of images: Celts hacking away at each other; houses burning; the girl Crystal bending over to look at the catalog, each move of hers sharp and clear.

He powered past the low-growing bushes that would later be heavy with blueberries. They had been cut way back so that it was easier to spot any bears that might be scrounging for scraps of food, although most cottagers were pretty careful about putting their garbage in the bear-proof bins. The black bears in the area were pretty harmless—unless you interrupted their feeding or they thought you were a threat to their cubs.

J.J. turned off the road onto his driveway. Even though his family's cottage was only a few yards away, you couldn't see much of it because of the tangle of saskatoon and chokecherry bushes and skinny poplars. Grandpa had said that he was darned if he was going to spend his summer mowing two lawns, the one in Winnipeg and the one here.

Years earlier, his grandparents had sold their house and bought a condo in Arizona, where they went to escape the icy Winnipeg winters. Then six months ago after sinking a hole in one on a golf course, Grandpa had died of a heart attack. Grandma was still in

Arizona. She said she was almost ready to come back to Kenora for a visit in the summer. In the meantime, she had told J.J.'s parents to feel free to use the cottage whenever they wanted to.

J.J. leaned his bike against the side of the toolshed. Painting the shed was one of the jobs he had to take care of this summer. His dad believed that just because you were at the lake didn't mean you could slack off. Already Dad was talking about clearing out all the brush and making a lawn, but Mom wanted to leave it the way it was.

Running up the wooden steps to the porch, J.J. could already smell cooking. "Hi, Dad. What's for dinner?"

His dad, wearing shorts and his favorite John Lennon T-shirt, was putting a package wrapped in foil onto the barbecue. He looked up with a big grin as he said, "Hi, Jason. Guess what we're having for supper?"

"Fish?" You could count on eating fish almost every day as long as his dad could catch them.

"Good guess, Jason. How do walleye and roasted veggies sound?"

"Great. Is Mr. Stevens here yet?"

"Not yet. You might see if your mother needs any help in the kitchen."

"Okay." He opened the screen door and breezed through the living room, with its rows of shelves lined with books, old issues of *National Geographic,* and games like *Monopoly* and *Snakes and Ladders* that Grandpa used to play with him. Everywhere were reminders of Grandma: a patchwork quilt she'd made from Grandpa's old ties, thrown over the sagging couch; her paintings—mostly of trees and the rocky shores surrounding the lake—which covered every available wall space; and year-old women's magazines, lying in a heap on the big wooden table surrounded by six mismatched chairs.

He noticed that there were only a few sticks of wood left on the hearth. Dad would be after him to clean out the ashes from the fireplace and saw some more logs. In the spring, nights could be pretty chilly at the lake.

The old wooden floor squeaked under his new Nike sneakers as he walked into the kitchen. His mom, dressed in green capris and a flowery top, was just taking a pie out of the oven. She laid it down on an oven mitt lying on the beige counter and brushed back a few strands of hair, almost as red as his—she called it auburn—that had escaped from her ponytail. As she turned around, he noticed that a dab of flour lay on one pale cheek.

"Rhubarb. Your favorite," she said, smiling at him as she held out her arms.

J.J. felt tears prickle his eyes. She was going in for an operation soon—some female thing, not fatal, his dad had said in his usual blunt way—but the recovery time would take some months.

Awkwardly—he still wasn't used to being a few inches taller than his mom, although she was almost as tall as his six-foot dad—he hugged her harder than he had intended and felt her flinch. "Sorry," he muttered, stricken by the thought that he might have hurt her.

His mother laughed and ruffled his hair. "Don't be silly. I'm fine. How did things go today?"

"Okay."

"Just 'okay'?"

When Mom looked at him that way with her hazel eyes that seemed to bore into him, it meant that she really wanted to know.

"Well, Mr. Stevens asked me to hold this pin and well . . ."

"You saw something?"

"I guess."

"You don't have to tell me if you don't want to, Jason."

He'd talked to his mom about most things, but this was different. "It was so weird!" he blurted out.

"Why don't you tell me all about it."

J.J. sat down heavily at the pine table. Then the words came out in a rush until he had told her everything.

His mother took a deep breath and sat down beside him. "We'll talk more about this later, Jason, but you're not weird—unless Grandma and I are, too. When I was a little girl, Grandma used to take me into Mr. Stevens's shop. She would tell me not to touch anything, but one time I saw this meerschaum pipe with an amber stem. The bowl of the pipe was carved in the shape of a horse's head. I still remember how real the yellow mane looked and how the nostrils flared.

"When I picked it up, I saw a man with a bushy moustache dressed in what looked like leather shorts—lederhosen, I think they're called—smoking that pipe as he sat on a rocky hillside. I was so scared I almost dropped the pipe. Grandma was not amused, but Mr. Stevens couldn't have been nicer. He came over to us and asked if I was all right and then offered me a cookie."

Out on the porch J.J. could hear voices. His dad was talking to someone.

His mom stood up. "I think Mr. Stevens is here. Don't worry about this ability of yours. Like your red hair, it runs in the Morgan family—you, me, and Grandma," she said with a grin. "Now how about setting the table? I think the plates with the sunflowers on them would look pretty."

At dinner, his mom seemed in the mood to reminisce. She and Mr. S. talked about how a number of the older people who had built cottages in the neighborhood were dying and new people moving in. His dad didn't say much; he seemed okay with letting those two do most of the talking.

Mr. S. leaned back in his chair and wiped his mouth with his paper napkin. "I'm going on a buying trip to San Francisco in the middle of June sometime, so I won't be needing Jason that week," he said.

Mom gave him a quick look. "That's interesting, Nicholas. A letter came to me the other day from Caleb Morgan, a cousin of mine in San Francisco. He's invited Jason and me to visit him at his home there. I gather he's pretty well off since he's inviting other members of our family to stay with him, too. Let me go get the letter and read it to you and see what you think."

While she was gone, his dad asked Mr. S., "You ever hear of this Caleb Morgan?"

"I have, Kevin—if he's the same man who is a well-known developer in San Francisco. Whenever I'm in town, I like to poke around in an antique store owned by a friend of mine whose shop is located in the Morgan Office Tower. Might be the same Morgan who is Diana's cousin."

"Here it is," said his mom, walking into the room and waving a letter in her hand.

"I would be interested in hearing it, Diana," said Mr. S.

Dear Diana,

Let me introduce myself. I am Caleb Morgan, your mother's cousin. I would like to invite you and your son, Jason, to visit me at my residence in San Francisco. Your mother as well as cousins of yours will, I hope, be visiting also. Since my home is fairly large, there will be no trouble in accommodating all of you.

You must be wondering why I am extending this invitation to you and others of the Morgan family. It has come to my attention that there is an urgent family matter that I wish to discuss with all of you. I will be happy to explain everything after you arrive.

San Francisco is particularly lovely at this time of year and offers many interesting pursuits. In the meantime, I am enclosing two airplane tickets for you and your son.

Yours sincerely,
Caleb Morgan

She folded up the letter and placed it beside her plate. "What do you think, Nicholas?"

"It sounds like a good opportunity to visit San Francisco."

"There's just one problem—I can't go."

"And I can't go, either," put in his dad quickly. "Diana's having an operation, and I'm staying with her in Winnipeg. We'll return to Kenora afterward for the summer."

Mr. S. looked at J.J.'s parents and said, "If you would allow it, I'd be happy to accompany Jason to San Francisco."

"I'd really like that, Mr. Stevens!"

His dad frowned and held up a hand. "Hold on, Jason. We haven't said yet if you can go. I'm not sure I want you going off to stay with some man we've never met—even if he says he is a cousin."

"But . . ."

Diana smiled and tapped the letter as she said, "I think it would be okay, Kevin. I phoned my mother, who said she had met Caleb once before when she worked briefly in San Francisco."

"And what did she think of Caleb?"

"She thought he was rather conceited, talked a lot about himself, his plans. He wasn't rich then, but very ambitious. Not a bad guy, though. He showed her around San Francisco a few times; then she never heard from him again until she received the same invitation."

"I suppose," his father said in that way that meant he had made up his mind about something, "that Jason might go if Nicholas is willing to accompany him to San Francisco."

J.J. found he was holding his breath. Mr. S. smiled at him and said, "It would be my pleasure."

"That's settled then," said his mother with satisfaction. "Who wants pie?"

CHAPTER 6

Marjory Morgan Bennett St. Ives, Cornwall, England, June 1, 1992

It was the kind of Cornish morning that she loved. In her garden overlooking the bay, Marjory lingered over a cup of tea. The damp mist softened the harsh outline of the flat-topped cliffs by the sea so that they looked soft and insubstantial. The cries of seabirds as well as the slap of waves against the cliffs had a soothing quality that made her love this place.

"You're up early, Aunt Marjory."

Dear Geraldine. How pretty she looked in her jeans and heavy red sweater, although her niece did look a little peaked with dark shadows under her green eyes this morning and the freckles on her nose standing out starkly against her pale skin. It would be enjoyable to have her spend a few days here. After their little tour of some megaliths, Charles, Geraldine's fiancé, who had traveled with them, had left—rather suddenly—to return to work.

"Would you care for some tea?"

"Please," said Geraldine. She sat down in a wicker chair and said awkwardly, "I wanted to say that I hope we didn't offend you when you told us about your vision of the woman you saw. Please don't think that I didn't believe you. You've never yet lied to me, and you're just about the smartest person I know."

"Smarter than Charles?" asked Marjory playfully.

Geraldine frowned and said stiffly, "Charles is a pompous twit."

"You seem upset. Is everything all right?"

Geraldine bit her lip and then admitted, "Not really. Just after Charles dropped us off here yesterday, he broke up with me."

"I'm so sorry, my dear. May I ask why?"

Geraldine drummed her fingers on the arms of the chair. "He said there was a distance between us, that I wasn't ready to marry him, not fully committed to him."

She stared unseeing at the sailboats dotting the harbor. Then she went on. "But I don't want to talk about Charles right now. I just want to thank you for treating me to this little holiday and to apologize for my attitude about your moving here to St. Ives—in a former fish-loft, no less!"

An excellent location, Henrietta used to say, because the light was so good here that all the artists were moving into these places, thought Marjory. Her cousin had painted some wonderful scenes of the old houses climbing the hill, the church with its high, square tower, and an Iron Age fort with its small round huts.

Geraldine brushed some strands of hair off her face and asked, "It's really pretty here—St. Ives is picturesque and charming with those quaint little shops and the views—but how can you live in such an out-of-the-way place away from all your friends? You used to love the museums, plays, and restaurants in London."

"I understand. I left a perfectly good flat in London where I'd lived all my married life—forty wonderful years with your uncle—to come here."

"Was it worth it, Aunt Marjory, all those years with Uncle David and then to lose him?"

"Love is never wasted, Geraldine."

"I wonder. The men in my life keep leaving me—first my father by dying—and now Charles." She stopped, unable to go on.

"Even with all its ups and downs, life is a precious gift, not to be despised."

The two women sat in silence for a time until Marjory said, "I feel very fortunate to have made new friends and found new interests."

"Like the megaliths."

"Quite so. Now there's something I'd like to talk to you about. An elderly cousin of mine is asking his Morgan relatives to join him there in his home for two weeks. He's even sent me an airline ticket. How would you like to come with me?"

"Where?"

"San Francisco."

"It might be a good idea. I was really excited by the last book I've just finished editing. The author said that if I was ever in San Francisco, I should look him up. This would be the perfect time to get away. So much has been happening the last few days," she said bleakly.

Like getting dumped by Charles, a young man old before his time, so set in his ways. Marjory would never forget what had happened on the holiday the three of them had just returned from. She had been following the track that wound its crooked way through the gorse up to the quoit, a massive tomb built with huge stones individually weighing tons, capped by a gigantic stone slab. Remembering what—or rather whom she'd seen there—made Marjory catch her breath. Afterward, wanting the company of her niece, she had hurried back to the caravan. Geraldine had instantly known that something unusual had happened.

"Are you all right, Aunt Marjory? You look so pale."

"Quite all right, dear." She really had received a jolt, but she hadn't wanted to upset Geraldine, who tended to worry too much over everything.

"What happened?"

"I saw someone."

The Boyfriend—she couldn't help thinking of him as one of those stock characters in a morality play for he always seemed to be playing a role—was staring at her as though she had just come down with an acute case of advanced senility, although she was only 61, not old for this day and age.

"Who was it?" Geraldine asked.

"A woman. She just appeared. She hadn't been there a second earlier. You know that place on the track, how nothing bigger than a rabbit could hide there in the gorse."

"How was she dressed?" asked Charles.

You had to give him credit. He was all business when it counted. Gone was the tentativeness, that air of constantly re-inventing himself that alternated between upper-class hauteur and diffidence. Poor boy wins scholarship to Oxford, graduates with doctorate, and becomes a lecturer in history at the University of London. Very satisfying in some respects, but he seldom looked happy—even though he had been engaged to Geraldine for some time.

"The woman was dressed very simply in some kind of long blue dress fastened with a cord. She wore a twisted gold necklace—I think it's called a torque—and a gold bracelet around her right arm. Her long fair hair fell to her waist. Oh, and she was holding out her hand to me."

"An admirable description, Mrs. Bennett. You say it was a torque she wore?" asked Charles, his tone respectful now. He obviously hadn't expected her to know anything about his specialty, Celtic history.

"Quite sure. In a museum I saw the exact same thing, a solid, tubelike thing that went close around the throat."

"Did she talk to you, Aunt Marjory?"

"No, Geraldine, she didn't. After she held out her hand to me and smiled, she vanished."

"Sounds like you've seen a real, live ghost!"

Twenty-nine and still her niece retained a childlike enthusiasm. Better that than the world-weary airs that some of her contemporaries affected.

Marjory remembered the solemn, quiet child she had first met when her brother had married Geraldine's mother, Helen, a widow. It had taken a while with trips to museums and the seaside to win the child's trust. One day, just before they were going on some excursion or other, Geraldine had blurted out that she wished her friend could come with them.

Only too glad that at last her niece was making friends, Marjory had answered, "Of course, as long as she receives permission from her parents."

"She doesn't have any."

"She must have a guardian."

Geraldine had turned pale and fidgeted in agitation before whispering, "She lives in heaven where my real daddy is."

Marjory thought back to the time when Geraldine had been so ill that the doctor had warned the family that she might die. Had she experienced what some called a near-death-experience before being resuscitated? Researchers had found that after what they called an NDE, people were different, some more psychic. Was this what had happened to Geraldine? Could she be seeing something or someone real, not a purely imaginary friend?

"I expect people see a lot of weird things out here, what with stone circles and enormous stone graves positively littering the English landscape." Turning to Charles, she asked, "Perhaps you've heard of the Dragon's Project?"

Frowning now, his lean frame slightly stooped and looking down at her from his superior height of six foot plus, Charles replied stiffly, "Vaguely. Weren't they investigating megaliths? I believe they used psychics."

She was quick to note the hint of disdain in Charles's tone of voice, as though the mention of the word *psychics* had left a bad taste in his mouth.

"They used scientists, also, to take measurements and monitor the energies at the sites. Professor John Taylor of King's College, London—where you lecture—and a Dr. Balanovski found magnetic anomalies with a magnetometer at a standing stone near Crickhowell in Wales. Some unusual signals were also found when monitoring with ultrasound at the Rollright Stones in Oxford."

"A fault of their equipment, perhaps?" suggested Charles.

Marjory shook her head decisively. "That was ruled out. Radio signals behave oddly, too, in the vicinity of the monuments.

People have seen strange lights and heard sounds that can't be explained."

"Has anyone else had those kinds of experiences?" asked Geraldine.

"Yes, three people, one of them a scientist, saw some amazing things at the Rollright Stones."

"Such as?" Charles was definitely challenging her. She saw Geraldine throwing him an irritated look.

Mildly, Marjory said, "Someone saw a gypsy caravan pulled by a horse—a caravan that hadn't been there a minute earlier. Many other people have seen unusual things."

"You're full of the most fascinating stories," said Geraldine.

"Hardly surprising. I was a reference librarian before I retired," she explained to Charles. "Old habits of researching information die hard, but now I can please myself and look up what I like, for example, megaliths in which I've become very interested."

Charles was thawing. He no longer looked quite so dour.

"Has this project come up with any explanation for these oddities you've just mentioned?"

"Several, but nothing definitive. Some scientists believe that people have these experiences here because these sites have a higher radioactivity than the surrounding countryside, or special magnetic backgrounds. It seems that the megalith builders may have understood something of this and used these areas to induce trance states. For instance, some of the stones have cuplike depressions where one can recline with one's head resting on the stone. In this way, by putting certain areas of the brain in direct contact with the stones, altered states can be induced."

Geraldine shivered. Rain-laden wind had begun blowing over the bleak countryside where the few stunted trees provided no shelter. And it had grown dark, too.

Marjory asked, "Would you like to go back to the caravan?"

"Yes, I think so. It's getting rather cold out here."

It was warm inside the caravan. The little circle of light cast by the lantern helped her understand better how the first Neolithic settlers in the region must have cherished their fires, which warded off not only prowling beasts but evil spirits, too.

Humanity seemed so puny in the face of the elements. It was a wonder the race had survived. Was it their felt inadequacies that had made them so determined to dominate the earth, to prove their right to be here?

Geraldine interrupted her reverie by asking, "How about a nice cup of tea, Aunt Marjory?"

She looked up with a start to see her niece looking with some concern at her. "Why, yes, I'd love one."

Charles was staring off into space, a distracted look on his face. For a few moments, she wished she were tucked up in her little cottage in St. Ives, but then she wouldn't have seen the woman.

Geraldine began fiddling with the tea things and then said, "About that woman you saw. I've been trying to puzzle it out, why she appeared to you. Could there be a special reason why you saw her?"

She might have known that Geraldine wouldn't leave the matter alone. Ever since childhood, she would get hold of something and wouldn't let it go until she was satisfied that she had learned everything about it that she could.

"Are you asking why it was I and not someone else who saw the woman, or why that particular person appeared on the road?"

"I'm not sure. Maybe both. Is there anything more you can tell us about her?"

Her niece was sharp and very intuitive. Somehow she had sensed that there was more information. It was only a small thing.

"A name came to mind: Bryanna. I have no idea who she might be—or might have been," Marjory corrected herself.

After a few moments of silence, Charles rubbed his chin and asked, "If the woman you saw was a Celt, what was she doing near the quoit? That tomb was built much earlier, in the Neolithic period. So what connection, if any, would a Celt have with it?"

Marjory shook her head. "I can't say, but I've read that people in later times may have used the stone circles for religious ceremonies."

"But this isn't a stone circle like Stonehenge, which, I grant you, early peoples may have used for astronomical calculations such as indicating the equinoxes. The structure here was used as a grave."

"So the lady was just another day-tripper, like ourselves," said Geraldine flippantly.

Charles flushed in irritation. He opened his mouth to say something and closed it as Geraldine put a restraining hand on his arm. A moment of awkward silence ensued before Geraldine announced, "I bought some crisps to go with our tea, if anyone would like some."

Charles brightened visibly at this, and Marjory was grateful for her niece's tact.

Later that night as she settled into her bunk in the rented caravan, she had remembered the letter Caleb Morgan had sent her. Why had he invited her to his home? What was so important that she had to leave her comfortable life here and involve herself in goodness knew what?

Yet she had to go. Caleb's letter had a sense of urgency about it that she could appreciate because after seeing Bryanna, she, too, had felt an urgency licking along her nerves.

"Aunt Marjory?" asked Geraldine softly, recalling her aunt to the present in St. Ives. "Thank you so much for asking me to come with you to San Francisco."

Marjory patted Geraldine's hand. "We'll have a good time, just like we used to do when you were little and we went all over together."

Geraldine nodded assent, but under her thick sweater her thin shoulders shrugged as though in disbelief.

CHAPTER 7

Dan Morgan   San Francisco, Friday, June 19, 1992

"Thank you for treating us to a wonderful lunch," said Laney, smiling at Caleb, as they were leaving the restaurant on Pier 39.

"My pleasure," said Caleb with an old-fashioned politeness.

This was the life, thought Dan, looking beyond the pier at the sailboats scudding along before the freshening wind. He didn't give a damn about streetcars or any of the other tourist attractions of San Francisco. He was enjoying being here with his daughter, Laney—thanks to Caleb, who had sent them two airplane tickets—and not having to worry about a thing.

So far, it had been the perfect vacation. Since they'd arrived a few days ago, Caleb had relentlessly played tour guide and host extraordinaire, escorting them in the morning to the little shops along Ghirardelli Square and then to his office building. From the gleam in his eyes and the way he had strutted around, you could see how proud he was of his tower.

For a guy in his 60s, Caleb sure had a lot of energy. He'd hustled them around like someone half his age.

Once or twice, he had caught Caleb looking speculatively at him and at Laney. She seemed to have wound Caleb right around her little finger. She had that effect on men, even older ones, it seemed. When Caleb looked at Laney, his gaze softened and even his voice got a touch gentler. He must have been a terror in his day. Probably still was.

With a faint smile on her face, she said something or other to J.J. (Laney had said that the boy preferred to be called that), who looked ill at ease with his hands jammed into his pockets.

Dan sighed. It seemed so long ago, he thought, since he'd been that age, but reliving his youth was something that didn't really appeal to him. Growing up had been tough at times. His father had been in the military and moved his family often. That meant new schools where the other kids all knew each other and he was always the odd one out. They didn't pick on him—he was tall and strongly built like his father, and they found out that, while he wouldn't pick fights, he wouldn't back down from them, either.

"It's quite the view, isn't it?" said Marjory.

"Sure is."

He cleared his throat. Aunt Marjory reminded him of his high school English teacher, Miss Crawder, tall and thin like her with short gray hair. You wouldn't have dared to mouth off at her like some of the kids did today with their teachers. She'd have put you in your place fast, but she was never mean, just really smart and absolutely determined to see that you learned the basics of English grammar and essay writing.

He'd been an okay student simply because there wasn't too much else to do. Because his family never stayed long in any one town, he quit trying out for football. Ditto for girls. After a while, he learned not to mind that everyone, except for the one or two buddies he'd managed to make, left him alone.

"I thought it would be nice if we could have a little chat and get to know each other."

"Sure, why not?"

His tone must have been too hearty. He could see that in her hazel eyes, so clear and direct and compassionate, too—not something he was used to seeing. It gave him a funny feeling. He was so used to hiding his real feelings under a friendly smile: "Hi! How are you? How're the wife and kids? Me? Just great. Couldn't be better." Better not try that routine with this lady.

"Such a lovely young woman, your daughter. Laney, I believe her name is?"

"Ah, yes, Mrs. Bennett."

"Please call me Marjory. Where are you from, Dan?"

"Minneapolis. Great city with beautiful lakes." Before Dan had split up with Laney's mother, Pam, they lived near Lake of the Isles in a handsome old house that Pam's father had given them for a wedding present. She and Laney still lived there, while these days he was bunking with an old Marine buddy—a temporary arrangement that would last for only another month.

"From your accent, I'd guess that you're English," Dan said, filling the silence.

"That's right."

"What part of England?"

"After my husband died, I moved from London to St. Ives, Cornwall. If I may ask, what do you do, Dan?"

"I used to do cost assessments for a construction company. I'm looking for other work now." Yeah, ever since Pam had run to Daddy—his boss—and complained once again about her marriage. His father-in-law had fired him and replaced him with Pam's brother. Shortly after, Pam had filed for divorce.

"That must be dreadfully hard for you. Work is so important to most people. We often define ourselves by what we do, rather than in terms of who we are."

Dan shrugged. "Too true. But I'll find another job. Jobs are always available for anyone who wants to work and isn't afraid to get his hands dirty." Except that it was getting harder to get a job. He was getting sick of going in and seeing the eyes of the interviewers shift as they gave him the old lines: "No openings . . . put your application on file . . . keep you in mind . . ."

He was almost ready to give up. It was Laney who kept him going. He owed it to her to act like a responsible parent.

"Life does seem very unfair at times, Dan, but maybe your luck is about to turn."

"You mean Caleb's going to cut us in on some kind of deal?"

Marjory permitted herself a small smile that softened the rather angular planes of her face as she said drily, "I rather doubt if my cousin has anything so altruistic in mind. He strikes me as a man who has definite reasons for whatever he does."

Geraldine, who had been walking alone, came up beside her aunt.

"You've met my niece Geraldine, of course," said Marjory.

"We've said hello."

The hand she extended to him felt soft and fragile as bird bones.

"Call me Gerry," she said.

The tiny freckles sprinkled across Geraldine's nose gave her a pixieish look.

"I've enjoyed talking with you, Dan. I think I'll go chat with Caleb."

"Nice talking to you, too, Marjory."

That left Gerry and him.

Without looking at him, she walked over to the wooden railing and began staring out to sea. She had a nice profile—kind of lean like her aunt's—with a straight nose and small chin.

"You ever been to America before?" asked Dan, coming over and standing beside her at the railing.

"Once, not recently." She turned and looked at him with green eyes laced with sadness. "After I graduated from university, Aunt Marjory and Uncle David treated me to a trip to New York."

"Lucky you. I was there once after I got out of the Marine Corps, but the city was too noisy and pushy to suit me. Some great clubs, though."

"I didn't frequent the club scene when I was there, but I did visit the Met, which had some fascinating exhibits. The costumes of Catherine the Great of Russia were superb."

"I liked the Natural History Museum with the rainforest exhibit and the dioramas."

Gerry nodded and went on. "I enjoyed the plays, too. There was a Neil Simon one that was particularly amusing."

She didn't look as though she laughed much.

"Have you ever been here, to San Francisco?"

She shook her head.

"Me, neither. Minneapolis is my town."

A lonesome look on her face, Gerry stared at some windsurfers scudding over the waves and a ferryboat with its top deck crowded with passengers. Gulls screamed overhead.

She didn't look much older than Laney, thought Dan, certainly younger than his 42 years.

"So what do you do for a living, Gerry?"

"I edit books. When my boss discovered my interest in metaphysical matters, he sent books like *How to Become a Psychic in Ten Easy Lessons* my way."

Nice to see that she had a sense of humor.

"Sounds interesting."

She nodded stiffly, as though she hadn't really heard him.

"Some days it hardly seems worthwhile getting up," Dan said pensively.

Startled out of her reserve, Gerry really looked at him.

On an impulse, he asked, "How'd you like to grab a bite to eat tomorrow, just you and me, Gerry?"

"I have to see an author in the morning, Dan, but thank you for asking." She attempted a smile and walked away.

At least she didn't actually say no, thought Dan. He could hear Caleb telling Marjory as he pointed to the slate-green water, "About 150 species of fish live in the Bay. Great white sharks have even been spotted here."

Leaning over the railing of the pier, her ponytail blowing in the breeze, Laney exclaimed, "Look! Sea lions!"

Thumbing through her guidebook, Marjory said, "Apparently the first male showed up here in 1989."

"We'll cruise by them when we get to my yacht," said Caleb, who began pushing his way through the crowd of tourists sauntering along the pier. His relatives dutifully followed him.

"There she is," he said, pointing with satisfaction to a large white yacht. "She has twin engines that can go up to thirty knots and four cabins, which sleep eight. I sometimes bring clients out here."

A man dressed in white slacks and shirt hailed them from the gangplank. "Welcome aboard."

"This is Joseph, my captain," said Caleb. "Let's go up to the flybridge."

He led the way up to an open area with spacious seating.

"Take us out, Joseph," ordered Caleb.

"Yes, Mr. Morgan." Standing at the helm, Joseph started the engines and began easing the yacht out of its berth between two sailboats.

"Nice," said Dan, running a hand over the highly polished teak railing that ran along the side decks.

As they were moving slowly past the dock area, Joseph remarked, "Mr. Morgan, a man came to inspect the safety equipment."

Caleb said sharply, "I didn't ask for an inspection. Who was this so-called inspector?"

Flushing under his deep tan, Joseph replied defensively," I don't know. He was wearing a company uniform and said you had sent him."

His bushy eyebrows climbing right up into his hairline, Caleb frowned and said, "I should have been contacted earlier about this."

"There wasn't time. He came about half an hour ago and left just before you came aboard."

Marjory darted a look at Joseph. She was looking older than she had a few minutes ago.

"You feeling a little seasick?" Dan asked her.

The normally clear hazel eyes were clouded as she said in a low voice, "No, no. It's just I'm getting a very bad feeling about this."

A tremor of unease ran down Dan's spine. His expression must have given him away because in the same low voice, Marjory added, "You feel it too, that something is wrong."

Gerry looked at her aunt with concern.

Sensing something was up, J.J. and Laney drifted over to them. "What's going on?" asked Laney.

"I don't know. Maybe nothing," said Dan, putting a hand on his daughter's shoulder.

"Where did this guy go?" demanded Caleb.

"Near the locker with the life jackets," replied Joseph meekly.

With an angry jerk of his shoulders, Caleb turned and went below, followed by his relatives.

He began throwing open lockers. Suddenly, he went very still.

Dan peered over Caleb's shoulder. What he saw made him suck in his breath.

Caleb put out a hand to touch the object. "Don't touch it!" yelled Dan.

"What is it?" asked J.J., crowding in close behind him.

"Bomb," said Dan tersely. He still had nightmares about the ones exploding in 'Nam, which was why, after his tour of duty was over, he had refused to accept any job having to do with his specialty—disarming the damn things.

Peering at a clock connected by wires to what looked like a battery, Caleb said urgently, "There's only ten seconds left!"

Marjory paled and put a gnarled, veiny hand to her throat, while J.J. froze. Laney let out an involuntary, "Daddy!" After she'd said it, she looked embarrassed. Then he could see the fear creeping into her eyes. That was what he feared most at this point—panic. He'd seen it kill more than one man.

"Couldn't we get off on one of the life rafts?" asked Gerry. Except for a muscle twitching in her cheek, she appeared very calm.

"Dad, why don't we just throw it overboard?" interrupted Laney, fighting hard to keep her voice calm.

"Not a good idea."

Laney's voice went up a notch. "Then what are we going to do?"

"Two seconds left . . . zero." Caleb's voice was flat.

No one moved. Time seemed to slow down. Dan forgot to breathe.

Dumbfounded, Caleb looked at him. "We're still alive!"

"I know, I know." Dan pointed to the bomb. "You'd better tell Joseph to stop the yacht. Now . . . and very gently! And bring some wire cutters."

"I hope you know what you're doing."

"In the military, I used to disarm bombs. Now go get those wire cutters!"

To his credit, Caleb didn't argue, just left, taking the stairs two at a time and bellowing for Joseph.

"Here," Caleb said, breathing heavily when he returned and slapped the wire cutters into Dan's hand.

Dan snipped some wires. "Now the bomb can't go off."

A ragged cheer went up.

He glanced involuntarily at Gerry. The freckles on her nose were standing out starkly on her skin, which made her look even paler than usual. She had one arm around her aunt.

Caleb was clenching his fists. "Someone will pay for this!"

His voice cracking with an effort to appear cool, J.J. asked, "Why would anyone want to kill us?"

"Oh, surely not!" protested Gerry. "What possible reason could anyone wish to do us harm? We just arrived the other day and don't know a soul here."

Marjory cleared her throat. "Maybe this has nothing to do with us." She turned to Caleb and asked, "Do you have any enemies who might want you dead?"

"Dear lady, I have many enemies, but none, I think, who would actually go to the trouble of killing me—at least as far as I know."

His curiosity temporarily getting the better of his fear, J.J. edged closer to the bomb and asked, "I don't get it. Why didn't the bomb go off?"

"After the timer counts down, the mercury in the glass thing needs to be joggled hard enough to complete a circuit. Then the battery activates the detonator, causing the C-4 to explode."

"What's C-4?"

Dan pointed to what looked like a brick of modeling clay. "We used a lot of the stuff in 'Nam. It's pretty safe, won't go off by itself. Sometimes we even burned it to make a fire for cooking food. There's enough C-4 here, once it's activated, to have blown us out of the water."

"Why is there a timer as well as a switch?"

"The IRA used to build their car bombs this way. The timer would be set to give the bad guy enough time to safely place the bomb and get away. After the timer counted down to zero, the bomb still wouldn't go off until there was enough sudden acceleration—could be a car or, in this case a yacht—to move the mercury to the end of the glass thing. Then boom!"

The group let out a collective gasp and edged away. The yacht was idling now, not going anywhere.

"I've told Joseph to call the police. Is it safe to stay aboard?" asked Caleb.

"I think we're okay as far as this bomb is concerned."

"Still, it might be a good idea to get out of here and wait on the pier for the police," said Caleb.

Shortly after, the police came with a bomb disposal expert.

When the wearisome process of having statements taken from them was finished, the Morgans didn't feel in the mood for sight-seeing. At Caleb's suggestion, they went back to his mansion.

CHAPTER 8

Dan Morgan   Caleb Morgan's library, San Francisco,
Friday, June 19, 1992

. . . .

They were a pretty subdued lot, thought Dan, looking around the library where they'd gathered after finishing the evening meal that Caleb had ordered from a nearby restaurant because no one felt like going out.

"Something to drink, sir?"

"A beer would be fine, Cummings."

After the day's events, he could use a drink.

Dan shifted uneasily in the brown leather chair. Sitting near the fire, which was sending up showers of orange-red sparks in the huge white marble fireplace, was making him too warm, although the luxurious furnishings in the room with its maroon velvet curtains blocking out the chilly San Francisco night and hundreds of leather-bound books lining the walls—while a little too fancy for his taste—were something that he might get used to.

The others, sitting on leather chairs and a sofa, seemed to be holding up pretty well. Laney was talking to J.J., who looked more relaxed now. Dwarfed by the large armchair she was curled up in, Gerry had that faraway look on her face again. As if aware of his scrutiny, she darted a quick look at him, then turned her attention to Caleb, who had stood up and was clearing his throat.

"I've talked to the police again, but it's too soon to tell who the bomber was, or his motive for placing that bomb on my yacht. In the meantime, we'll just carry on as usual. I hope you're all comfortable and have had enough to eat and drink."

"You've been most hospitable, Caleb," said Marjory. "And I for one do not intend to let the events interfere with our visit here."

A murmur of agreement went around. But was the danger really over?

"Thank you, Marjory," said Caleb smiling, the light from an ornate standing lamp throwing his weathered face into relief. His bushy white eyebrows drew together, giving him an ominous look that must have intimidated plenty of business opponents. He stopped and again cleared his throat. For a minute there, Caleb looked downright uneasy, but he recovered himself quickly and went on. "Last year, a firm specializing in genealogical research looked up my, ah, our family tree. One of the things that came to light was a memoir, written by our ancestor, Jeremy Morgan."

Dan groaned inwardly. Not another guy who was nuts about his family history! Personally, he didn't care where he'd come from. The important thing was where he was going next.

"You're probably all wondering what this has to do with you. I ask you to bear with me for a short time."

Dan sat up straighter and tried to look interested as Caleb threw him a glancing look and then began reading from a battered-looking volume bound in a dark, stained leather:

San Juan Mission,

June 1683

I, Jeremy Morgan, having arrived at the age of 52 years and in rapidly failing health, do hereby set down a brief account of my life. So fantastical a journey, which led me from the civilized world to the depths of the wilderness in the New World, would scarcely be believed. If it had not been for God's grace, I should have perished after taking ship from New Amsterdam to the West Indies and from thence to a Spanish mission in the Californias.

After laboring long with the good brothers, I set out with Father Francis, who, in a dream, received a call to venture north and set up a mission. A converted Indian was our guide into the vastness of the land, on which no European had ever set eyes. We settled finally at the place that the good Father had been shown in his dream, a land of wild beauty near the sea.

My life began in a remote place by the sea in Norfolk, England, on—so I am told—a wild, wet night on the thirteenth of September in the year of our Lord 1631. The taking of my first breath was the occasion of my mother's taking her last, leaving my father and older sister, Susanna, bereft. To his credit, my father, a man of some distinction in those parts, did not blame me for this misfortune, but neither, thereafter, did I see much of him.

Caleb paused. "I'm not a man who believes in the supernatural," he said, "but this Jeremy person appeared to me twice in visions. He even monkeyed with my elevator, making it go out of control until I promised to ask all of you to visit me in San Francisco."

Laney and J.J. were staring openmouthed at him. Gerry was sitting up straight now and looking at Caleb with a wide-eyed interest.

"I'd like to hear you read some more from the memoir," said Marjory, breaking the awkward silence.

Pleased with her show of interest, Caleb said, "If you insist," and turned to the memoir again.

Between my sister and me sprang up a bond that I would have sworn was stronger than death, for she became my constant companion. Many were the long hours we spent roaming the moors, gathering the purple-headed flowers and screeching like wild young things as we raced across the cliffs rising like mighty towers above the sea.

Until I was 12, I was as thoughtless a boy as you might find anywhere, until Jacob de Ruyter literally dropped into my life. It happened in this fashion.

The day of his coming was a gloomy day in early October. I remember Will, who looked after our horses and did odd jobs of work around the estate, scowling at the leaden gray sky and predicting a rare great storm that night. And so it happened. Glad I was to be behind stout walls when the wind was keening like a soul pursued by the Furies.

Then we heard a thundering at our door and men's voices calling out. So fierce was the storm that our superstitious servants feared to open the door, thinking it was the devil himself trying to get in. My father had to go down and draw the great bolt that barred the door. A small company of men rushed in, water pouring in sheets off them, and carrying a man who looked to be more dead than alive, so still and white he was. After examining the man, my father pronounced him still to be breathing and ordered him brought into the parlor, where he was divested of his heavy clothing, rubbed with cloths to dry him, and wrapped in blankets. Some Madeira wine was administered to the poor wretch, who began coughing and heaving up a quantity of water in his lungs.

At this juncture, my father noticed my presence and ordered me to tell Molly, our elderly housekeeper, to fetch some hot soup and one of Father's nightshirts for our visitor.

As you may have guessed, I was aflame with curiosity to know the identity of our visitor. Later, I discovered that the Dutchman Jacob de Ruyter—for so he was named—had grown weary of his country's incessant warfare with Catholic Spain, which had been fighting to take over the Protestant United Provinces. (The southern provinces, the Spanish Netherlands, were already under Spanish rule.)

In addition, Jacob's parents and two sisters had died of the plague, which had killed about 20 percent of his countrymen in Amsterdam. Longing to leave the scene of so much heartbreak and see something of the world, he had resolved to visit London.

In the course of his journey, his ship had been blown off course in a great storm. Foundering off our inhospitable coast, the ship had gone down with all hands lost, except for him. At this point, my father, seeing the man's labored breathing and unhealthy pallor, forbade any further questioning, thanked the men for their part in the rescue, and sent them home after giving each one a coin.

In the morning, I was up early, surprising Molly, who usually had to shake me awake before I would get up for my lessons, which I took with the village lads in the local school. I rushed into the parlor, where I found Jacob de Ruyter sitting in my father's heavy oak chair, his broken leg swathed in bandages.

The barber-surgeon, a portly man with greasy, thinning hair and displaying that air of authority that all medical men seemed to exude, was just finishing packing his bag of instruments and saying to Father, "I have splinted your guest's leg and bandaged it. It should heal in six weeks or so. For relief of pain, I will leave some wintergreen. Tell your cook to brew a potion with it for your guest to drink."

Father thanked him for coming and escorted him out of the room. I was left alone with Jacob. I had not been shy the previous night about looking at his corpse-like figure—in those parts death was accepted with a certain phlegmatic stoicism—but I was not prepared to greet a gentleman only a few years my senior who, apart from a certain pallor, seemed none the worse for his misadventures.

Up to that time, I had lived a rather secluded and uneventful existence. When school finished each day, it was still early enough to go roaming the hills with Susanna or, more rarely, play with one of my schoolmates. But my father did not encourage "mixing with the lower classes." He was keenly aware of his position as a Morgan, a family who, in preceding generations, had elevated themselves to a position of some wealth and prestige. Now, however, we had fallen on hard times.

Father had invested heavily in buying tulip stocks. When the stocks crashed in February in the year of our Lord 1637, my father lost a great deal of his fortune. He had little money left to keep the estate in good repair.

This was the state of affairs when Jacob came into our midst. He smiled kindly at me and said, "You must be Master Jeremy. Your father has spoken of you with great pride."

My father? I thought he was scarcely aware of my existence. He spent most of his time reading in his library or out riding the one horse left in the stables, which had once housed a dozen.

"Your father has kindly asked me to stay on here until my broken leg has mended. In return for his hospitality, I have offered my services as a tutor—such as they are—for I have not been so trained in this occupation, but have been well-educated in the things that gentlemen should know—so there will be no necessity for you to attend the village school, which your father thinks that you have outgrown. I hope this meets with your approval?"

He was asking for my consent, although we both knew that it mattered not a whit now that Father had made his decision. I supposed that under Jacob's supervision I would no longer have to work very hard at my studies. Although I did not know it then, my days as a heedless youth were over. Under the guidance of Jacob, I would be initiated into the mysteries of

Greek, Latin, and other studies befitting the education of a young gentle-man. Susanna, too, was allowed to partake in these studies and proved to be superior to me in her grasp of them.

Around this time in Father's library, I chanced upon a manuscript dealing with alchemical studies. I was dazzled by the prospect of learning from the manuscript how to turn base metals into gold. After much dis-cussion, I persuaded Father to allow me to buy the flasks, stirring rods, a mortar and pestle, charcoal, and various other materials needful for con-ducting alchemical experiments.

Jacob was loath to see me begin these experiments, warning that few—if any—had ever been successful in turning base metals into gold.

"But the great Paracelsus did agree that it was possible to make gold," I argued.

"But of an inferior sort," Jacob was quick to reply. "He tried through his experiments to discover cures for illnesses."

"If I am not to repair my family's fortunes by making gold, what is the use of alchemy?" I asked. "I have little interest in finding cures."

Jacob laughed and then turned serious. "What the true alchemist seeks is to discover the secrets of the universe by delving into his soul, where hidden abilities lie. The transmutation of the baser elements in one's self is what mystical alchemy is all about."

When my tutor's leg was pronounced healed, my father prevailed upon him to stay an indefinite time with us, for by this time Father had found in him so congenial a companion that he was loath to see him go. It mattered little to my father that Jacob was a Protestant, for Father—whatever his faults—was of the opinion that each man should make up his own mind as to how he should worship. Our family had been Catholic for generations and still was, although it was growing very risky to practice one's faith. In secret we attended mass, celebrated by the priest who had lived in our house. He had a special room—a "priest's hole," as it was known—but be-cause of the perilous times for those of the true faith he had taken leave of us a month ago and gone to a monastery in France.

Oliver Cromwell, a militant Puritan and the general of Parliament's New Model Army, for years had been whipping up sentiment against the king, who had been raising taxes without the consent of Parliament, until the whole country was divided. Generally, we Catholics supported the king, while Protestants supported Parliament.

Cromwell's army had soundly defeated the Royalist forces and was keeping the king a prisoner on the Isle of Wight. Would we have a monarchy still under Charles Stuart, or perhaps a republic, or—an even worse fate—would Cromwell proclaim himself king?

Many were the evenings that Jacob and my father sat by a crackling fire and discussed these and other matters of great import. Sometimes they argued: Father staunchly upholding the divine right of kings to govern as they pleased—in his estimation, Charles I was within his God-given rights to raise taxes without the consent of Parliament for as long as he pleased—while Jacob argued for the right of men to put checks on the power of kings.

Both agreed that the Dutch and English were making the world a vastly different place by setting up colonies in the New World, which had led to new beverages like coffee, which Father noted had become all the rage in coffee shops in London.

Dan moved uneasily in his chair. While they were sitting listening to Caleb drone on, someone could still be out there planning another way to get rid of them.

Caleb stopped reading and said, "If anyone cares to, you can take the memoir and read it for yourself."

"May I look at it?" asked Gerry, standing up.

As Caleb handed the memoir to her, she said, "Thank you, Caleb. I'm rather tired, so I'm going to call it an evening."

She wasn't the only one who seemed tired, thought Dan. J.J. could hardly keep his eyes open, and Laney was yawning behind her hand. Even though the attack had been foiled, the whole thing was bound to affect them all.

"Tomorrow I have some business to attend to, so feel free to wander around the city by yourselves. If you need anything, ask Cummings," said Caleb, nodding to his butler, who was standing by the door, hands laced over a gently swelling paunch.

Dan hurried to catch up to Gerry. He felt like a high school kid again. He'd ask her out for lunch once more. If she gave him the brush-off, that would be it. "Gerry," he called out. "I know you're meeting with an author tomorrow, but would you like to do something after? Cummings told me about a great little place that serves Chinese food."

Gerry hesitated, then squared her shoulders and said, "Why not?"

Dan's heart lifted. "Could you make it to the Golden Dragon in Chinatown by eleven thirty? I hear it gets really busy around noon."

"I'll be there." Her smile sent a wave of warmth through him.

Laney was dawdling in the hall. Dan put an arm around her and walked with her down the long hallway, carpeted with a heavy maroon plush carpet that hushed their footsteps. They passed little tables holding expensive-looking vases filled with hothouse flowers and gilt-edged mirrors that reflected their passing.

"So what do you want to do tomorrow, Laney?"

"Shop. I want to get something for your birthday, which is coming up soon, and I think I know exactly what to look for."

"Not by yourself."

"Oh, Dad, I'm not a kid anymore!"

"We could go together."

Laney shook her head. "What kind of surprise would it be if you saw what I bought for you?"

"Then take J.J. with you."

"But he's such a kid! You trust him and not me?"

"J.J. is only two years younger than you, and besides, this is your first time in San Francisco. There's safety in numbers. Go ask him."

Laney grinned at him. "I already did. I just knew you would have a fit if I went by myself and you'd worry all the time."

"That's my girl. Why don't you and J.J. have lunch with Gerry and me?"

"I don't think so, Dad."

"Okay, but don't spend too much on my present. You'll need your money later for college."

"Okay, Dad, but I'd like to get a swimsuit, too. That is, if I can find one that looks good on me. I've put on a few pounds here." She slapped her thighs. "Why did I have to get Mom's build? It looks great on her, but big hips and a fleshy bod went out in the fifties."

"You look marvelous to me, kid. Besides, how you look isn't the most important thing."

At the door to her bedroom, he gave Laney a hug and said, "You're a great kid—a fantastic trumpet player, a swimming champ on your high school team, and smarter than your old man."

"Oh, Daddy, how you exaggerate!" said Laney, rolling her brown eyes expressively and giving her shoulder-length light brown hair a toss.

"Look who's going to college in the fall—on a scholarship, no less."

"Four years," moaned Laney, "and then off to more school to learn how to be a vet."

"You'll love it. Think of all the people you'll meet."

"I can hardly wait!" said Laney, her eyes dancing with excitement.

His spirits rose. Maybe his streak of bad luck had come to an end. He had a gut feeling, the kind he used to get in 'Nam—they called it situational awareness—before the action would heat up that something very important was going to happen, something that would change their lives forever.

Even though he wanted very much to tell his daughter how much he loved her, he felt awkward about sharing his feelings.

So he contented himself with saying, "Time for your beauty rest, Laney. Tomorrow's shaping up to be pretty busy."

"And don't worry about me, Dad. After all, I'll have my trusty sidekick with me."

Laney planted a firm kiss on his cheek. "Have fun!" she called out, throwing him a teasing look.

His little girl was definitely growing up, Dan mused as he went into his bedroom. He felt restless, though, and started pacing around the room. The notion wouldn't go away that someone was trying to take out the Morgans. He hadn't mentioned this to anyone else; he didn't want to scare them.

Could someone be trying to make some quick bucks by killing Caleb? But that didn't make any sense. Holding him for ransom would be the way to go—unless someone had a definite grudge against him. But why wait until his relatives were with him?

No point trying to hash out the problem now. He was too beat. Quickly shucking his clothes, he fell into bed and yawned hugely. San Francisco was turning out to have more excitement than he'd bargained for.

CHAPTER 9

Carlo Hauptman   San Francisco, St. Francis hotel,
Friday, June 19, 1992

Leaning forward in an armchair in the living room of his suite and jabbing a finger at the two men standing in front of him, Carlo yelled, "You told me there would be no problems!"

Sean, the older of the two men, seemed unruffled by Carlo's outburst. "The plan was good. We watched the Morgans go into the restaurant. Mick stayed with the car while I boarded the yacht. No problem getting the captain to let me on. I hid the bomb in a locker. It should have exploded."

"You were sloppy!"

His black eyes cold, Sean merely looked at him. "I am never sloppy," he said.

"Then what happened?"

"They must have discovered the bomb before they left the dock area. The yacht needed to accelerate before the mercury switch would cause the bomb to explode."

"I'm not interested in your excuses!" Carlo raged. "And you're supposed to be the best—ex-IRA—I'm paying you enough to do the job right!"

What was he going to say to Papa? His plans were ruined. Carlo remembered the time when he was six years old and had tripped over the cat and accidentally spilled hot coffee all over his father. Papa, his eyes burning like hellfire, shouted at him and raised his hand to hit him. Then Mama came in. Papa stopped shouting and acted as though nothing had happened. He didn't even seem to care anymore about the spilled coffee, just turned away and waved his hand indifferently at Carlo. That had been the pattern of their relationship.

After Mama died, no one had much time for him, certainly not Papa, who was always so busy.

He thought constantly about his father. It was important to please him, but what could a small boy do for such a one? Only be ready to serve him instantly.

And so he had grown up, hanging on to Papa's every word.

After Carlo's expensive education at Harvard, Papa had allowed him to learn the business. "A sacred trust," he'd called it.

He had tried, really tried his best. But it was hard to win Papa's approval.

What would his father say about his failure to have the Morgans killed? Papa had been very clear: Nothing could be allowed to interfere with the task at hand. Nothing else mattered.

Mick, the younger man standing next to Sean, shifted from one foot to another. A fox-faced runt with a pointy chin and nose, his none-too-clean clothes hung on his skinny frame, thought Carlo contemptuously. What a contrast to Sean, whose corded muscles showed that he obviously was familiar with the inside of a gym.

"Just so we're perfectly clear about this," said Carlo. "You'll have to try again or find another way to eliminate the Morgans—and it must be done within two days' time!"

"The mechanic where the old guy gets his Lincoln serviced said that the car has to be cleaned and ready to go on Sunday. Maybe we could set something up for then."

Sean shot a disapproving look at Mick and said, "Forget it. We don't have time to make another bomb and set it up properly."

Barely containing his rage, Carlo ordered, "Then find another way!"

"That wasn't part of the deal. We did what we said we would do." His ramrod-straight posture and glacial stare made Carlo realize that the man wasn't going to change his mind.

For a heartbeat the two men stared at each other. Then Carlo said petulantly as he stood up, "All right. Have it your way."

Sean nodded. "The money," he said.

Carlo went to the safe, took out a bulging envelope, and said as he handed it to Sean, "It's all there."

Without counting the money, Sean took the envelope and put it into the pocket of his navy windbreaker. Then he and Mick walked out of the suite without speaking.

Alone, finally, Carlo took a deep breath. He wasn't cut out for this kind of rough stuff. He shivered slightly as he remembered the way Papa had looked, his eyes fiercely alive and his mouth twisting. "The window of opportunity to destabilize this timeline will be open for one day only, June 21. You must kill the Morgans before they have time to access this window and ruin my plans for the future!"

Carlo's gut rumbled. The tension was getting to him.

It wouldn't be so easy now to eliminate the Morgans; they would be on their guard. But it had to be done—and he would have to do it himself. There was no time to make other arrangements.

Only two days. That was all the time left. He would never get another chance. Papa had been very clear on that point.

But he would succeed. Afterward, Papa would look at him, not praise him—that was not Papa's way—but give him that certain look of respect, which would be enough.

Carlo smiled. When this was all over, how he planned to celebrate! It would be exciting to see the changes occurring because of the death of the Morgans. For a brief moment he regretted the necessity of killing them—after all, he was a civilized man. He would carry out his obligation. Soon. Carlo went to the safe and took out the case. Opening it, he began assembling his gun.

CHAPTER 10

Geraldine Morgan   Caleb's mansion, Friday, June 19, 1992

Standing in front of the door to Marjory's bedroom, Geraldine looked fondly at her aunt. "After I visit my author tomorrow morning, I'm going to meet Dan for lunch. Would you like to join us?"

"No, thank you. Don't worry about me, dear. I plan to take in some of the sights around town. Now off you go and get a good night's sleep."

Her aunt still treated her sometimes like the five-year-old child she had been when her mother, a widow, had married Marjory's brother. Over the years, a close bond had developed between her and Marjory, who had treated her as though she were of her own blood and not her brother's stepchild. She could always talk to Marjory about things that she was reluctant to talk about even with her own mother, such as sometimes dreaming about events that later happened.

"Do you have any idea what is really going on, Aunt Marjory?"

Her aunt pursed her mouth, a sure sign that she was seriously considering her niece's question. "No, but I have a feeling that we are about to find out. Soon. And don't worry; we'll be fine."

How could her aunt be so optimistic when they had become involved in an adventure that was catapulting them into something that went way beyond anything they had ever experienced?

However, she didn't want to burden her aunt with her fears so she smiled at her and said lightly, "'To sleep, perchance to dream'?"

"Perhaps. Geraldine, if you would like to talk about Charles . . ."

"Not yet, Aunt Marjory."

Her aunt looked at her and nodded.

"I'll be okay. I just need some time to adjust. Thank you again for asking me to come with you. I've already told Caleb how much I appreciate his inviting me to stay here in his home with the other Morgans."

"Everything is working out very well. Good night, dear."

Geraldine's throat closed up with emotion. Without speaking, she turned and walked down the lushly carpeted hallway and into her bedroom, where she sat down in a dark green velvet wing chair. She felt so exhausted: her broken engagement, escaping death by a hairbreadth, and now the revelations from Caleb.

Geraldine moved restlessly in the chair. She was very glad now that she had come on this trip. She wanted to put as much space as possible between her and Charles.

After dinner, when Caleb had started reading Jeremy's memoir, the mention of his sister, Susanna, had made the hair on her arms stand up—a kind of sign telling her to pay attention. What was that all about? More mysteries.

After putting on her reading glasses, she began reading where Caleb had left off.

I was in the midst of an alchemical experiment when Father, with Susanna close behind him, flung open the door. "You and your sister must hide yourselves!"

Startled, I dropped the flask I was holding. Ignoring the shattering of glass, Father said, with an urgency that I had never before seen him display, "There is no time to lose. Alf has spotted Cromwell's men on the track. They will be here momentarily."

He hurried me down the stairs where our housekeeper, Molly, was wringing her hands. We swept past her, urged on by Father, who pushed us into the priest's hole. A faint smell of incense and candle wax still lingered in the air. The thought of the many masses that had been celebrated here was oddly comforting.

"You will remain here until the invaders leave."

"But, Father, I must help defend our home."

"They are too many for us, my son. Hide here with your sister. If I am arrested, take the gold hidden here—enough to provide for you both for a short time—and get you away to London to my sister's home. Here, I have written your aunt Arabella's address."

As Father spoke, he pressed a bit of paper into my hand. Then he went over to the wall on which hung a crucifix, in front of which stood a table bearing a small altar. He pressed a cunningly wrought design of a flower, which swung open. Thrusting his hand into the crevice, he withdrew a small velvet bag in which one could hear the clink of coins. His face resolute but pale, he put the bag into my hands.

Then he looked at my sister and said, "Take this, Susanna. It was your mother's rosary." Emotion choked his voice as he added, "She prayed every day for you—for all of us."

At this juncture, we heard a mighty pounding on the door and the voices of men demanding entrance. Throwing an agonized look at us, Father hurried away. After that, we heard a loud altercation, then the sound of much stomping about and coarse voices being raised.

As my sister bowed her head, her fingers desperately fingering the wooden beads of the rosary, I could hear her whispering, "Hail Mary, full of grace." It was not until our solitary candle had burned down and all was quiet that we heard a tapping at the door of the priest's hole.

"Master Jeremy," came a whisper.

I opened the door to find Molly, a terrified look on her face, and her brother Alf beside her.

"Oh, Master Jeremy, they've taken your father and everything they could lay their hands on, including the joint of beef I was going to serve you for dinner," she wailed, putting her apron to her eyes.

"Did they hurt Father when they laid hands on him?" demanded Susanna.

"They pushed him about somewhat, but he were walking by his self when they took him," said Alf, his burly frame fairly quivering with outrage.

"And I heard the captain of the men—a shifty-looking lot he were—boasting that Cromwell himself had promised him this house."

"You and Miss Susanna must away from here," said Molly, wiping the tears from her eyes. "Alf will help you."

"I give you thanks for your offer, Alf, but we both will ride to London."

Alf shook his shaggy head. "Cromwell's men, the Roundheads, took the horse, but there be another way to get to London. I make weekly deliveries of vegetables there," he explained. "You can ride with me in my wagon."

"Would that not be dangerous, what with highwaymen infesting the roads?" I asked.

Alf laid a finger alongside his nose and said with a sly look, "Ned and me have a bargain."

At my puzzled look, he said patiently as though to a child, "He be a cousin of mine. I pay him what I can when I go to town. He's never robbed me yet."

"Alf will see that Miss Susanna comes to no harm," said Molly hastily. "And she can wear a bodice and skirt of mine—they're clean—just so she's not bothered on her way to London. And you, Master Jeremy, could wear something of Alf's."

I almost laughed aloud at the thought of my slender sister wearing Molly's overlarge clothing and saw a fleeting smile touch Susanna's lips as she, no doubt, had the selfsame picture occur to her. Then I felt a throb of gratitude for the help offered by these two who had labored so long and faithfully for our family. "Alf, you have hit upon a favorable plan to spirit us away. But now as I think on it, it seems the best plan is for me to find passage on a ship to Amsterdam, where I may bide for a while with Jacob de Ruyter. When he left here, he said that anytime I wished to visit him, he would welcome me as a guest."

"But that's dangerous! Pirates roam those waters!" protested Susanna.

"Fear not, sister. Now go with these two and leave as soon as you can. Here is the address, which Father gave me, of Aunt Arabella. She will keep you safe."

"But why will you not come with me?"

"I would not impose upon our aunt. It will be safer for her, also a Catholic, to take only a female into her household, than if she gave me shelter, too. Questions would be asked. No, I will go to the coast, which is not overly far. Many ships carrying cargoes of grain and fish sail from ports round about there."

Susanna stared searchingly at me and then thrust our mother's rosary at me.

"Susanna, why do you not wish to keep this?"

Her voice was fierce as she looked at me with perfect calmness and said in measured tones, "Have her prayers changed ought of our circumstances? Take it. Perhaps you may find some use for it!"

I was horrified. Susanna had never been overly religious, but she had always dutifully followed the tenets of our religion. Had she now lost her faith? From the bottom of my heart I pitied her, but I found nothing of comfort to give her.

Taking her hand for the last time, we walked around the house where we had been born. Benches and chairs were overturned, my laboratory turned into rubble, and Susanna's Bible box—left to her by our mother—missing. The day being far spent, we retired to bed. The next morning after packing the few possessions that remained to us, we bid each other a mournful farewell. My last glimpse of my sister was of her sitting proudly beside Alf in the wagon in front of a great heap of turnips.

After an uneventful journey by ship, I came to the place where Jacob lived in Amsterdam. His house fronted on a canal, one of many, which are to the Dutch as roads are to the English. The high gabled house, very tall and somewhat narrow, was built (as is common here because of the spongy soil) on pilings made of long stout beams and of brick, with five casement windows opening onto the narrow street. De Ruyter was inscribed, together with the family coat of arms, on the pediment above the front door.

I was received with much goodwill by Jacob, who expressed to me that I had arrived at a most convenient moment, for he was that afternoon about to pay a visit to an alchemist who had just come lately into the country. "A countryman of yours, Gordon McCorrister, who appears to have made some marvelous discoveries."

That he was no countryman of mine but a Scot I did not deem worthwhile to point out to Jacob since it would have been of no avail to explain the niceties of the situation to one who was not an Englishman.

We hurried on foot through very narrow cobblestone streets, which wound around canals on which floated boats carrying, I was told, foodstuffs and painted in an array of colors: green, black, red, and blue. If it had not been for my guide, I should have been lost very quickly. I felt certain to be deafened by the clanging of so many bells from church towers and by the clattering of carriages driving at breakneck speed. We had to constantly make shift to dodge these conveyances.

After some time of walking in this fashion, we halted in front of an imposing residence, which Jacob informed me was the property of a certain wealthy merchant who owned a sugarcane refinery, the raw sugar being brought from a faraway place called the West Indies.

The merchant himself, a certain Nicholas Coolhaas, a rotund gentleman, greeted us at the door and embraced us after the fashion of the Dutch. He bade us enter and introduced us to the Scotsman, a man lean to the point of emaciation and dressed in breeches and coat, which had seen much wear.

Bowing deeply to us, McCorrister muttered a few words of greeting made virtually incomprehensible by his thick Scots dialect. He set to work immediately with his experiment. Pouring what I recognized to be quicksilver into a crucible with sulphur and other ingredients—the names of which he refused to tell us—he began stirring them together. Coolhaas, fairly quivering with eagerness, bent close to the alchemist, who then began heating the mixture. Jacob, too, stared fixedly at the bubbling crucible.

And I? Something about the entire matter made me uneasy. If McCorrister had ready access to such quantities of gold as he might wish to make, why were his boots worn and his clothes of an indifferent cut and cloth?

"Look, 'tis gold," whispered Coolhaas, pointing in awe at a yellow lump congealing in the crucible.

His weathered face breaking into a grin revealing a missing front tooth, the Scotsman boasted, "Did I not promise to make you a fortune?"

"I would like to examine your equipment," I said boldly.

Fixing me with a malevolent look, McCorrister said, "You doubt that gold lies there in front of you?"

"Not at all," I replied, "but I have some doubts as to how it got there."

"Then I'll be off. There be others who will be overjoyed to partake of my secrets."

"Not so fast," said Jacob. "Tell us your suspicions, Jeremy."

"I would like to examine this," I said, seizing the stirring rod.

The Scotsman yelled and lunged at me. Moving surprisingly fast for a man of such heft, Coolhaas stepped between the man and me. "In my house, mynheer, you will behave like a gentleman or be thrown out."

Speaking fast, for I sensed that the Scotsman would not long be still, I explained, "I have read of some charlatans who stuff gold into hollow rods. When they stir their mixtures, the gold falls into the crucible, making the unwary think that a miracle has been performed."

"And this rod?" inquired Coolhaas, looking very grim.

"Is hollow, sir."

"That proves nothing!" yelled McCorrister, cursing me roundly.

Jacob glanced significantly at Coolhaas. Abruptly, the two of them laid hands upon the rogue, who, possessed of surprising strength for so small a man, kicked and yelled as he was dragged from the house and thrown out into the street.

Upon returning, Coolhaas shook my hand solemnly and declared, "I am in your debt, mynheer, for saving me from the loss of a goodly amount of guilders. The rascal was trying to get me to buy some rare ingredients, which he said were necessary to make gold. It was a scheme that would have filled only his pockets." Looking at me earnestly, he added, "It would be my great pleasure if ever I could be of service to you."

It was a matter of the space of only a few weeks before I had occasion to benefit from the Dutchman's good offices. In the meantime, we became fast friends. Over dinners spent with him and Jacob, the merchant took me into his confidence, telling me of his extensive business interests: his ships that carried sugarcane from the Indies to Amsterdam and his sugar works that rendered the cane into sugar.

His colorful stories of a virgin wilderness where a man might make his mark stirred my imagination to fever pitch, so that one evening over our brandies I exclaimed that I must see for myself what manner of place this New World might be.

The world I had known had been abruptly ripped from me, my father—probably dead now—and my sister lost to me because of the hated Cromwell. Many a time I thought of writing to Susanna, but in the end I did not. She would be better off forgetting about a brother who, without money or even a home, could not provide for her. Aunt Arabella would see to Susanna's needs and marry her off to some suitable young man. For these reasons, I believed myself free to make my fortune in the New World, which must prove more hospitable than the old one.

Coolhaas was not so sanguine about my prospects. He tried to stifle my enthusiasm by saying that the New World was a place only for the stout of heart and body. Dangers abounded from aborigines, wild animals, and even the bitter winters that some said could freeze a man's blood within a very short time if he should go unprotected.

At last, seeing it was impossible to dissuade me from my course, he said, "I have a ship lately come into harbor, on which you may, if it please you, take passage to the West Indies. My agent there has a son whom he wishes to be tutored. If you are interested, I will recommend you for the position to him."

I was agreeable, and so it came to pass that shortly thereafter I set sail in one of the merchant's ships bound for the New World.

Of that long and bitter journey I will say little, except to say that I had never seen more at one time of human suffering. The passengers suffered miseries from brackish water and maggoty food, which was hardly fit for pigs, never mind human beings, and from being crowded together—the sick with the well—with no privacy for weeks on end. By the end of seven weeks, some of the youngest children had died. To see their poor little bodies thrown overboard was enough to set the strongest man to weeping.

I admit to spending most of my time in the only cabin besides the captain's in a kind of semi-stupor from drinking the rum and wine and partaking of the provisions, which Coolhaas had thoughtfully provided for my comfort.

When I sought to allay the pangs of my conscience by sharing some of my food with a child and his mother (a young woman whose bearing and features reminded me of Susanna), the captain called me a bloody fool for not saving what I would need later. As Providence would have it, both the woman and her son died.

My health, although taxed by the voyage, remained good. With thanks to God, I landed in the West Indies, where I speedily sought out the gentleman to whom Nicholas Coolhaas had given me a letter of introduction. My plan was to earn some money by tutoring the agent's son and, after I had *learned somewhat of the country, seek out other possibilities for earning a livelihood. Little did I know then what difficulties awaited one so naive as I was.*

The writing stopped. Geraldine took off her reading glasses and drew a slow breath. She had hoped that Jeremy's memoir might give her some clue as why, according to Caleb, Jeremy had insisted that the Morgans meet together or else face the extinction of their timeline. That sounded so far-fetched. The one good thing, though, was the opportunity to visit San Francisco.

And then there was Dan, not really her type, but an intriguing man, competent in his own way—look how he had taken charge on the yacht and defused that bomb—but not someone she would ordinarily have been interested in. Not that she was really interested, just . . . intrigued.

He was so different from Charles, who had led her to believe that he wanted to spend the rest of his life with her, and then left her because he said she was having trouble fully committing herself to him. But she was 29 years old, not some silly teenager prone to gushing over a man.

To be honest, though, she did find it hard to trust men. Sometimes that puzzled her. She had never had reason to distrust the men in her life—not her father nor the boyfriends she had dated. So what was wrong with her?

Some other time she'd try to figure it out. It was getting late. Wearily, she undressed and climbed into the old-fashioned four-poster bed that some Victorian lady might have slept in.

Just before she fell asleep, a face swam into her mind. "Susanna," she murmured and fell into the dreaming dark.

CHAPTER 11

Susanna Morgan   London, April 2, 1648

Clutching the piece of paper in her hand, Susanna looked up at the gabled wooden house and shivered in the cool breeze. This was the right address. Would Aunt Arabella receive her kindly? After knocking and waiting a few minutes, a young woman in a plain brown dress and white cap opened the door and looked suspiciously at her.

"I am here to visit Lady Arabella. Please tell her that it is her niece, Susanna Morgan, who begs to speak with her."

"She don't live here no more," said the girl.

"Do you know where she lives now?"

"No."

The servant began closing the door.

"Please, I must know. I have journeyed a long way to see her."

With a note of glee in her voice, the girl said, "Cromwell's men took her—to the Fleet Prison, the butcher's boy said. Now a good Puritan owns this house. So be off with you."

So even Aunt Arabella's position in society had not saved her from the persecution of Catholics that was taking place now all over England. How must she be faring, locked up in that grim stone tower built on an island in the Fleet River, a place of pestilence and disease and reeking of the rotting carcasses that the slaughterhouses dumped into the river! And where was her father?

Suddenly, the sulphur- and smoke-laden air seemed overpowering. Susanna longed for the pure air of the countryside, not this pestilent place where the foul stench of overflowing privies and cesspools—each house was built over one—assaulted her senses. She must return to the inn where Alf had dropped her and decide what to do. Wearily, she turned away.

"Miss Susanna."

A tall, well-set-up young man in the livery of a junior footman was standing on the basement steps and beckoning urgently at her.

"Miss Susanna?" he called again.

"Yes, and you are?"

"Fletcher, miss, one of Lady Arabella's footman—that is, until the present lot barged in," he said indignantly. "They kept the staff on and so I stayed," he said apologetically.

Walking over to him, she said, "I remember you. You are the son of one of my father's tenants and had just begun working for her ladyship. The day I arrived and took tea with her, you dropped a whole plate of biscuits."

"And you were bending down to help me pick them up . . ."

"When my aunt bade me stop. I don't know what shocked her the more, your dropping the biscuits over her expensive Turkey rug or my trying to help you."

A pleased smile spread across the young man's face as he smoothed back a lock of his carrot-red hair. He dug into his pocket and brought out a much-crumpled piece of paper on which she saw a hastily scrawled address in her aunt's handwriting.

"Lady Arabella feared that Cromwell's men were coming to get her, so she wrote this address and told me to give you this if she was taken."

"To the Fleet?"

Fletcher nodded. Tears gleamed in his eyes. "She treated me good, never a bad word to anyone."

"Whose address is this?"

The footman shrugged his shoulders. "A friend was all she would say."

"Thank you, Fletcher. I appreciate your loyalty to her lady-ship." She dug out a coin and gave it to the young man, who accepted it hesitantly and then burst out, "If I could ever be of service to you, Miss Susanna . . ."

"You already have."

But she would not throw herself on the mercy of a stranger. Not until she had exhausted all other means of support.

A fortnight later, her situation had worsened; her money was almost gone. When she had applied for jobs as a servant, she was told each time that she needed a reference, but who would furnish her with one? Jacob had left and her brother had gone to stay with him in Amsterdam. Her former neighbors in Norfolk were Protestants, who would certainly not vouch for her, and even if they were so willing, a reference from a Catholic would bring a world of trouble down on both them and her. Since she had little skills in needlework, no one would hire her as a seamstress.

She was about to go upstairs to her room in the inn when the innkeeper's wife, her beefy arms planted on her ample hips, blocked her way.

"I wants me money now," she said in a loud voice, jutting out her pudgy jaw.

Susanna drew her shawl more tightly around her and said stiffly, "I will have it for you tonight."

"Now," said the woman, holding out a grubby hand.

"I don't have it now."

"Then I'll sell yer clothes, the fancy ones yer got upstairs."

Little did the woman know that she had already sold them, except for one gown, her favorite russet-colored one, the hue of the ripe apples in her father's orchard. "I could work for you in the inn," offered Susanna.

The woman gave her an incredulous look. "Yer hands. Soft as a baby's bottom they be. Yer never done a day's work in yer life!"

Susanna's protestations died on her lips as the innkeeper came and stood beside his wife. "Best you go now," said the innkeeper in a gruff but kind voice.

Staring at the couple, Susanna left without a word. In a daze, she walked down the narrow street, barely managing to avoid coaches bowling rapidly along and wagons heaped high with produce from the country. A lady of ample girth, her face adorned with beauty patches of stars and crescents, was borne in a sedan chair carried by two stout fellows, who nimbly avoided piles of refuse. Ragged street urchins darted back and forth among the clot of pedestrians. A chimney sweep carrying brooms, and his apprentice, who could not be above the age of five, hurried past a girl with a tray slung around her neck, who was monotonously calling out, "Pins, straight pins." Above the din, a man's strident voice could be heard: "Brooms, good brooms."

Panic seized her. Where was she going to go? What was she going to do? A man bumped into her. When she whirled about, a young dandy in stained breeches and doublet, coming out of a tavern, swept off his tall hat and leered at her. She shuddered and began to run.

Out of breath, she stopped and shrank against a grimy wall. Her hand clenched the paper with the address that the footman had given to her. It was the only avenue of help left.

She hailed a hackney and, after climbing into it, gave the address of her destination to the driver, a burly man huddled in a stained coat missing several buttons. He grunted at her and whipped the horse into a fast walk, that seemingly being the fastest pace the poor creature could go.

They arrived in an affluent part of London, where stately houses stood near the Thames. The hackney drew up with a flourish to the address that Aunt Arabella had written down. Susanna paid the driver with her last few coins, and, her heart beating wildly and her mouth dry, she knocked at the front door.

A footman dressed in scarlet livery with gold buttons marching down his waistcoat opened the door. "Whom may I say is calling?" the footman asked from his superior height of six feet.

Summoning an air of confidence and wishing that she had worn her best gown, Susanna replied, "I am calling at the request of my aunt, Lady Arabella, who bade me contact her friend."

The footman wrinkled his forehead; then his brow cleared as he asked, "Would you mean Lady Hastings?"

"Indeed, the very one," said Susanna, guessing that the lady must be her aunt's friend.

"Come in. I will see if she is at home. And you are?"

"Miss Susanna Morgan, niece to Lady Arabella."

A few minutes later, a small plump woman wearing a finely wrought lace collar over the bodice of her bottle-green gown entered the room. Lady Hastings looked keenly at her and then dismissed the footman. "Come into the library," she said as she led the way into a large room with books filling shelves that reached to the high ceiling. Upon thick carpets of a rich burgundy hue stood elaborately carved furniture and chairs covered in velvet. A new style of clock, taller than she was, its pendulum majestically swinging back and forth, stood in a corner.

Indicating that Susanna should sit, Lady Hastings demanded, "Now tell me why Arabella sent you here. Is she well? I have not heard from her for several weeks."

"When I went to her house, I was told that she had been sent to the Fleet."

Lady Hastings drew a quick breath and exclaimed, "So Cromwell has struck again! That presents a problem. And what of you, Miss Morgan?"

Susanna felt her eyes fill with tears. With as much dignity as she could muster, she explained briefly what had happened to her and Jeremy.

"So you have nowhere to go?"

"Yes."

Lady Hastings pursed her lips as she looked meditatively at her and said, "You may stay with us, but I warn you to say nothing of the fact that you are Catholic. My husband, Lord Hastings, is a member of Parliament. He suffers me to practice my religion in secret but has commanded me not to inform others of my religion.

"I will tell him that you are my niece from a distant branch of my family who has fallen on hard times. Yes," she said brightening, "your family's estate has been sequestered and you had nowhere else to go. That is close enough to the truth to be believable and will explain why you have brought no clothes."

It was a clever idea. She had known of several families whose estates had been seized by local committees who were now able to settle old grievances. Sequestration was Parliament's way of cutting back the power of the Royalists to support the king, and was especially appealing when Parliament kept the rents and incomes of these very same Royalists.

"You must be hungry. I will order some refreshments and have a room prepared for you." Then, frowning at Susanna, she added, "I will provide you with some gowns. What you are wearing may have been suitable for the country, but not here in London."

"Thank you, Lady Hastings. I appreciate what you are doing for me. I would not have come here unless I had nowhere else to go. I would not be a burden. If I could be useful in some way . . ."

"Perhaps you may be," said the countess, eyeing Susanna speculatively.

Booted feet came clumping down the hall. The door to the library was thrown open by a servant. The countess sprang to her feet. "Lord Hastings, may I present my niece, Miss Susanna Morgan. She is come lately from the country where her parents have died and left her in dire straits. As her only living relative, she has appealed to us for help."

The count was a querulous-looking man with a long nose and the petulant face of one who was perpetually dissatisfied. Of indeterminate middle age, he leaned heavily on a cane, which she perceived was more useful than ornamental, as his legs dragged when he walked.

"A niece, you say."

"From a distant branch of my family," continued her ladyship.

Lady Hastings seemed to have no qualms about lying and did it so smoothly that no one would know that she was less than honest in attributing kinship to a woman whom she had met only moments ago.

"If it pleases you," Lord Hastings said, turning to his wife and giving her an irritable look. Then, bowing to Susanna, he said, "Welcome to my house, Miss Morgan."

"Thank you, my lord."

The next day, Lady Hastings's maid brought Susanna an armful of clothing, which consisted of shifts and gowns that had been cleverly mended—her ladyship's castoffs. But she was a pauper now and could expect no more, thought Susanna bitterly, even though she acknowledged to herself that the gowns were finer than any she had ever worn.

The week passed slowly. Susanna spent much of the time alone in her room thinking of Jeremy. Had he reached Amsterdam safely? Was he staying with Jacob? When would she see him again? An ache filled her heart. How she longed for her father and Jeremy, for the safety and security of her own home, not this stranger's house, however grand it might be.

She saw little of Lady Hastings, except for those few days when the weather was fine and they could stroll about the garden. Peppering Susanna with questions about her family and about her religious convictions, her ladyship took in everything and missed nothing. Of herself, she revealed little.

Dinners were exceedingly dull. Lady Hastings would prattle on about their two daughters and their husbands and children, while without fail, Lord Hastings would complain about everything from the inadequacies of the servants to the vagaries of the weather.

On the night before everything changed, Susanna dreamed that she was delivering a present to someone. Her feet dragging, she felt so tired, so lost. Nothing was familiar. When she looked down at her hands, they were empty, the present gone.

Then, as dreams do, things changed abruptly. A dark shape was pursuing her. She tried to run but was powerless to move her legs. A hand clapped her on her shoulder. She struck out at the entity, waking suddenly to find herself chilled to the marrow of her bones and entangled in the bedclothes.

It was only a dream, but it felt like a presentiment. Once, when she was little, she had blurted out to Molly, the housekeeper, a dream about men breaking into their house. Molly had given her a strange look and then told her that she had once overheard Susanna's mother talking about a similar dream with the master. Her mother, very upset, had implored her husband to take care.

"But don't you worry none, Miss Susanna," Molly had said as she lifted her onto a stool and gave her a piece of cake. "Your father won't allow no bad men to break in here."

But her dream had been true. Bad men *had* broken into their house and taken her father. Now her dream was warning her about something else.

Too agitated to sleep, she wished now that she had kept her mother's rosary, even though she had lost faith in its efficacy. It was almost dawn before she could calm her mind and sleep. She woke up to the sound of rain on the window and a pale light filtering through a gap in the heavy brown curtains. She dressed quickly and tried to arrange her hair in some sort of order, but her thick brown hair stubbornly resisted.

An impatient knock at the door startled her. In a rustle of maroon silk, Lady Hastings swept regally into the room. "You have slept well, I trust?" she asked politely.

Without waiting for an answer, she sat down and asked, "Are you comfortable here, Susanna?"

"Yes, Lady Hastings. I am grateful—"

The countess waved away her thanks and said, "We must talk. You indicated earlier, Susanna, that you would be willing to be of use here. I have need of a favor."

"I should like to be of service, your ladyship."

"Well, then," said the countess, "there is somewhat you might do—not for me, but for our king—if you are willing."

"I hardly know, your ladyship, that there is ought I could do."

"I have found you to be a person of good sense. The favor I ask is well within your compass."

"Then I shall do it."

The countess drew a letter out of the bodice of her gown. "Take this to the address I shall give you and give it into the hands of the gentleman whose name I shall tell you."

At Susanna's look of bewilderment, the countess added, "I shall be at an important dinner tonight with my husband and do not have an opportunity to deliver this letter myself. If you feel you are not capable of performing this small service for me . . ."

If her ladyship could not take it herself, why did she not send a servant with the letter? Something felt wrong, but her benefactress, used to getting her own way, was not one who would easily brook a refusal.

"Of course, I would be pleased to be of service."

"But you are doubtful," said the countess, staring at her and tapping her foot on the floor. "Do you consider yourself a good Catholic?" she asked.

"Yes, I do, but what has that to do with your request?"

"And you are loyal to Charles Stuart, our king?"

"Indeed, yes, your ladyship."

"Then for love of God and king, I ask you to deliver this letter to a gentleman. Much may depend upon this."

A tide of equal parts excitement and fear began rising in Susanna. Events were bearing her onward to some inexorable fate that she could not resist. Her carefree days of roaming the countryside with Jeremy had left her ill prepared to endure days of inactivity, bound by the wishes of others.

"I will do as you wish, your ladyship."

"Very well, Susanna," said the countess briskly. "Hold yourself in readiness for tonight, then."

That evening after a servant had brought her a light supper, which she took in her room, Lady Hastings came to her door. "A coach I have hired is waiting downstairs for you. Here is the letter. Deliver it to the gentleman at this address." She looked searchingly at Susanna and added, "This is a matter of great import, or I should not ask you to do this."

"I understand." But she did not. What was so important that this letter had to be delivered now? There were so many factors here that she did not understand. She wished that she had paid more attention to what was happening in the political realm.

She knew only what was common knowledge: that Queen Henrietta Maria, Charles I's wife, had been forced to flee to France when Parliament's army had defeated the Royalists and captured the king. Prince Charles's efforts to liberate his father had failed, so he, too, had fled to the continent. All other attempts of the king to escape his captors had had a similar outcome. What had this letter to do with any of this?

A sudden dread seized her, and she had to force herself to walk downstairs. Her steps dragging, she walked out into a light mist. A man was waiting who helped her into the coach, which bore no coat of arms or other insignia to tell to whom it belonged. The driver, whose face was hidden by the collar of his greatcoat, whipped the horses into a canter.

They drove for perhaps half an hour through twisting streets until the coach drew up in front of a house of modest proportions in one of the new squares that were being built in London. The driver waited silently on top of his perch until Susanna realized that they had come to her destination. She gathered her skirts around her and cautiously stepped down from the coach. She walked up to the front door and knocked. A young maid opened the door, asked her name, and told her to come in. She left Susanna in a comfortable room with a fire, but even the heat of the room could not warm her. Prickles of fear ran through her. She was a fool to have come. Her dream had warned her. Fury rose in her. Must she play the helpless victim once again?

A young man of cheerful countenance with a short cloak slung over one shoulder and dressed in a silver-colored satin doublet over a linen shirt tucked into blue breeches entered the room. "Ah, Miss Morgan, Sir Gilbert at your service. I believe you have something for me."

She thrust the letter at him. If he was surprised by her silence, he was too well-bred to show it. "You must be cold. Have a seat by the fire. Would you like a glass of Madeira?"

"Thank you, no. It is growing late." And she was alone with a man she did not know. Reluctantly, she sat down. Her nerves crawling, she could scarcely contain her impatience to be off.

Sir Gilbert tore open the letter and read it quickly. He was evidently pleased by what he had read, for he gave her a big smile that revealed small white teeth with a gap between the two in front, giving him an air of boyish mischievousness. He sat down opposite her and dropped the letter onto a small table made of inlaid woods. Stretching out his legs, he discreetly admired his tan leather boots with the cuffs.

He beamed at her as he leaned forward and said, "So, Miss Susanna, I had hardly hoped for so lovely a messenger. I understand that you have come lately from the country. Do tell me something of yourself."

"My parents are dead, so Lord and Lady Hastings have kindly offered me the protection of their home." She fell silent. She would tell as little as possible about herself.

Sir Gilbert was leaning forward and eyeing her with frank interest. "And how long do you propose to stay with those two?"

"What do you mean, sir?" she asked sharply.

The air of boyish good humor was gone as he said, "You may not know that my lord and his estimable wife are clever and well skilled in the conduct of great affairs. Be careful that you do not become enmeshed in their intrigues."

"I know little of politics, sir."

"Of that I am sure," said Sir Gilbert drily.

Rising from her chair with as much dignity as she could muster, Susanna said, "Thank you for your hospitality, Sir Gilbert, but I must be gone."

Before he could answer, they heard a loud knocking at the door. The maid burst in, her eyes wild with fear.

"It's all right, Nancy," said Sir Gilbert, snatching up the letter and stuffing it into his doublet. "Go to your room."

Seizing Susanna's hands, he commanded, "Come with me."

"No, not until I know what is going on."

"Certain death if we stay, but that will not happen if you come with me."

He swiftly led her out of the room and up a winding staircase, which led to the roof.

It was cold and a light rain was falling, which made the roof tiles slippery. Sir Gilbert grabbed her hand and pulled her around the corner of a chimney. A heavy thudding rang loudly through the still air.

Susanna shivered and pulled her cloak more tightly around her. "Will they not search here for us?"

"Ah, but we are not staying here." He released her hand and peered around the chimney. "As I thought, they have broken down the door and are now inside."

"But who are they? Why are they looking for you? What have you done?"

"That would take too long to tell, but if we are discovered, it will go hard for us."

Susanna planted her feet, looked into the man's eyes, and said, "Tell me now or I do not move."

"They are Roundheads . . ."

"Cromwell's men. Why are they interested in you?"

Sir Gilbert's voice was cool as he answered, "I am a Royalist, endeavoring to set the king free from his captivity at Carisbrooke Castle on the Isle of Wight."

Susanna drew a sharp breath. "And the letter?"

"Bade me be ready to go to the king's assistance this very night."

"But you can never make it to the Isle of Wight."

"We can and we will."

"We!"

"You are compromised now and cannot return to his lordship's home. But we must be off," he said impatiently as he grabbed her hand.

They crept across the roof until they came to a locked door. Sir Gilbert pulled out a key from his pocket, unlocked the door, and led her down a dusty spiral staircase. They heard shouting and the maid's terrified cries.

Susanna was sure that Sir Gilbert must hear the pounding of her heart in her chest. Then she heard a quiet sigh of satisfaction from him as they exited into a back garden, where the sodden grass and leaves dragged at her skirts.

Sir Gilbert gave a low whistle. A man emerged from the gloom and tugged at his cap. Without a word, they followed him into the stables, where a horse, already saddled, whinnied softly.

Sir Gilbert vaulted into the saddle and stretched out a hand to Susanna. With the assistance of the servant, the two men hauled her up on the horse, so that she was riding pillion behind Sir Gilbert, who guided the animal to the back of the stables and into the woods.

Except for the soughing of the wind in the trees, there was little sound as well as little light, but from time to time the clouds would clear briefly for the moon to shine through. As she leaned against the back of the man bearing her away from harm, she wondered how this was going to end. Not well, she feared.

They had journeyed for some time in this fashion when they came to a road. Sir Gilbert halted the horse.

"What . . . ?"

"Shhh."

She could hear the swift flow of a river and smell the rank odors of decomposing offal blowing in on the wind, which had strengthened and was sending cold fingers under her cloak. The moon broke through the clouds and turned the river into molten silver.

Now she spied a boat lying at anchor and felt the man's excitement as his muscles tensed. As he urged the horse forward, three men burst out from behind a low stone wall shouting, "Hold, in the name of Parliament!"

Sir Gilbert laid about him with his sword, injuring two of the men. The third man fell backward as the terrified horse reared.

They plunged down an embankment and slid to a sudden halt. "Take the horse and go!" shouted Sir Gilbert as he leaped to the ground and began running toward the boat.

Susanna nearly fell off her mount. She righted herself and grabbed the reins. Several bullets whizzed harmlessly over their heads. The animal bolted.

When she heard no one following them, she pulled the panting horse to a walk. Now where was she going to go? She could not return to the home of Lord and Lady Hastings. Not when her ladyship had knowingly sent her into danger.

Her fury rose as she remembered how Sir Gilbert had lied to her about taking her with him. Instead, he had left her alone. Now she had no one and nowhere to go. She had been a pawn, and pawns were expendable.

The horse was walking docilely enough now, although occasionally it would prick up its ears and turn an unquiet eye on her. She had no notion as to where she was, except that she was riding along a footpath that ran near the river. Dim shapes of houses in the distance reared out of the darkness. The lapping of water together with the country sounds of crickets and the rustling of small creatures soothed her senses and lulled her, along with the gentle rocking of the horse . . .

The rocking stopped. She looked up. The horse was munching grass. Nearby was some outbuilding behind a house. Rain had begun to fall. She left the horse where it was and lifted the latch on the door of the small building. She went inside and felt her way along the dark interior until her feet encountered something soft—straw. She pulled out a quantity of the stuff and spread it on the dirt floor. Too tired to stand any more, she sat down, wrapped her cloak tightly around herself, and promptly fell asleep.

The noise of crows screeching awakened Susanna. She stood up and eased her way over to the door. Opening it carefully, she looked around. Her horse had gone. The first light of dawn was vanquishing the darkness. People would be rising, coming outside. She had to leave.

After brushing bits of straw off her skirts and cloak and smoothing her hair, she walked quickly down to the Thames. Reaching the top of some steps leading to the river, she could see watermen ferrying people to the other side of the river. Cries of "Oars! Oars!" came from other watermen looking for customers.

From her vantage point she could see shops and houses, many of them several stories high, huddled tightly together on London Bridge. In the fast-moving current, watermen were skillfully guiding their boats through the narrow openings of the bridge's arches, which held back the flood tides from the ocean. Barges loaded with grain, vegetables, and wood moved toward docks situated along the Thames.

Did she have the courage to drown herself, especially in this murky water reeking of its burden of noxious offal from privies and slaughterhouses? Footsteps sounded behind her.

"How beautiful the river looks. See the way the light moves, always changing," observed a deep voice.

A tremor of fear stabbed her. Thieves and killers were everywhere. A lady alone stood a good chance of being raped and killed and her clothes stripped off her and sold.

She turned around and took a good look at the man. From his dark cloak of some rich material and well-brushed hat with a high crown, it was obvious that he was a gentleman. She swallowed and strove to make a light reply, but words would not come.

Seeing her distress, he said in a gentle voice, "I have observed you at the inn where I occasionally take my meals. It has come to my notice that you may be in some difficulties."

She nodded.

"The innkeeper's wife was most unkind."

His compassion broke down her inhibitions; she began to cry. The man slipped a handkerchief into her hand and held out his arm. "I would be honored to have your company over a meal," he said.

Scarcely knowing what she was doing, she allowed him to lead her to an inn, where a serving girl seated them at a table in an alcove. Some finely dressed ladies in silken skirts and jackets, accompanied by fashionably dressed men in boots, breeches, jackets, and hats with plumes in them, sat on benches around tables loaded with food and drink. A fiddler was playing a merry tune. The smell of roast beef from the joint roasting in the enormous fireplace set Susanna's mouth to watering.

"Allow me to introduce myself. I am Paul Kerchoff, at your service."

"And I, sir, am Susanna Morgan."

After ordering roast beef with vegetables and a pudding to follow, Paul told her that he was a merchant doing business in London and abroad. In turn, she found herself pouring out her tale of Cromwell's men taking her father, Jeremy's escape to Amsterdam, her flight to London, and her discovery of her aunt's incarceration in prison. She omitted her most recent adventures. After all, he was a stranger.

When the meal came, Susanna found herself digging eagerly into the food.

They spoke little until they had almost finished their meal and Paul offered, "If you will allow me to be of service, I will send my man to inquire of your relatives."

"I bid you thanks," Susanna said, "but why would you do me such a kindness?"

"I, too, know what it is like to feel every man's hand turned against me when agents of the Czar hunted me across Europe."

"Why would they do such a thing, sir?"

"Because in Russia I spoke out against the injustices I saw daily around me: injured war veterans forced to beg in the streets, children starving and subject to the most wretched conditions, and the nobility riding roughshod over everyone."

"Are things much better here?" asked Susanna bitterly.

"You English have a parliament that bends even kings to their will. Given time, matters may change for the better in Russia, but nothing save a revolution will break the power of the Czar. That is the difference. But come, we have done here. Where should I take you?"

Susanna drew a long breath. What should she tell him? She had nowhere to go.

Her chin lifted defiantly. "I have no particular place to go, sir. I was hoping to find a position, but so far have been most unlucky in that regard."

If he was shocked by her words, he did not show it. His dark eyes held such kindness—and something else—an admiration. "It is difficult for a woman alone."

"Yes," she whispered. She felt a quickening of interest in this man. He was no foppish Royalist or a petulant lord.

He laid a hand over hers. "You are very welcome to stay with me. Until you find a position," he added hastily as Susanna shifted suddenly in her chair. "I might be able to help you in that regard. As a lady's maid or a governess, perhaps?"

"Perhaps."

"If that is not to your taste, I may be able to find you something else."

"You are very kind."

"Then that is settled," said Paul briskly as he rose from his seat and held out his hand to her.

His hand was firm, curling around hers in a grasp that was at once comforting and intensely moving. She drew a sharp breath. It would be best if she kept a firm rein on her emotions. Even though she found the man appealing, he might turn out to be one of those men who took advantage of women. Like Sir Gilbert? She felt an enormous relief that he had not taken her with him. He was nothing like Paul. As he paid the bill, she admired the breadth of his shoulders, the way he held himself.

They went outside where his coachman was waiting. They said little as they journeyed to the outskirts of London until they came to a substantial-looking house set in a small park of several acres. Paul's house was exquisitely furnished with elaborately carved oak furniture and colorful Turkey rugs.

"Susanna, this is my housekeeper, Mrs. Zeman," said Paul, beckoning to a thin middle-aged woman of plain looks, with a rigid stance and pursed lips. A look passed between her and

Paul—not exactly that of master and servant, but not a look between equals—something between the two.

"Take care of Miss Morgan," said Paul. "I must go out again on business."

The housekeeper nodded, then showed Susanna to a plainly furnished bedroom and called a maid to bring some covers for the bed.

"I shall have cook prepare a posset for you. It will be served in the parlor."

Susanna thanked her and then, as she had nothing to unpack, waited a few minutes and went downstairs into the parlor.

It was a pleasant room with a fire crackling on the hearth. Shortly after Susanna had sat down on one of the padded chairs, Mrs. Zeman glided into the room and set a posset on a small table beside Susanna. With the fire and the hot drink of milk, sherry, and spices warming her, Susanna felt herself relaxing for the first time in days.

Then the housekeeper did an astonishing thing: she sat down, too. In any other household, she would have been severely reprimanded or even lost her position.

"You are in trouble," Mrs. Zeman murmured.

Susanna was dumbfounded. What kind of household was this that a servant should be so forward?

As if reading her mind, the housekeeper gave her a tight little smile. "You will find matters different here. You are not the first person in difficulties to be brought to this home," she said. "There have been others. Mr. Kerchoff has a kind heart. I was the first that he rescued. If it had not been for him, I should have died." Looking at Susanna she said, "These are troubled times. The Thirty Years' War is ravaging the countries of Europe even as the civil war in this country is wreaking havoc upon many. It is no shame to be brought low through no fault of your own."

Susanna's eyes filled with tears. She found herself blurting out to this woman—just as she had to Paul—the circumstances that had brought her here.

"You are safe now," Mrs. Zeman said softly. "We will talk again soon," she added as she stood up.

Who were these people? Susanna felt embarrassed that she had disclosed so much of herself to a servant, but then Mrs. Zeman did not act like a servant.

Her eyes growing heavy, Susanna fell asleep.

She awoke to the sounds of someone coming into the room. It was Paul. As he greeted her, she noted his look of weariness.

"Mrs. Zeman has been seeing to your comfort?" he asked, going over to the fire and rubbing his hands together.

"She has been most kind," said Susanna cautiously. After a pause, she added, "She told me that you rescued her."

"It was a terrible time for her and many other Jews in Poland. Even though King Wladislaus IV was not hostile to Jews, many Poles resented them because of their money and influence and accused them of being killers of Christ.

"I had met Miriam once in the course of doing some business with her father. A few years later, I encountered her coming out of a shop. She looked fit for the boneyard, so emaciated and ill she looked. I might have passed her by without recognizing her except for her eyes, which still had a certain fire to them, a look of dauntless refusal to give in. She told me that she had been put out of her lodgings a week past because she could not pay the rent. I told her that I was leaving town that night and invited her to come with me. She has worked for me ever since. Her services have been invaluable."

"Truly, she has suffered, but Jews are not allowed to live here, not since they were expelled from England by King Edward in the thirteenth century!"

"So they were, but some, mainly Spaniards and Portuguese, live here secretly now. They fled from the Inquisition in their native lands. Even though they became New Christians, people still thought of them as crypto-Jews, killers of Christ."

"But how . . . ?"

"Many of these are rich merchants who pass themselves off as Catholics. Since some of them perform certain secret services for the government, they are allowed to stay."

Susanna's mind reeled. She remembered when her father had taken her, Jeremy, and Aunt Arabella to the playhouse to see *The Merchant of Venice.* How the audience had booed Shylock the Jew with his hooked nose and beady eyes, who had insisted upon his pound of flesh!

She looked up to see Paul gazing steadily at her. "You are offended?" he asked.

She sensed that the answer was important to him, so she answered carefully, "I have never met a Jew before, but if you have seen fit to make one your housekeeper, that is your prerogative."

Paul nodded gravely. The silence stretched out. "I have given some thought to your situation," he said. "By your leave, I will ask Mrs. Zeman to teach you such skills as you may need in the future."

"Thank you, sir," was all that Susanna could find to say.

"And now to dinner," said Paul, leading the way into the dining room, where a varied repast had been set out for them.

After they had finished a satisfying meal, Paul asked, "Do you play chess?"

"I have some small skill there, sir. My father taught me how to play."

"Then, if you are agreeable, we shall have a game."

When they had finished a game, which Paul handily won, he said, with a glint of laughter in his eyes, "You have an unconventional way of moving your pieces, but for all that, you may make a fine player yet."

"Many thanks, sir, but I acknowledge that you are far superior."

He laughed and admitted, "Perhaps so, but are you teachable?"

"I think you may find me an apt pupil," said Susanna softly, looking up at him. A log fell, sending a shower of sparks upward and illuminating Paul's face. He was looking intently at her. Warmth that had nothing to do with the fire on the hearth surged through her.

Paul parted his lips as if to speak, then thought better of it. "I have some letters to write. If there is anything else . . ."

"No, I . . . I am quite comfortable here."

He stood up, bowed, and left the room.

The next morning after Susanna had finished her breakfast, Mrs. Zeman joined her and said, "The master has left town for a few days. He has asked me to acquaint you with some housewifely skills."

Why had Paul not told her of his leaving? But then he probably gave no more thought to her than he would a lost puppy that he had rescued. And what sort of "skills" was Mrs. Zeman going to teach her?

"Do you know how to make a posset or a syllabub?"

When Susanna shook her head, the housekeeper said, "There is nothing like a good hot drink to ward off the chill of winter. We will begin with a syllabub."

Mrs. Zeman led her into the kitchen, where the cook was dozing in a chair and a scullery maid was washing dishes. With a flick of her fingers, the housekeeper dismissed them. She pulled out a pot into which she poured cider, sugar, and a little nutmeg. "Now stir that while I pour in some cream," she said to Susanna, who reluctantly took the proffered ladle.

Was she reduced to being a servant now? Angered, Susanna stirred the liquid so hard that some of it splashed out of the pot.

Mrs. Zeman merely pursed her thin lips at this show of temper. She lifted the pot onto the large wooden table standing in the center of the room. "Now we let the syllabub stand for two hours," she said.

"Sit down, Susanna," said the housekeeper, pointing to a wooden chair. "You may think me unkind, but it is to your advantage to learn those things that would gain you favor in the eyes of an employer."

"But what can I do?"

"Can you sew?"

"No."

"Then being a lady's maid or a seamstress is out of the question. I gather that you have never cooked?"

Susanna shook her head.

"Can you read and write?"

"Yes, I can. And I even know some French and Latin."

"Then you might become a governess or teach in a village school, but one must have references for that."

Susanna heaved a great sigh. "Nothing seems quite suitable," she murmured.

"Suitable! You are without family or fortune. You must take what you can and be thankful, else it's the streets for you, my girl."

"I will never, ever resort to such a thing, of that you may be sure!"

Her dark eyes flashing with anger, Mrs. Zeman said, "Like you, I once had a family and bright prospects. Then my father died, his partner absconding with all his money. My suitors left, looking for girls with fortunes. My mother and I were forced to leave our house and live in lodgings. We took in sewing, barely keeping body and soul together. Then my mother began coughing up blood and died. Alone, I could no longer afford even our meager lodgings. I slept in the streets for a week. That is when the master found me. You are fortunate that he takes an interest in you."

"Maybe I will marry," said Susanna defiantly.

"Yes, you might—you're pretty enough—but you would still need to know how to bake bread, make preserves, and know which herbs are good for certain illnesses so that you may treat your family . . ."

"Isn't that what servants are for?"

Mrs. Zeman smiled thinly. "If ever you should be fortunate enough to marry well, you will be expected to organize and supervise the servants. In addition, you might help your husband with his accounts."

Susanna brightened. This was something she might learn to do. Mrs. Zeman dampened her enthusiasm by saying, "I will teach you how to keep accounts, but first you must learn the housewifely arts."

A week passed, with Susanna reluctantly learning somewhat of cookery from Mrs. Zeman. She had just baked a loaf of bread, which was deemed "at least edible," when suddenly they heard the clatter of boots in the hall and men's voices.

Soldiers! They had found her! Fear swept over Susanna in a great roaring tide. Then a torrent of anger swept away the fear. Was she never to be safe again?

Susanna ran into the hall, skidding to a halt in front of Paul and an older gentleman. She could feel the blood rushing to her head. Darkness filled her vision. She staggered. Then she felt Paul's arms around her, steadying her.

"I thought . . . soldiers," she whispered.

She could hear Paul calling for Mrs. Zeman and saying, "She has had a shock; take her up to bed."

Then he was gone, and the housekeeper was leading her by the hand upstairs, putting her to bed, soothing her as one would a child, and she was sobbing in great wrenching gasps that she could not control.

Time passed. Worn-out, she stopped sobbing. Then Mrs. Zeman was helping her to sit up and telling her to drink. Obediently, she swallowed, and then the blackness came again.

Susanna awoke slowly out of a dream in which Paul figured prominently. Remembrance of the events of the day before rose vividly in her mind. She wanted to dive under the bedcovers and never get up. What must Paul think of her, in an apron, her hands covered with flour, and nearly fainting in front of a strange gentleman. She must never allow herself to be so overmastered by emotion again.

A quick rap on the door, and Mrs. Zeman marched into the room. "You are up, I see," she said. "The master has been asking after you. Come down when you are dressed."

Susanna sat up in bed and asked, "Who was the other gentleman who was here last night?"

"Mr. Antonio Carvajal, a merchant whose ships trade from the continent to the Indies, a man of great wealth, one not to be trifled with, but withal generous to the poor. And," she added drily as she drew the heavy curtains open, "from all accounts he is happily married with two fine sons."

Susanna dressed quickly and went downstairs.

Paul saw her and rose to greet her. "I trust you are feeling better?" he asked.

"I am much recovered," she said, feeling a sudden shyness in his presence. She shoved down the delight she felt. His inquiry was only the customary politeness he showed to all.

"Please convey my apologies to your visitor for my unseemly behavior last night."

Paul waved away her apology. "I have seen it happen thus," he said, "that when the danger is passed, some slight thing may provoke an individual to temporarily lose control of himself. It may be that the mind becomes so overheated that it can no longer function as before. I am glad that you are over your difficulty. Now come along and let us do justice to the fine repast that Cook has prepared."

The days fell into a rhythm, with Mrs. Zeman teaching Susanna the many things required to run a household. Paul and she spent many evenings playing chess and backgammon and discussing the affairs of the day. He treated her with courtesy and something else—respect for her as a person of intelligence.

Several times Mr. Carvajal came to dinner. The conversation then was lively, with the two men discussing the latest *Mercurius*, the paper that held forth on various political opinions, and the latest discoveries in medicine and exploration.

It was nearing Christmas when Paul joined Susanna in the parlor, where she was warming herself in front of a fire. She turned and noticed that he was looking gravely at her.

"I have some news of your relatives," he said. "The information you gave me previously was correct. My agent found that Lady Arabella had, indeed, been taken on Cromwell's orders to the Fleet."

"Is there a way to have her released?"

"I am much afraid that would be impossible. She died of a fever shortly after she had been brought there."

"And my father?" asked Susanna in a low voice, her hands twisting in her skirt.

"I am so sorry. Your father also was taken to the Fleet, where he died a week after his arrival. That is why it has taken so long to find information about them. And then I was not sure if you could safely stand the shock of it."

Susanna put a hand to her mouth, stifling a sob.

"How did he die?" asked Susanna in a low voice.

"The jailor was loath to speak of the matter, but some coins from my man loosened his tongue. It seems that one of the thieves imprisoned there tried to steal your father's boots. When your father resisted, he was thrown against a wall and died shortly thereafter. As to your brother, he left Amsterdam for the New World."

Paul put an arm around her. "Susanna, stay here as long as you desire."

"I would not be a useless burden to you?"

"Never useless. Do you not realize how I feel about you?"

"But I have no family, no fortune."

"I have more than enough for both of us. I have loved you since the day I saw you." Paul lifted her chin and smoothed back her hair as he said softly, "You are a woman of uncommon intelligence and independent spirit, but you are alone and need a protector. I would like to be that one."

Susanna drew back and asked in a tight voice, "What precisely, sir, are you proposing?" Did he think her a wanton, a woman who would agree to be his mistress?

"That you become my wife. I made up my mind some time ago, for an assortment of reasons, not to marry, but I did not count on meeting a woman such as you. You need not give me your answer immediately. Take as long as you need to think on this matter."

Emotion clogged her throat as a torrent of feeling swept over her.

Mistaking her silence for rejection, Paul said, "If you feel an antipathy towards me because of my religion, I would not hold you against your will."

Startled, Susanna asked, "What do you mean?"

"Surely you must have guessed. I am a Jew."

Things she had wondered about fell into place: Paul making a Jew his housekeeper, the fact of his going out punctually every Saturday at the same time, never going to church. Now she understood.

"You didn't know." He let her go, taking a turn about the room as he ran his fingers through his dark hair, graying at the temples.

"Your faith does not offend me," Susanna said in a low voice. "Catholics and Protestants are locked together in a civil war that is tearing apart our country. Neither side is practicing the virtues of Christian love and forbearance. I have seen nothing of this vileness in you. On the contrary, you have treated me well." She took a deep breath and added, "I will marry you, Paul."

A great gladness filling his eyes, he drew her to him. "My love," he said and kissed her.

CHAPTER 12

Geraldine Morgan

Golden Dragon Restaurant,
San Francisco,
Saturday, June 20, 1992

"Sorry I'm late," said Geraldine as she rushed over to the table where Dan was seated.

He stood up immediately and helped her take off her coat. "Not a problem. I was a little early. I hope you like dim sum. Cummings said the food was good here."

He looked quite handsome, wearing a navy blazer over a white shirt and tan slacks. "I've never tried dim sum. I'll take whatever you're having."

A waiter, a young Chinese man pushing a cart loaded with food, came over to their table.

Dan pointed to a tureen of steaming soup. "For starters, you might like the hot and sour soup."

The waiter ladled out their soup into small white bowls, which he put on the table, and then left. Gerry took a sip of her soup. "I like it," she said.

"I missed breakfast because I went early to the gym," explained Dan. "I haven't exercised since we got here and thought I'd better do it while I had a little free time. So what did I miss?"

Gerry put down her spoon. "Well, we all got to meet Mr. Stevens. Jason works for him in his antique shop in the summer. I gather that Mr. Stevens is supposed to accompany Jason around San Francisco, but Jason had other plans."

Dan grinned. "Yeah, like shopping with Laney. I wouldn't let her wander alone in San Francisco, so she got J.J. to go with her."

Gerry smiled back and said, "He seems like a nice boy. He suggested that Mr. Stevens accompany Marjory around town."

Dan's grin got wider. "And what did your aunt think of that?" he asked.

"She didn't seem to mind at all. In fact, I think she was quite pleased. Oh, and Caleb, who was just leaving for his office, invited Mr. Stevens to dinner."

"Sorry I missed all that, Gerry. And how was your author meeting?"

"Interesting. He was friendly and full of all sorts of stories that weren't in his book."

"What was his book about?"

"Reincarnation. He'd worked for ten years to find actual proof."

Dan looked skeptical. "What kind of proof?"

"He found children who remembered their past lives and interviewed them and their parents."

"But how did your author know that they weren't just telling stories? Kids do make up things. They don't know any better."

"Their stories checked out. He located their past-life families, who vouched for the truth of the children's stories."

Dan moved uneasily in his seat. Gerry could tell he didn't believe her. Maybe he was one of those people who wouldn't change his mind no matter how much evidence you gave him.

"Lots of cultures believed in reincarnation: the ancient Celts, Druids, North American Indians. Even today, Hindus, Buddhists, and quite a few people in the U.S. believe, too," said Gerry.

The waiter came around with the food cart again. Dan eyed the selection of food and said, "Cummings said that the squid with Chinese broccoli was pretty good. You want to try that?" he asked.

"All right."

After their waiter had left with the cart, they ate in silence. Then Dan put down his chopsticks and said, "Look, I never really thought about past lives before, but I'm willing to accept that we don't know much, if anything, about what happens after we die. Did this author of yours ever say *why* we have to keep coming back to earth?"

"It's usually about learning lessons."

"So it's not about punishment for what a person did previously?"

Gerry shook her head. "No. We act out of ignorance according to what we think is best for us at the time. By paying attention to what we do, we can choose not to repeat the mistakes of the past."

"Like what?"

"Well, if you were a killer in the past, for example, you might find yourself in situations now where you have opportunities to learn how to care about people."

"I guess from what you say that soldiers have a lot to learn."

"I'm not saying that the military are bad people," said Gerry defensively.

"I hope not. I was once in the Marines and found that many of them were just as moral as anyone else—some of them more so than the general population. And a lot of us signed up because we thought it our duty to defend our country. Someone has to do it."

"My author was talking particularly about people who *enjoyed* killing. You must have met some of those," said Gerry more sharply than she had meant.

"Some," admitted Dan. "But far fewer than you might think."

Gerry flushed. "I didn't mean to sound rude. How long were you in the Marines?"

"I did one four-year tour of duty. I learned a lot."

"What sort of things—that is, if you don't mind talking about it."

"Oh, things like situational awareness."

"What's that?"

"Our commanders taught us to become aware of everything going on around us. Being good at it could mean the difference between getting back to camp on your own two feet or being carried there by your buddies. Often I'd get hunches about situations we were in, like where the enemy was, how bad it could be."

"That sounds like a very useful ability."

"Essential. They say there are three kinds of people: the good guys, the bad guys, and the clueless. Most people fall into the last category. You see them walking around, not paying attention to anything around them . . ."

He stopped, a faraway look in his eyes as he fiddled with his chopsticks.

Gerry rushed in to break the awkward silence and said, "I also learned that a wound you might have received in the past could result in a birthmark."

"Interesting. On my right arm just above my elbow, I have a birthmark—a big one. So you think that could be an old war wound?"

"Or maybe you fell off a horse."

Dan laughed as he sprawled back in his seat. "I've never been crazy about riding horses. Fast cars are more my style. I've got this 1973 Barracuda I've almost finished restoring, but anything's possible, I guess."

He was really quite handsome when he smiled. And he seemed so comfortable in his own skin, no affectations, so up-front.

"Often people reincarnate with people they've known before."

"The same people each time?" Dan asked, sitting up straight and leaning toward her, his eyes probing hers.

Gerry drew a quick breath and said, "That's right."

Dan's mouth turned up at the corners in the beginning of a smile. "Now why would that be, I wonder?"

He really paid attention to what she said, not like some men, who seemed more interested in themselves than in her. It was a refreshing change, but was it all just an act? Gerry gave an elaborate shrug. "Because we have things to learn from one another. And because sometimes the group has a common purpose."

"Sort of like us Morgans all meeting together to do . . ." Dan waved his hands expressively.

"You could be right."

"So," said Dan, a teasing glint in his eyes, "do you think that you and I might have had a past life together?"

As Gerry looked at Dan, she suddenly knew what had been tugging at the back of her mind, the thing that she had refused to acknowledge ever since that dream she had been having about Susanna.

In a gentle voice, Dan said, "It's okay, Gerry. I shouldn't have asked that."

Unwillingly, she looked at him. His eyes were brown, not black, but the feeling in them was the same, a love that wouldn't let her go . . . Was he the reincarnation of Paul? Then that would make her the reincarnation of Susanna.

Gerry stood up. "I should leave. I have things to take care of."

"I've upset you. I'm sorry."

She shook her head, reaching blindly for her coat. Dan was ahead of her, putting it on around her shoulders. Struggling for control, she shrugged into it.

"I'm tired, didn't sleep much last night after reading Jeremy's memoir." Especially because of her dreams about Susanna and Paul.

Dan stood as if undecided, then asked quietly, "Could I call you a cab?"

"No thanks. I'd like to just walk for a while by myself."

Opening her purse, she found her sunglasses and jammed them on, then rummaged around for some money.

Dan put a hand on her arm. "I'll pay. My treat," he said. "Take care, Gerry. I'll see you at dinner."

"Thank you," she said and walked away.

CHAPTER 13

Jason Kramer

Caleb's mansion,
Saturday, June 20, 1992

"Thanks for coming shopping with me, J.J.," said Laney as they walked after dinner into the library.

"No problem."

It was the first time he had been allowed to go off on his own in a big city. Well, not quite on his own, but close, with no adult to supervise him. Laney wasn't really an adult, although she thought she was, but she was okay—didn't boss him around—and he did have fun. After shopping for a bathing suit, she had helped him find a scarf for his mother, and then he had helped her find a watch for her father.

Would he ever get the chance to visit San Francisco again and take in some of the sights, maybe with someone his own age like Crystal, Davis's friend? She was smart—definitely not an airhead—and kind of cute.

J.J. flopped into a wing chair, wondering if he dared to stretch his legs out over the side of it, and then decided not to, not in front of his relatives.

Dan was looking at Gerry like she was the sexiest thing alive. Too bad they were cousins.

Marjory and Mr. S. were quietly sipping their drinks. They must have really hit it off earlier. He had overheard them at dinner talking about their visit to the antique shops in Jackson Square.

Mr. S. was excited about buying some earrings made out of human hair. He was sure that they would sell very well in his store in Kenora.

Cummings was pouring Caleb a shot of brandy.

Beside J.J. stood a small table that held Jeremy's memoir, which Gerry had put there after supper. J.J. picked it up. The binding felt dry and cool to his touch. Thin spidery writing covered every inch of the brittle paper. His fingers began to burn. He tried to wrench his hand away, but a mighty force seemed to be gluing them to the page. He opened his mouth to shout—and fell into another time and place.

In disbelief, he gulped and rubbed his eyes, but the man standing in front of him was shockingly clear. He was wearing stockings and breeches and a reddish-colored cloak, which reached just below the tops of his boots. His long hair was neatly tied back in a ponytail.

"Who are you?" blurted out J.J.

"Your ancestor, Jeremy Morgan, at your service. Now pay attention, Master Jason. There is something you must do."

It's just like school all over again, thought J.J. resentfully. Fixing Jeremy with what he hoped was a good imitation of the Terminator's hard stare, he asked, "Why?"

"Because if you refuse," said Jeremy enunciating each word precisely, "much of your world will know cruel oppression at the hands of one who knows no mercy."

J.J. blinked and then let out a strangled yell. It was like the time in Mr. S.'s shop when he'd gone traveling out of his body and looked back into Celtic times. All around him was clear blue sky and nothing holding him up as far as he could tell.

"That which you term your 'consciousness' is here with me. Your body is taking its ease back in Caleb's library," said Jeremy's voice from beside him.

"How can I be separated from my body?"

"Consciousness can be anywhere it is needful for it to be. Time and space are not the barriers you view them to be."

Jeremy sounded like one of those far-out quantum physicists. Since there wasn't anything he could do about his situation, he might as well enjoy the view, even if it was the product of what had to be his hyperactive imagination.

And what a view! He could see the outline of California, the tips of mountain ranges poking up through huge clouds of dirty gray smoke.

"Where are we?" asked J.J.

"San Francisco in 1992 in an alternate reality."

"What happened here?" J.J. whispered, for the land was burning: towns, villages, fields, everything torched.

"You see before you a conquered country," said Jeremy. "The Great Oppressor, in league with the Japanese, dreams of world conquest. His armies are victorious everywhere and now shake the New World as a farmer might shake an apple tree. None dare oppose him except some few. And so the land burns.

"Disease kills as many as force of arms. Three persons in five fall prey to smallpox. Of those three, one dies, one becomes horribly disfigured, and one is only slightly marked. It is the custom during particularly bad outbreaks for the corpses to be burned."

J.J. shuddered. Now he could see what was left of farmhouses, their chimneys broken and red tiles jutting out from gaping roofs. In some cases, only burned-out shells remained. The towns were in even worse shape, with whole blocks of buildings wiped out and only piles of rubble to mark where they had stood. A few people were scavenging in the ruins. They dived for cover when what looked like jeep-type vehicles painted brown drove slowly down the street.

They moved swiftly to the south. "Los Angeles," said Jeremy.

The structures of the megalopolis, familiar to J.J. from movies, were not there, only a string of small towns that showed the same signs of devastation as the towns farther north.

"Behold, the Spanish territories," said Jeremy. "They were established here until the Japanese overtook them. Rather than build great manufacturing enterprises, these outposts ship the fruits of the land to the mother country, which uses these resources to manufacture goods and then ships these goods back to the colonists."

Now they were moving inland, soaring over mountain peaks that stuck up above a jumble of rock and wastelands of cactus and sage in lonely deserts where nothing moved for miles.

Foothills began to appear and then high, broad plains where vast herds of animals moved slowly. They dipped down closer.

"Bison!" exclaimed J.J. "So many of them!"

Now he could make out some dark-skinned men and women on horseback, expertly cutting out some of the animals from the rest of the herd.

"What are they doing?"

"Indians in the west joined with other Indians from all across this great land to create a federation of Indian nations. They supply quantities of meat, hides, and the by-products of bison to the rest of North America, even shipping their products to foreign markets."

Below them, J.J. could see a train pulling into a station surrounded by acres of corrals that contained bison standing, patiently awaiting their fate.

Abruptly, J.J. could feel himself streaking faster and faster eastward, the empty plains giving way to a patchwork quilt of neat farms.

There was nothing resembling the great cities of his time, cities linked together by a network of roads in a nonstop urban sprawl. Here were smaller towns where slow-moving vehicles, about the size of Volkswagen Beetles, puffed along dirt roads. Women in long dark dresses and scarves on their heads walked sedately from shop to shop, most carrying baskets into which they put their purchases. Men were dressed in pants and coats of the same dark material as the women.

"Their forebears were the early Puritans," said Jeremy answering the boy's unspoken question.

"Don't they believe in having fun?"

J.J. could hear a snort of laughter from Jeremy as he answered, "The Master of Hell was associated with fun. In Puritan New

106

England it would be a grave error to associate oneself with the Horned One. Religion is a sober affair. Everyone goes to the meetinghouse on Sundays."

"What happens if you don't?"

"Few people would patronize your business, bullies would set upon your children at school, and ladies would scorn to be seen with your wife."

"So they didn't really have a choice."

"You say it very true, Master Jason. No War of Independence, offering the right to live free from whatever class of society into which one was born, occurred. No masses of immigrants seeking to conduct their lives in the manner they chose flooded into the land. No great nation promoting individual freedoms and responsibilities— the likes of which the world has never known—arose.

"It happened in this manner. After Metacom or King Philip, the name given to the Indian leader, and the tribes who joined him laid waste to the English colonies, the French under Count Frontenac swooped down from the north upon the colonies and took control of the area.

"After the burning of their towns, the widespread killing of their people, as well as the repressive policies of France, the Thirteen Colonies never built up a great nation. And so the matter has stood ever since.

"Thus, when the armies of Hitler enslaved Europe in the 20th century, there was none to stop him. England, France, and all their allies eventually succumbed to the Great Oppressor, who, along with his ally, the Japanese, established a great empire extending throughout the whole of Europe, right up to the borders of Russia. Now he looks across the sea to the Eastern Seaboard of North America.

"There are cycles in time. The Hindus wrote about yuga cycles, each one of which lasted for thousands of years and had various characteristics. The Mayas also were aware of various cycles of time, as were the North American Indians. We are shifting now into another cycle. Soon the present cycle will close permanently.

"A distinct possibility exists that other forces will be able to shift the present timeline into what will become a nasty future."

"So, what has this to do with me or the other Morgans?"

"More than you think."

"But how?"

"Each of you has a talent, such as your ability to pick up impressions from objects. At other times you may have an intuitive knowing of the appropriate thing to do."

"I still don't understand how this works."

"You are at a particular point in time—a kind of window or opportunity—where, with some help, you will be able to project your consciousness into a former body of yours that lived at a particular turning point in history. This will allow you to effect the changes necessary to prevent the other forces from altering the present and future."

"What happens if we can't?"

"Then the timeline in which you now live will not manifest."

"Would that be so bad? Life isn't so great now for a lot of people." Like his mother, who had to have an operation and had lost her dad, and especially for the people living in third world countries.

As if reading his mind, Jeremy said, "And yet, my young kinsman, you live in a time where you have choices and opportunities undreamed of by those in other periods of history. Would you, for example, give up the industrial potential, which sometimes creates pollution, and forgo certain experiences that hold a great richness of expression for human beings?"

"Uh, I guess not."

"As I did mention previously, there are certain periods where, depending on the choices that individuals collectively make, the stream of human events may go one way or another. Colonial America was one such turning point. There are others."

"I don't get it."

"Each person is connected to a field of consciousness and, therefore, connected to each other. Carl Jung called it the *collective unconscious*. So what each person does, or even thinks, has an effect on everyone else. By your thoughts and actions, you Morgans can affect the direction in which humanity will go."

"They're never going to believe this, not in a million years!"

"Leave that to me, Master Jason. I charge you to tell them what you have seen and then bid them go to the San Juan Mission south of San Francisco. Advise the abbot that you have come for the box left there by Jeremy Morgan. You will find further instructions in the box."

J.J. opened his eyes and found his hand gripping the memoir.

Mr. S. was already out of his seat. Putting an arm around him, Mr. S. asked, "What's the matter, Jason?"

J.J. wanted to sink down into his chair. Everyone was staring at him. Then Laney slipped over to his side and whispered, "You okay?"

"Yeah."

"What happened to you, young man?" asked Caleb, frowning.

"Uh, well, I had a kind of vision. I met Jeremy and . . ." His voice trailed off.

This was going to be worse than he thought. Dan was staring at him skeptically, but then Marjory was saying, "Why don't you just tell us what happened, Jason?"

He gulped and said, "Jeremy said we're supposed to go to the San Juan Mission and pick up a box that he left there. And then we're going to travel back in time."

Dan whistled and leaned forward in his chair as he asked, "Did he tell you *how* we're supposed to go back in time?"

"Uh, no."

"Doesn't seem possible."

"I belong to a physics club at my high school. A physicist came to talk to us once. Someone asked this guy about time travel. He said it was theoretically possible. The math equations show that what he called 'the arrow of time' can go backward as well as forward."

"But no one has ever done it," said Dan, leaning back and crossing his arms over his chest.

"Not necessarily," said Marjory. "Cases do exist where people appear to have gone back into the past. A few years ago I came across a book written in 1902 by two Englishwomen who had toured Versailles just outside Paris the previous year. They saw a woman in a large hat and full-skirted dress, who was sketching. Later, they saw a picture of the woman, whom they identified as Marie Antoinette, wife of Louis the Sixteenth.

"Apparently, these two ladies had wandered into another time period, the 18th century, just before the French Revolution. And there were a number of other anomalies, including a footbridge they had walked over that no longer existed in 1901 but had been there in 1789 and a door that they had seen a footman closing, but which had been bolted shut for years before the ladies' visit."

"Could the ladies have been, ah, mistaken or just looking for their fifteen minutes of fame?" joked Dan.

"I think not," said Marjory. "Both were highly respected academics. Eleanor Jourdain was the principal of St. Hugh's College at Oxford, and Annie Moberly was the headmistress of a school for girls."

"Do you remember, Aunt Marjory, when we visited Bond Street in Liverpool? A clerk told us about something similar that had happened there," said Gerry.

J.J. began whistling a tune.

"Isn't that 'Hey Jude'?" asked Gerry.

When his relatives all looked at him, J.J. could feel himself flushing and said, "My dad's always playing old records by the Beatles. He said they grew up in Liverpool."

The tense atmosphere relaxed and everyone smiled, even Caleb, whose lips twitched briefly.

"So what happened in Bond Street?" asked Laney.

Gerry sat up straight, her face animated as she said, "We were shopping there and dropped into Dillons bookstore. The clerk, who was helping us find a book, mentioned that several days earlier a woman had been waiting in the shop for her husband to join her. When he came in, he looked confused. He told his wife how after they had split up to do some shopping he noticed everything had become really quiet—no traffic noises. He found himself suddenly standing in the middle of the road, where a 1950s-type van with *Caplan's* written on it had almost run him down.

"The other strange thing was that when he peered in the front window of what he was sure was the bookstore, he could see women's shoes and handbags for sale; the sign over the entrance read *Cripps*. As he walked into the shop, the interior suddenly changed back into a bookstore. It was later found that a clothes shop called *Cripps* used to be there."

"What about the van?" asked Caleb.

"In the 1950s, there used to be a company called Caplan's, which used white vans."

Mr. S. scratched his head as he asked, "Have any other strange phenomena occurred there?"

"Yes, I believe there have been other incidences in Bond Street of what some call *time slips*," said Marjory.

"So perhaps there is a possibility, after all, of time travel," he said reflectively.

There was dead silence, except for Caleb's putting down his glass a little too hard on a table.

"Getting back to the present," said Caleb, "I told you all yesterday about my visions of Jeremy and how when I didn't call the family together as he asked he caused my elevator to go berserk. Now the boy has seen him, too."

"I have been dreaming, also," said Gerry quietly. "About Jeremy's sister, Susanna. It was very . . . real, not like a dream at all."

"I think you should know that J.J. has a gift for psychometry," Mr. S. said. "By holding a Celtic pin, which had been dated back to the time of the Romans in early Britain, he picked up impressions of some events that happened in that period of history."

"And just before we came over here, Aunt Marjory, you saw a Celtic woman, Bryanna!" exclaimed Gerry.

Dan was shifting uncomfortably in his chair. "I don't doubt that your experience was very real to you, J.J., but time travel, alternate timelines? It sounds right out in left field."

J.J. did know how Dan felt. Even after what he'd seen, it was still hard to accept.

"There may be a way of determining the truth of the matter," said Marjory. "I think we have to go to the mission and find that box."

Everyone nodded in agreement while Caleb said, "I agree. You'll all enjoy the ride out there—the scenery is really spectacular— so be ready to leave tomorrow morning at ten o'clock."

The others nodded in agreement and then filed out of the library.

CHAPTER 14

Susanna Morgan   Near London, May 1, 1649

A soft May breeze was bending the heads of the roses and ruffling her hair as Susanna sat in the small garden at the back of Paul's house. In the months she had lived here, life had flowed in quiet, even channels, its small pleasures, like sitting in this rose garden, soothing, thought Susanna as she surveyed the herb and vegetable garden.

Her heart lifted with excitement when she thought of her forthcoming marriage with Paul. She had begged him to wait until he had found news of Jeremy, whom she wanted to attend their wedding, or, if that was not possible, to at least find out where he was and if he was safe.

Paul's good friend, Mr. Carvajal, whose ships regularly plied the trade route to the New World, had promised to help find her brother. As she rubbed her belly, she hoped Jeremy would be found soon. Her feelings for Paul had grown so strong that she had given herself to him. It was right after they had heard of the execution of the king on January 30, 1649. She had fallen into a depression, during which Paul's loving attentions toward her had made her fall even more in love with him.

She remembered that evening as they had sat beside a dying fire, their hands touching, his smile, and his deep voice saying good night, all culminating in her returning his chaste kiss on her cheek with a kiss that was neither proper nor chaste. But she had never regretted it, although she could not entirely dismiss an underlying unease that sometimes disturbed her sleep.

She heard the crunching of gravel at the front of the house as a coach came to a stop. It must be Paul returning. She would tell him now, this very night, about the babe growing in her belly, that she wanted to marry him very soon, whether or not Jeremy was found.

A few minutes later Mrs. Zeman, who had become more of a friend than a servant, came running in. "Susanna, come quickly! The master has met with an accident!"

"How?"

"He was knocked down in a street by a runaway hackney."

Without waiting to hear more, Susanna ran into the hall and found two men carrying an unconscious Paul. She directed them into Paul's bedroom. After they had laid him on the four-poster bed, she dismissed them with a coin each.

"Call a physician," she ordered the housekeeper.

"I have done so already," said the woman quietly. She then left.

Susanna turned to Paul. He lay with his eyes closed, his left leg at an awkward angle.

"Paul, speak to me."

He looked so peaceful lying there. She bent down and kissed him. He did not stir. She put a hand to his nostrils. No breath. His chest was still.

An overpowering numbness overtook her. She fell into a chair. Sometime later a physician came and confirmed the worst: Paul was dead. Now he would never know about the baby. Now they would never marry. After they led her away to her bedroom, she lay down, her grief so deep that she could not even weep. Mrs. Zeman came in, offering a posset, but Susanna turned away. There was no comfort anywhere.

How long it was she did not know before she arose. The household was quiet. Paul was well out of the world's troubles, she thought bitterly, but as an unmarried mother she would be a target for the malicious. She must get away from this place—and soon—before her condition became obvious to all.

Going to Paul's desk then, she pressed a spring that opened the secret compartment, which he had directed her to open in the event of his death. She drew out a letter addressed to her and dated a fortnight after she had agreed to live with him.

My Dearest Susanna, You are perusing this letter because I have died. I hope that we have had many happy years together. Know that your presence has made me the happiest of men. Do not grieve overlong for me, but go abroad as soon as may be possible, for as you are a Catholic and living in the household of a Jew, there are those who may wish to do you harm.

Tears blurred her vision. Angrily she wiped them away. She had no time to grieve. She had to plan how she was going to survive, she and the babe growing in her belly. She could depend only on herself. It was her good fortune that the money Paul had left her would make her a rich woman.

She spent hours that night wrapping each coin and sewing it into her petticoat. It was early morning when Mrs. Zeman ushered in Antonio Carvajal.

"My dear Susanna," he said, wrapping her hands in his two big ones. "I hope you will pardon my intrusion on your mourning. I wanted to let you know that I will help you in any way possible."

"I thank you for your kindness, sir. Please come into the parlor."

As they sat down next to the cold hearth, Mr. Carvajal asked, "It may be too early to inquire, but have you thought about what you might do?"

Susanna shivered. "I must get away from here. My brother, have you found him?"

"My agents tell me that they tracked him as far as the West Indies."

"I would go find him. He is my only living relative."

"The voyage would be a long and arduous one—especially for one in your condition—taking at least six weeks."

Startled, Susanna asked, "How do you know about my 'condition'?"

"When Mrs. Zeman came to me last night and gave me the news about Paul, she expressed her opinion that you were pregnant. She is very concerned about you."

That explained the knowing looks the housekeeper had been giving her lately.

"Jeremy is the only one left of my family. I would brave anything to see him again," said Susanna in a low voice.

"Then if that is truly your resolve, I will arrange passage for you on one of my ships." He paused and, looking keenly at her, asked, "Have you given thought as to what you might do when you reach the colonies?"

Susanna shook her head.

"I have a plan," said Carvajal. "I have a good, stout house in Salem where my agent lived until a month ago when he died. You could live there if you would consider taking over his job. Mrs. Zeman has given a good report of you. She says that you have an uncommon facility with accounts and a level head. I have need of both. I would, of course, pay you a fair amount for your services. What say you?"

"Your plan has merit," said Susanna slowly. "I should not wish to stay in England, not when Cromwell is so fierce against Catholics."

"You have nothing to fear from that quarter."

"Why not, sir? My father and aunt were both seized by the Roundheads and thrown into the Fleet, where they died. Why should I not suffer the same fate?"

"I do have some influence with Parliament."

Susanna looked at Carvajal in astonishment. "Of what nature is this influence?"

Carvajal shrugged his shoulders. "I have done some small favors for Cromwell."

"But I understood you to be a Catholic?"

Carvajal gave her a wry smile as he said, "We Jews survive by doing what we must—as did Paul."

"He would never . . ."

"Why do you think that Parliament gave me, as well as four other London merchants, the army contract for corn? Was it not because I had increased trade with Spain by bringing cochineals, dyes for cloth, from the Canary Islands where I once lived? My ships trade as far as the East and West Indies, Brazil, and Syria. Cromwell may suspect I am a Jew, but he dislikes Papists more and doesn't mind profiting from the taxes I pay on my profits—and the information I bring him about what is happening in various parts of the world. Knowledge is power, Susanna. Cromwell knows that and is prepared to deal with anyone who can supply that knowledge."

"And Paul, too, worked for Cromwell?"

"He worked for himself and occasionally brought me information. Don't let this distress you, Susanna. Paul did what was necessary to survive, and in the process made a small fortune."

Her mind reeled. She had loved Paul, thought him so upright a man, loved him for his kind heart and his good works, and all the time he had worked for that wretch who had killed her father and aunt and ousted Jeremy and her from their home. But she dared not tell any of this to Carvajal, who was coolly assessing her, trying to divine her thoughts. She could dissemble also.

"I had not known of these things, sir."

"I should not have expected you to. Come, Susanna. I need an agent and you need a place to live. Obviously, you cannot stay here. In Paul's will, which I witnessed before you appeared, this house is to become an orphanage. But if you are willing, one of my ships will take you and your housekeeper to Salem on the coast of New England. I have already spoken to Mrs. Zeman about this. She would be willing to accompany you."

Susanna's nails dug into her palms. So once again others were deciding her fate. But this would be the very last time. "Very well, sir. I will go."

"Ah, good, Susanna. You will find Salem quite different from here, but I see a brilliant future for the colonies. An abundance of wood, fish, and other resources are to be had over there."

"I should like to discuss the terms of my contract with you, the kind of goods you export and import, and the exact nature of the duties that I am expected to perform."

The merchant looked at her with respect. "I shall be most happy to oblige you. Paul said that you were a woman of good sense. Let us begin."

After they had finished their discussion and Mrs. Zeman had ushered out Mr. Carvajal, she returned to the parlor, where Susanna was pacing the floor.

"Susanna, I hope you do not mind my accompanying you to Salem."

"You are determined to do this? Mr. Carvajal has told me that the voyage will be arduous. If it will be so for me, how much more arduous would it be for one of your age?"

In a voice that was softer than usual, the housekeeper said, "I have been through events much more *arduous* than that."

"I would not uproot you from your home."

"Jews have no home, except with the people they care for."

"I have no home to offer you," said Susanna bitterly.

"Mr. Carvajal has provided you with one—if you will but accept it."

"I have told him that I will take it, and the position as his agent."

"A wise decision, Susanna."

"Since I have no family or home, it is the only course left to me."

"It is a difficult thing to bear, I know, but does not your Christian religion tell you that it is by trials and tribulations that one is strengthened?"

Susanna rounded on the housekeeper. "What care I for that, or for a God who allows such things to happen? The man I loved is dead. Sometimes I wish I were, too!"

"It is men, not God, who are responsible for the ills of the world," said Mrs. Zeman tartly. "Put aside thoughts of death and live for the sake of the babe growing in your belly. You will get through this, Susanna, and I will help you."

"Very well. I am pleased that you are coming with me, but I had to be sure of your determination to do so."

The next few days passed in a whirl of activity. Mrs. Zeman looked after the arrangements for Paul's funeral and packing for the voyage.

On the day of their departure, Susanna did not look back as the coach drove away from Paul's house. What might have been was of no concern to her now, only survival. With difficulty, for the gold she had sewn into her petticoat was no mean weight, she walked onto the ship. Six and a half weeks later, she found herself in New England.

It was a simple matter to pass herself off as the widow of a merchant, a Charles Morgan. And now here she was, her own mistress, living in the small town of Salem, where her neighbors were friendly but respected her need for privacy. In turn, even though she was done with religion, she respected the Puritan dedication to work and the stern philosophy that had impelled them to leave comfortable homes for the hardships of the wilderness. In this place, exposure to common dangers and hardships bestowed equality on them all. Here she would build a new life.

Carvajal's house, although much smaller than Paul's, was adequate. Someday, Susanna vowed, she would own her own house and land. By good fortune, the law decreed that widows might own their own property. For instance, Margaret Hardenbroeck had taken over her late husband's shipping business in New Amsterdam and become quite rich. Another independent woman, Anne Bradstreet, was an author who had written verse and was widely known as America's first female writer.

In Salem, no one would dare question her right to act as agent for so important a merchant as Antonio Carvajal. In time, she would own her own business and run things her way.

CHAPTER 15

Dan Morgan   South of San Francisco
                              on the coastal highway, June 21, 1992

They'd been driving south for almost half an hour, and Gerry had said nothing. Earlier that morning at five minutes to 10 A.M. everyone—except Gerry—had been seated in the limo, while Caleb had been looking at his watch and muttering to himself. Two minutes later, Gerry had arrived. Cummings was right there to hand her into the only seat remaining—beside Dan.

"Sorry to keep you waiting," she'd said.

"Just on time, young lady," Caleb had said gallantly. "We can leave now, Cummings," he'd said to his servant, who had started the engine and driven out into the heavy San Francisco traffic.

Without looking at anyone, Gerry had taken her sunglasses out of her purse and put them on.

The steady stream of traffic didn't stop some drivers from taking chances in passing them on the two-lane Highway 1 as they headed south. With the Pacific Ocean thundering against the rocky cliffs on their right, where twisted pines clung precariously, and the hilly country to their left, there was no room for mistakes.

Marjory smoothed down her navy print dress and said, "Last night Jeremy said that we would go back in time into our *previous* bodies to rectify certain situations. It sounds very much like reincarnation. You edited a book about this, didn't you, Geraldine?"

Gerry nodded but said nothing.

Dan stole a quick look at her and said, "Gerry and I talked about this yesterday. She mentioned that people often reincarnate with others that they've known before."

"Do people have to be related to each other?" asked J.J.

"Not necessarily," said Gerry slowly, taking off her sunglasses.

Her eyes looked tired, and there were purple shadows underneath them.

I've fallen in love with her and she's my cousin, thought Dan. What do I do now?

"I was wondering," said Marjory, "if Nicholas is supposed to be included in this task that Jeremy wants us to take on."

"You mean the one where we save the world, our world?" asked Laney.

That was his girl, always the diplomat, trying to smooth over situations.

"It would be my pleasure to help," said Nicholas with a smile. "I guess we'll find out today. This is the twenty-first of June, when, according to Jeremy, the window for cementing this present timeline in place will close."

"I don't get this reincarnation thing," said Laney, wrinkling her forehead. "I mean, how do we know it's true?"

"I remember reading about the famous American actor named Glen Ford," said Marjory. "When he was hypnotized in 1975, he recalled a past life at Versailles at the court of Louis the Fourteenth as a cavalry officer named Launvaux. He was killed in a duel over a woman. Strangely enough, Mr. Ford now has a birthmark below his breastbone, the very same place where he was killed by the thrust of a sword. And the amazing thing is that during his regression he spoke flawless seventeenth-century French, a language unknown to him.

"After being regressed to another past life when he was a music teacher in eighteenth-century Scotland, he could play the music of composers like Mozart and Beethoven. In this lifetime, Mr. Ford cannot play a note of music."

Nicholas straightened his bow tie and said, "I'm speculating here, but it strikes me that at least some of you Morgans, like Jason, seem to have unusual abilities. As Marjory has implied, you might have developed these in previous lifetimes. This might indicate why you have been asked to take on this task."

"How perceptive of you, Nicholas. You could be right," said Marjory looking around at the others.

"I don't," said Laney, "have a special ability, I mean."

"Not true," said Dan. "You pick up right away on other people's feelings, and even those of animals."

"And Aunt Marjory has the Sight. She saw this woman, Bryanna, from Celtic Britain," said Gerry.

Marjory smiled at Gerry and said, "Gerry has been having particularly vivid dreams about Susanna, whom Jeremy mentioned in his memoir."

"What about you, Dan?" challenged Caleb, who had been listening intently.

"I get hunches, mainly."

"Hunches?" asked Caleb, his eyes boring into Dan's.

"Yeah." Like the feeling that the driver of a certain Chevy van, which had been following them for some time, might be planning something bad for their health. But he didn't want to mention anything that might disturb the rest of them.

"One of my buddies in the Marines mentioned a rumor going around that after hearing that the Soviets were using psychics to steal information from the U.S., the CIA had recruited some guys from the military for a special program. After being trained, the 'remote viewers,' as they were called, would be given certain co-ordinates and asked to draw pictures of what they saw. But this is all classified stuff, so you won't be able to find out anything yet." Dan looked straight at Caleb and added, "We know that you have been having visions."

Caleb turned beet red. His left foot began tapping on the floor of the car. Laney looked with concern at him but said nothing. Obviously Caleb wasn't happy about being reminded of his ability.

"It looks as though I'm the odd man out," said Nicholas in a light tone that held an undercurrent of anxiety.

"Perhaps you have another purpose in being here," said Marjory, who was sitting beside him.

Nicholas turned sideways in his seat and looked inquiringly at her.

"Maybe, for some reason, your presence is needed. Perhaps at some point in the past you were with some of us and have to go back to a turning point."

No one spoke, seemingly mulling over what Marjory had said. Dan looked at his new watch again. Laney had insisted on giving it to him as an early birthday present. Found it on sale, she'd said. Even so, how many kids would buy such an expensive present for their dads? But Laney had always been a generous person. What had he done to deserve a great kid like that?

Now Cummings was turning left onto a side road, which a sign said led to the San Juan Mission. Farmhouses and clumps of trees dotted the rounded hills. In the distance near some buildings clustered around a church with a bell tower, grapevines marched up the hill.

Shortly after, Cummings brought their car, the only vehicle there, to a stop in a car park. It felt good to get out of the car and stretch his legs.

Laney climbed out of the car and turned her face to the sun. "Um, that feels great," she said. "It's a lot warmer here than in San Francisco."

"It gets warmer as you go inland," said Caleb, loosening his tie and striding over to a monk working in the flower bed that ran along the front of the quadrangle with its roof and large arches shading a walkway.

Gerry stepped gracefully out of the Lincoln, then stopped a little distance from the others and began digging into her purse.

Dan drew alongside of her and asked, "You had a bad night? Sorry," he said quickly. "That didn't come out right. I mean, I notice things."

Gerry took a deep breath and said, "I had some more dreams about Susanna. I think I might have been her."

"Well, if reincarnation is a fact, we all had to be somebody," joked Dan.

"If you put it that way. The thing is, I might have met you there."

Her look—part longing and part something he couldn't quite define—made him involuntarily move close to her. This time she didn't pull away.

In a low voice he asked, "How did we know each other?"

In the distance he could hear Caleb talking to the elderly monk.

Gerry heard them, too. "We should go," she said, shutting her purse and walking away to the others clustered around Caleb and the monk.

"Visiting hours haven't started yet," said the elderly monk, hauling his short, compact frame up with some difficulty.

"I'm here on business. It's important that I see the abbot right away."

Caleb obviously didn't care whose feathers he ruffled. The monk seemed to take it in stride, though. His weathered face showing no reaction to Caleb's imperiousness, he said, "I'll go talk to Brother Jude, who handles our business affairs. In the meantime, won't you all please come inside and sit down."

He led them into a dim, cool room with a flagstone floor and walls hung with religious paintings. A simple rectangular wooden table stood in the center of the room. A hanging lamp gave out just enough illumination to see. Nicholas and all the Morgans except Caleb, who was pacing back and forth, sat down on the wooden benches arranged around the room.

"Kind of bare, isn't it?" said Laney as she looked around.

"Yes, just the essentials," agreed Gerry. She looked very appealing in a yellow sundress covering just enough of her to be ladylike and revealing enough to encourage sexy ideas.

They hadn't waited more than a few minutes when a very tall man walked into the room. His dark robe hung loosely on his skeletal frame, and his sandals were a little too small for his large feet.

"Good morning. I'm Brother Jude. The abbot is very busy right now. If you would tell me who you are and what you want, I'll do what I can to help you."

"I am Caleb Morgan, and these are my relatives. I must talk to the man in charge," said Caleb, drawing himself up to his full height.

"You will have to tell me first. Then I will decide whether or not it is a matter for the abbot's consideration," Brother Jude said.

Dan could tell by the way Caleb was chewing his bottom lip that he could hardly contain his frustration, but he was smart enough to realize that leaning on this guy wouldn't work.

"It's a private matter," said Caleb. "And urgent, very urgent. I must see him now."

"And does this matter concern all of you?"

Turning a little red, Caleb replied, "What if it does?"

Getting up from the bench where she had been sitting beside Gerry, Marjory walked over to the monk and said, "The abbot, we believe, has been entrusted with something that belongs to us. Some of us have come from long distances just to talk to him about this. We won't take much of his time, but, as Caleb said, the matter is one of great importance."

"Very well," said Brother Jude, his gaze flickering over his visitors. "I'll see what I can do."

His sandals slapping firmly against the floor, he left. After returning a few minutes later, he led them down a bare hallway with whitewashed walls into a room that wouldn't have been out of place in any office building. The abbot was working at the latest IBM computer model sitting on an oak desk in front of him.

He stood up and said, "I'm Father Lawrence. I understand from Brother Jude here that you are the Morgan family, who have come to retrieve a box left here by your ancestor, Jeremy Morgan."

As the abbot spoke, Dan looked him over carefully. Father Lawrence's robe only partially concealed a build that would have been a football coach's delight.

"May I ask how you learned of this box?"

"From a memoir written by a family member," said Marjory.

"I'm sure that must be very interesting," said the abbot politely. "A lot of people these days are investigating their family trees. However, I'm sorry to tell you that I know nothing of any box."

He was about to dismiss them when J.J. burst out, "Could it be in a cellar maybe, where everyone's forgotten about it?"

The abbot's face creased into a smile as he said, "We have no cellars here."

"It's really important, Father Lawrence, that we find this box."

"Yes, I'm sure it is, but I really don't see how I can help you. However, if you'd like to take a tour of our mission, Brother Martin would be happy to show you around."

"Thank you. You've been most helpful," said Marjory.

Brother Jude showed them out and took them back to the reception room where they'd waited earlier. "Brother Martin will meet you here very soon," he said and left the room.

"Silly idea to come here in the first place," muttered Caleb to Marjory.

"Welcome to our mission. I am Brother Martin," said a monk coming into the room a few minutes later. A regular Friar Tuck with a round cherubic face and a body to match, he was everybody's idea of what a monk might look like.

Leading them at a brisk pace over to a modern-looking building, Brother Martin said, "We run a small winery here. Thanks to some generous donors, we have all the latest equipment, which you will see shortly."

An hour later they had been shown, in more detail than Dan had ever wanted to know, exactly how the wine was produced. They had gaped at 15-foot-high redwood casks banded with metal in which wine was aged for a year before being put into oak barrels, and then toured the bottling room where automated equipment filled the bottles with wine.

"Dad, shouldn't we ask about the box?" whispered Laney, looking with concern at a quiet and withdrawn J.J.

"Why, Laney? What makes you think there really is a box?"

Too late, he realized he should have kept his thoughts to himself.

"Do you think J.J. was making it all up, lying to us?" she asked in a fierce whisper.

"No, but . . ."

Throwing a disgusted look at her father, Laney flounced away from him and over to the monk. Her voice was clear and carrying as she said, "Brother Martin, I expect there isn't anyone else here at the mission who knows this place the way you do."

"That's probably true," said the monk, smiling at Laney. "I've been over every inch of this place at one time or another."

"Then you might have seen an old box that was left here for us Morgans by a Morgan. It's awfully important we find it."

Under the combined stares of the eight of them, Brother Martin flinched, then asked guardedly, "What's so important about this object?"

"I'd like to see this infernal box now!" bellowed Caleb.

Offended, the monk drew himself up straight and was opening his mouth to reply when J.J. sent him a look of mute appeal and Laney cried, "Please!"

"I don't know if it's what you're looking for," said Brother Martin in a reflective tone of voice, "but there is a rather interesting box I came across some months ago. Come with me."

He led them into a small room where old ledgers were stacked neatly on shelves going from floor to ceiling.

"Our mission was founded by Father Francis, who received a dream that told him to go north and found a mission. This was in the seventeenth century, long before any other missions in California were founded. Some of these records go back that far." Reaching under the lowest shelf, Brother Martin brought out a small wooden box, hinged with brass clasps discolored with age. "Is this what you're looking for?" he asked.

Caleb took the box and opened it. Nothing in it but a yellowed lining that might have been cotton.

"Did you find anything in the box?" asked Caleb.

Brother Martin shrugged. "Nothing but a bottle of brandy."

"What happened to it?"

"The bottle was empty, so I threw it away."

Dan could see the disappointment in his relatives' faces as they looked at each other. After the big buildup they'd been given, it was a real letdown to discover that there was nothing to it.

Cummings, who had been trailing behind their party, glided up to Caleb and murmured, "You might, sir, like to take the box with you."

"What's the point?"

"A souvenir, perhaps?"

Caleb grunted something incomprehensible. He was being made to look foolish, and he didn't like it one little bit.

A look passed between Cummings and Brother Martin. Then the monk said, "You might as well take it," and handed the box to Cummings.

"Let's get out of here," said Caleb.

At that moment they heard the clatter of sandals. Brother Jude swooped into the room like a windjammer under full sail and said, "Brother Martin, the abbot would like to see you. He has some instructions for you."

Turning to the Morgans, he asked, "I trust you enjoyed the tour?"

"Oh, yes. Wonderful," said Marjory. "Your winery is as well run and efficient as wineries I've visited in Provence and Tuscany."

Looking gratified, Brother Jude inclined his head graciously toward her and said, "You must stop at our tasting room, but I'm afraid the younger ones of your party will not be allowed to sample the wines."

"Oh, that's okay," said J.J. quickly.

Brother Jude led them to another room made attractive by a stained glass window and some kind of ivy sitting on a ledge. "I'll leave you here with Brother Matthew," he said, nodding at a pleasant-faced young man, who looked hardly old enough to drive and was standing behind a counter made of rough stones for a base and a polished stone top.

"Ladies and gentlemen, would you care to try a chardonnay first?" the young monk asked.

When they nodded, he took down some wineglasses that had been hanging upside down from a rack suspended from the ceiling.

"Ah, very good," said Caleb approvingly after taking a sip. "Aromatic with a kind of lemony, citrus quality and a very long finish."

"Quite so, sir," said Brother Matthew, looking at Caleb with respect.

"Perhaps, Mr. Stevens, since you're in the antique business, you might find this article of some interest," murmured Cummings, gesturing to the box he'd placed on the counter.

"Why, yes, thank you."

Taking the box and examining it carefully, Nicholas said, "Probably of seventeenth-century manufacture."

"Are you picking up impressions from it?" asked J.J.

There was a twinkle in Nicholas's eyes as he said, "Why, I suppose I am."

"So you have an ability, too!"

Caleb, who had been listening, asked, "Is the box valuable?"

"Not particularly. The workmanship is rather crude. Wait a minute. What's this?" All the time Nicholas had been talking, his long white fingers had been exploring the box.

"Something seems to have been tucked behind the lining. See how it appears to be padded on one side only. Do you mind if I tear the lining?" Nicholas asked, looking at Caleb.

"Take the whole damn thing apart, if you like. It's no use to us."

Dan heard a collective indrawn breath from the other Morgans as Nicholas ripped open the lining and what was behind it fell into the box.

CHAPTER 16

Laney Morgan Restaurant near San Juan Mission,
June 21, 1992

"I'd like the fricassee of sweetbreads with lentils in a sherry wine vinegar sauce," said Caleb, speaking to the waiter as he pointed to his menu.

Not for her. She'd settle for a regular hamburger and fries. The restaurant was a pretty nice place. She liked the Spanish theme with paintings of senoritas in their flouncy dresses kicking up their heels in a flamenco dance. She almost expected to see a guitar player in a big sombrero come strolling through one of the arches.

They waited until the waiter had gone to the kitchen with their orders before they started speculating about what Nicholas had found.

"As a former librarian, this is more your department than mine," said Nicholas, handing a piece of paper to Marjory.

"Possibly," she said, putting on her reading glasses and smoothing out the yellowed paper.

"What does it say?" asked Laney.

Marjory didn't need any further prodding. "The letter is dated 1683 and begins, 'My dear kinsmen, As Providence would have it, I have been led, along with Father Francis, to this rustic and secluded spot where I am about to die.'"

"Skip all that folderol," said Caleb, "and give us the gist of it."

"Jeremy writes that he worked at the mission for some years. When he knew that he was dying from a wasting disease, he gave the monks a box containing a bottle of brandy and the instructions you are now reading.

"'I am spending these last years of my life in contemplation of the sacred mysteries as did the ancient Hermetic philosophers, who knew that it was by accessing inner wisdom that one could discover the hidden laws governing the universe.

"'And it was given to me to know that within certain cycles of time there exist windows of opportunity wherein the informed individual may travel to times in which the course of history may be altered.

"'Now there are those who would try to alter world histories for their own ends, disregarding the good of humanity as a whole. It is to stop those who would limit the choices of the many in order to favor a few that I would enlist you, my dear kinsmen, in this great project.'"

Her dad was rolling his eyes. This mystical stuff was beginning to get to him, but she could sense that he was impressed by the fact that they had actually found a letter written by Jeremy.

"But, Marjory, what does Jeremy want us to do?" asked Caleb in a kind of frenzy.

"He says that he made a decoction with herbs given to him by an Indian shaman. The lining of the box was steeped in this decoction, and then used to line the box. Each of us needs to cut out a piece of the lining about the size of our thumb—this will ensure that we ingest the right amount—and then put it on our tongue. The herbs impregnated in the piece will dissolve and enhance our natural abilities. At the same time, we must hold in our minds the intention to go back to the time where we will be most useful."

"You mean, we're going to take over other people's bodies, possess them?" asked Laney.

"It's our own bodies—the ones we used to have—I think," said Gerry.

"Laney, you can't be serious about going!"

That was her dad, still trying to protect her. "Who says I'm not?"

Interrupting her, Mr. Stevens said, "I'd like to be part of this venture."

"Why?" Caleb asked.

Mr. Stevens drew a deep breath and turned a little pale, but his voice was steady as he said, "My name isn't really Stevens; it's Holtz. I had the misfortune to grow up in Germany during the Second World War. I was a boy of sixteen when I was marched off to fight for the glory of *Die Fuehrer*. The things I experienced . . ." He shuddered and went on, "I wouldn't want anyone to go through it. I lost everyone I loved. My home in Dresden was reduced to a pile of rubble."

"Firebombed," murmured Marjory.

"Quite so. And that's why I insist upon being part of your group. If I can do anything, anything at all to prevent the Nazis in another time frame from winning the war and enslaving Europe, then I will do it."

Marjory said nothing, but laid a hand on Nicholas's arm and looked at him with a concerned expression.

"You're welcome to join us, Nicholas," said Caleb.

Just then the waiter returned with their orders. It wasn't until everyone had mostly finished eating that Marjory took out Jeremy's letter from her purse. "It seems that we're to go to the garden at the back of the mission. What he calls the 'window,' a kind of portal I gather, is located in the garden."

"And what do we do once we get there?" asked Dan, putting down his fork.

"Follow the instructions I just read to you."

"How long is this window open?"

"Apparently for one day, June 21."

"Which makes it today. But what do we do when we get to the past—if we do get there?"

No one had an answer for that. Would they all die if they couldn't do what Jeremy wanted them to do?

"Seems to me," said Caleb, "that Dan's right. There's an awful lot of information we don't have. But all we can do is to follow instructions and wait for Jeremy to pull the strings."

The others nodded their heads in agreement.

"That's settled then," said Caleb.

Laney noticed that, except for her, everyone had finished eating, while she was still picking at her fries.

"What's the matter, honey?" her dad whispered.

"Nothing."

"Must be something."

"Supposing something happens, Daddy, and we don't see each other again?"

Her father's concern tore at her as he tried to comfort her by saying, "Don't you worry, sweetheart. I'll come back."

"*We* will," she corrected. "If I'm old enough to fight and die for my country, I'm old enough to go with the rest of you, too."

"Laney, if this time travel thing does happen, my mind would rest a whole lot easier if I knew you were okay. Now please go along with me on this."

"Dad, I'm not ten years old anymore. You do what you want— I'm going."

He didn't like that, but she knew she was right. She wasn't a kid anymore. Up to now she had been absorbed in her own problems. Now she was ready to take on something way more important. In the past, girls her age had ruled empires. She could do what had to be done, too.

"Okay, Laney. I can't stop you, but remember: you've got a whole lot of living to do yet."

She looked at him with tears in her eyes. "So do you, Dad. So do you."

"Just 'cause I'm down sometimes, honey, doesn't mean I want to die. But I've had a lot on my mind."

Like being fired and her mother divorcing him. She felt how miserable he'd been. Mom had tried to convince her that the divorce was Dad's fault, but lately she'd been seeing a new side of her mother, how manipulative and feeling sorry for herself she was. And, yet, her mother was hurting, too. Maybe both of them were doing the best they could. But it wasn't up to her to fix their relationship—even if it could be fixed. All she could do was keep on loving them both.

Marjory was wiping her mouth with her napkin and saying, "I would be happy to cut a piece of the lining for each of us, Caleb."

"As you wish, Marjory."

Marjory took out a small pair of scissors from her purse. Nicholas silently handed her the box.

"Now let me see. Show me your thumbs," she said lightly. The tension eased as J.J. snickered while the others laughed.

When Marjory had finished giving out the thumb-size pieces of cloth to everyone, Caleb got up and laid some big bills on the small tray that the waiter had left.

Her dad seemed lost in thought.

"Let's go, Dad."

He stood up, pulled her gently to him, and held her for a long moment.

"Dad, people are staring."

"I don't care. They're probably jealous because they don't have such a beautiful daughter. I love you, Laney, and I plan on coming back and sticking around for a long time. After all, your kids will need a grandpa to teach them how to play football."

She brushed her hair over her shoulders as she said, "And I suppose I can expect you to tell me how to raise them."

"Absolutely."

They walked out into the brilliant sunshine glinting blindingly off the tiles of the restaurant's roof and the white stucco of its walls, over to the Lincoln in which the others were waiting.

CHAPTER 17

Dan Morgan   San Juan Mission garden, June 21, 1992

"What a pretty place!" exclaimed Laney.

Dan could see her point. Beds of roses ranging in color from red to pale yellow and the luxuriant foliage of bushes and trees encircled a small lawn.

A man with his back turned to them was loitering by a bush with bird-of-paradise blooms on it. Now he was fishing under his coat for something . . .

Catching his breath, Dan catapulted himself at the man. They fell to the ground. Then they were both clawing and jabbing, each trying to get the advantage. But although the guy was shorter than he was by a good three inches, he was wiry and hard-muscled—and drawing a gun.

Dan seized the gunman's wrist. Using reflexes he thought he'd forgotten, he brought the side of his other hand down hard on his assailant's neck. One last grunt and the man went limp.

There was a shocked silence. Caleb let rip a few choice expletives.

Dan got up. The whole fight—unlike Hollywood movies where the fight scenes went on forever—had only taken a minute or two. He felt sore all over, as though he'd been wrestling with a bear, and his head hurt where a lucky punch had landed.

Was the killing starting again? He picked up the guy's gun and on impulse checked his pulse. A little fast, maybe, but he'd live. Relief washed through Dan.

"How did you know he was going to shoot us?" asked J.J.

"I didn't, but I thought it was funny he was wearing that trench coat when it's so warm out."

Pointing shakily to the gun, J.J. asked in a tone laced with disbelief, "He was going to kill us all with that thing?"

"You better believe it! That's a thirty-two-caliber Czech-made submachine gun."

"It's not that big."

"But lethal. They don't call it the Skorpion for nothing. Put it on automatic, and you can let off 150 rounds per minute. Even on semiautomatic it'll fire sixty-five rounds per minute, enough to take us all out fast. These babies are real popular now in places like Africa, Europe, and South America."

There was a grudging respect in Caleb's eyes as he said, "You seem to be making a habit of rescuing us. It's fortunate for us all that you were so alert." Then, pointing to two wooden benches, he said, "Let's sit down over there and talk this thing over."

"Shouldn't we call the cops?" asked Laney in a worried tone of voice.

"I'll do that," said Cummings, who had been standing discreetly to one side of the benches. "But at the moment," he said, "I don't think our attacker is going anywhere. Until you return, I'll stand guard here,"

When they'd sat down, Nicholas asked, "Do you suppose that these attacks were meant to stop us from taking advantage of this 'window' that Jeremy talked about?"

"But how could anyone have known about all this? We only found out the other day," objected Gerry, who had sat down beside him. His heart constricted as he thought what might have happened to her if the gunman had successfully carried out his intent to kill them. She gave him a small smile and didn't pull away when he took her hand.

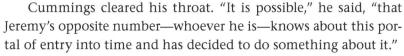

Cummings cleared his throat. "It is possible," he said, "that Jeremy's opposite number—whoever he is—knows about this portal of entry into time and has decided to do something about it."

"Like making sure we don't use it," said Dan.

Cummings nodded.

They were all silent for a moment as the implications of that registered. None of them looked too happy, and no wonder—they'd expected a mild sort of adventure and here it had turned definitely nasty.

Suddenly Caleb roused himself and said, "Well, let's get on with it. Are you all with me?" he challenged, his bushy eyebrows drawn together in a frown that made him look like a pirate.

With a bleak look, Marjory said, "It seems we have no choice. More than ever, it appears necessary to follow Jeremy's instructions."

After taking his thumb-size piece of the herb-soaked cotton out of his pocket, Caleb put it into his mouth.

Dan still had doubts about going back in time, but the two attacks on them were rapidly convincing him that someone was taking this whole thing very seriously. That probably meant that he should, too.

Their assailant wasn't moving, he noted. He looked at Cummings, a good guy to have their backs, who was standing guard with the assailant's gun. He nodded gravely. Reassured, Dan popped his piece into his mouth. The herbs in the cotton tasted slightly bitter, but not unpleasantly so.

Marjory put her piece on her tongue without showing any visible reaction except for a certain tightening of her lips afterward. Nicholas followed suit with a gusto that surprised Dan. Revealing his past must have been a real relief. Now it was J.J.'s turn. The boy's hand trembled, whether from nerves or excitement it was hard to say, but he, too, put his piece onto his tongue and clamped his mouth shut, while Laney closed her eyes and did the same. Gerry gave him a small smile before putting her herb-soaked piece into her mouth.

Then the light began to fade, the red, fuzzy-looking blooms of the bottlebrush tree and the vivid tints of flowers and the grass gradually losing all their color until they looked like one of those sepia-toned, 19th-century photos.

Everything was losing its substance, becoming two-dimensional: Laney, the trees, everything becoming only an outline in a landscape rapidly blurring and dissolving into nothingness. Was this what it was like to die?

Out of the void came a force that pulled him with such intensity that he felt turned inside out.

Then all sensation passed, as wrapped in a dreamlike state he passed into a strange country. He could see in the distance a massive hill upon which stood several large structures. At the base of the hill grazed cattle, small, rangy-looking creatures, compared with the hormone-filled and force-fed animals modern American industry had produced.

"Dad, we made it!" said Laney, who edged closer to him. Caleb, for once with nothing to say, was there with the others looking around in wonder.

Pointing to some round stone houses with thatched roofs, Marjory, a little catch in her voice, observed, "Surely this can't be New England. From what I've read, the early American settlers lived in frame houses and, later on, brick ones."

"Or log cabins," piped up J.J.

"The Swedes and Germans were the first to build them," said Marjory.

"I wonder if we're even in America," said Nicholas.

At this daunting remark, they all began scanning the horizon anxiously.

Then Dan saw a woman walking toward them with quick, firm steps, a heavy, golden thing around her neck and her hair streaming down the back of her blue robe. Stopping in front of them, she smiled gravely and said, "I am Bryanna, your ancestress, one of those in your lineage. As was common for children in Celtic Britain, I was sent away to a foster home. Tighearnach, the Archdruid, fostered me and taught me much. Eventually, I became a Druid priestess, one qualified to mediate disputes, school the young who would later become Druids, and to carry out religious rituals."

"Druids yet!" Dan barely managed to avoid blurting out. Next, they'd be talking to elves. He prided himself on having as open a mind as the other guy, but this was getting more than a little strange. Had the decoction of herbs that Jeremy had prepared for them been a kind of hallucinogen? He'd smoked grass every now and again, and once had even tried some of the heavy-duty stuff—practically everyone he knew in 'Nam had tried some form of drugs—but this was unlike anything he'd ever tried before. This was so real!

"I saw you once before in Cornwall, near the megalith," murmured Marjory.

A look of understanding passed between the two women. Bryanna nodded and then turned her attention upon the rest of them.

"Like Tighearnach who fostered me, I am part of an ancient tradition that included Hindu priests and the Magi, the priests of Persia. Our belief that souls never die, just take on new bodies, came from an even earlier priesthood who knew the Ancient Ones, those who long ago walked this earth as gods. Our oral tradition tells us that there will come a time when humankind will fall so far out of balance that life for all on this plane will hang by a hair.

"To succeed in your task, you must be prepared to learn the precepts of the One, who bids us live in harmony with all life and to follow our own inner wisdom. This inner guidance will tell you what has to be done. On this, the future of the human race may depend."

A ton of questions sprang to mind, but before he could ask even one of them, a powerful force swept him up.

"Welcome, kinsmen."

The change was so abrupt that for a moment Dan could only gape at the man who had to be Jeremy.

"We really did it!" exclaimed J.J.

"Where are we?" asked Dan.

"In transit to seventeenth-century New England," said Jeremy.

Dan looked around. Then it hit him. "Hey, where is my daughter? And where are the rest of them?"

"Elsewhere and elsewhen."

"Nobody said anything about separating."

Jeremy ignored Dan's interruption and went on. "A number of key points in time require each of you to go to different places and times, into bodies that you once inhabited."

"Yeah, we already talked to Bryanna," said J.J.

"Then you know the extreme importance of your task. Now let us to business. In June 1675, Metacom (or King Philip as the English call him), chief of the Wampanoag tribe, with the help of other Indian tribes, began conducting an all-out war against the colonists of southern New England. Metacom believed that the settlers were trying to dominate the Indians by encroaching on their lands and dealing unfairly with them in the English courts. During the many battles that ensued, the Indians destroyed some twenty-five settlements. If the Wampanoag sachem is not stopped, Count Frontenac from New France to the north will claim the Thirteen Colonies for France. Then there will be no American Revolution and, consequently, no United States of America."

"So what's your big plan? You want us to march up to this dude and tell him, 'You're history, buddy'?"

"Not at all, Dan. My plans do not incorporate murder."

"What can I do?" broke in J.J.

"You will save the life of the man who, more than any other, was responsible for stopping Metacom."

"But I'm no hero!" cried J.J.

CHAPTER 18

Little Running Horse—Jason Kramer Seneca village, south of Lake Ontario, July 10, 1675

As his voice echoed in his ears, a relentless force signaling another time shift propelled him forward. It felt like the day he'd gone swimming in Hawaii, when he'd been picked up by a huge wave and shoved with roller-coaster speed up onto the beach.

With a painful wrench that made his guts feel as if they were being turned inside out, he came gasping out of the void into a noisy confusion of dogs barking, children squealing, and someone chanting. He could smell the smoke of campfires and food cooking. Weights lay on his eyes, and he ached all over.

What really shocked him was the fact that his body felt different, shorter and more compact, the muscles weaker now from . . . from the sickness that had made him take to his bed over a week ago.

What sickness? How?

The questions raged in his mind, the turmoil threatening to pull him under in a whirlpool more dangerous than the one in Lake-of-Many-Waters.

A crazy montage of images raced through his mind: canoes holding paint-daubed warriors slipping through the calm waters of a river; cornfields where women were hoeing; masked men whirling around in a frenzied dance. They tore at the small point of sanity, the essence that was Little Running Horse.

No! No! Jason Kramer!

Panicking, he clawed at his eyelids, tumbling off the weights, small pink stones, and looked into the face of the demon looming over him.

Stifling the shriek that came bubbling up into his throat, he saw that the demonic figure was really a man wearing a black wooden mask, which had a crooked nose, a wide, lopsided mouth, and what looked like corn husks for hair.

Who . . . what was going on?

Reassuring answers came from his host's mind, calming his racing heart and his sudden attack of panicked breathlessness. The mask represented a spirit that could heal disease. The guy wearing it belonged to the False Face Society, an Iroquois healing group.

The Indian continued chanting and shaking a turtle shell rattle, winding up with a loud whoop that sent an involuntary shudder through J.J. Nothing to worry about, just a guy trying to drive away the evil spirits that were making Little Running Horse sick.

Then the Indian laid surprisingly gentle hands upon J.J.'s chest. Something like an electric shock surged through him, running down his spine and spreading instantly to his arms and legs. He fell into a kind of stupor in which he was only half-aware of being rubbed with something gritty and smelling like ashes.

The blackness came again, and then he awoke. Instead of a demon, this time he saw a girl about his own age. Her smile reminded him of Crystal. It felt weird to "remember" his past as Little Running Horse along with his 20th-century memories. Those memories of his host body told him that he was now in a Seneca village with this girl, Teya.

"Are you hungry? Would you like some soup?" she asked, giving him a friendly look.

The thought of food made him react like one of Pavlov's dogs. "Uh, sure."

Hey! How could he understand what she said? Without even thinking about it, he'd talked back to her in her own language. Good thing. It was bad enough being yanked back into the past, but it would have been impossible to do anything useful if he couldn't speak the language.

Teya went over to one of the fires burning on the dirt floor of the building, which was built like a rectangle. It had to be at least 70 feet in length, maybe longer. Enormous bunk beds, each one of which looked big enough for an entire family to sleep on, stood against the walls. He was lying on one of these lower bunks.

Jumbled together on the top bunks lay an odd assortment of things: hatchets, deerskin clothing, muskets, beaded belts—wampum was the name that came into his mind—knives, and a mask like the one that had frightened him earlier. Braided corn, kettles, and pelts of animals hung from the beams.

"Here, try this."

Teya thrust a wooden bowl, steaming with some kind of corn-meal mush, into his hands.

He was absolutely starved. His stomach felt tight as though nothing had been in it for days. The mush was hot and good. While he dug ravenously into it, the girl stood silently watching him.

"You feeling better?"

"Much."

The dizziness and weakness were passing off now.

"The strawberries are ready for picking," said Teya, her eyes full of warmth that J.J. found a little unsettling. "Soon we will be celebrating the Strawberry Festival. Are you well enough to go pick a few berries now?"

He felt a familiar affection for her. Had she been his girl? Images of him and Teya swimming, picking fruit, going to festivals together swarmed though his mind.

"Sounds like fun." It beat lying in bed waiting for more visits from a guy wearing a mask.

Teya reached up to the top bunk and brought down two baskets made of woven splints. "We should go now," she said in a low, urgent voice.

"Where are you going?" A muscular young guy, with a tattoo of an owl on his arm, deerskin breeches, and an impressive necklace of animal teeth, barred their way.

"To the river to pick strawberries," said Teya.

"Don't be long. When you return, I must speak to Little Running Horse."

Nodding, Teya gave J.J. a little push and walked quickly to the bark door. Once outside, the air was fresh and sweet. The girl slowed down, accommodating herself to J.J.'s slower pace.

They were in a regular little town, he saw, with longhouses spaced evenly along dirt streets. Enclosing the village was an enormous palisade of upright logs, tall as telephone poles.

No one stopped them when they slipped out of the village.

"Look how ripe they are! Try some," said Teya as she bent down to pick the berries.

J.J. didn't have to be persuaded. He loved fruit.

Teya laughed as the juice ran down his chin, her eyes crinkling with amusement.

"I didn't really ask you out here to pick strawberries," she said, "but to warn you about Kiontawakon."

She paused expectantly and looked at him.

According to Little Running Horse's memories, Kiontawakon was the tribe's shaman, the guy with the owl tattoo who wanted to talk to him.

"What's he up to?"

"I think he's jealous that we've lain together. He's spreading a rumor that you're a witch. Only a few believe that, but now that you've recovered miraculously, some might believe you are."

"Do you believe it?"

Teya tossed her head, her black braids flying. "Of course, not. I know you, and I care for you, but you must be careful."

"You got any suggestions?"

"You might say you had a dream about Kiontawakon."

"How's that going to help me?"

"If you told people your totem spirit came to you in a dream and said that *Kiontawakon* was the witch . . ."

"Oh, I see."

These people took their dreams—especially sick people's dreams—very seriously. If he said he'd dreamed that Kiontawakon was a witch, the Senecas might kill the shaman. Murder wasn't what he wanted on his conscience! But what if the guy really was trying to kill him?

"I don't know, Teya."

"Think about it, but not too long. In the meantime, let's gather some strawberries."

As he bent down to pick a cluster of berries, he reflected that things were beginning to seem like a bad dream. He had a hunch it was going to get worse.

CHAPTER 19

Kiontawakon — Seneca village, July 10, 1675

Kiontawakon was disturbed by what he had learned from the Stone Person, who spoke through a particular stone, but only to someone, like himself, who could hear. The entity had revealed the history of the world to Seneca shamans before him, how there had been three worlds before this one. The first World of Love had been ended by the jealousy of the yellow race, the second World of Ice by the carelessness and forgetfulness of the brown race, and the third World of Water, by the greed of the white race.

Shifting uneasily on the packed earth of the sweat lodge, he sprinkled tobacco over the dying coals of the fire. As he watched the brown shreds curl into ash, he was reminded of the times he had sat here with his teacher.

If only he could ask the advice now of that wise one who had gone to the gods many moons ago, leaving his student to carry out the rituals and ceremonies for their people.

Even now, in the seasons it had taken him to grow to manhood, the newcomers had worked their destruction among the Wampanoags and other peoples who had taught the English how to plant corn and to live off the land. It would have been far better if these palefaces had never come to the shores of this land.

If they were not stopped, things would grow worse, much worse. But it would take more than war parties of fierce braves, for like the tides of the Great Sea, those spawn of demons would only keep coming.

Kiontawakon ignored the whispers of the Stone Person telling him not to take the Crooked Trail leading to fear and destruction, a trail that would make him lose his connection to the Earth Mother, who taught that all humankind were part of a wholeness.

He had tried to walk the Path of Beauty as he had been instructed, tried to identify with all of humankind, not just with his own race. But he was afraid that doing nothing might lead to the destruction of his own people, the Seneca, Keepers of the Western Door. They were the farthest west of the tribes belonging to the Iroquois League, and the tribe that guarded the western frontier.

If he could not persuade the League to help the Wampanoag chief, Metacom, who was warring against the English, those whites would crush Metacom's forces and destroy the rest of the Indian tribes. He could not accept that, for it was possible that the whites could end this present world—the fourth World of Separation. He would do everything he could, even enlist the help of the dark spirits, to make sure that this would not happen. He would ask for guidance, too, from his totem and guardian spirit, the owl, a messenger of darkness and magic, whose help he now sorely needed.

The sweat rolling off his lean, muscular body, Kiontawakon began slowly rocking back and forth, allowing the rhythm of his body to calm his mind. Chanting softly, he took up his small drum and began thumping out the powerful beats that would send him into a trance, thereby allowing his spirit to slip into the Underworld. There he might enlist the help of the dark forces, who would help him oppose those whose very existence meant slavery and death for his people.

CHAPTER 20

Little Running Horse—Jason Kramer   Seneca village,
July 10, 1675

Kiontawakon had taken him to a secluded place where he had chanted some gibberish and then said, "Oh, Spirit, I command you to speak."

When he'd kept quiet, Kiontawakon, with that air of authority about him that let you know he expected to be obeyed, commanded, "Tell me your name, your real name."

Did that mean that Kiontawakon knew there was something wrong, that there was someone else in the body of Little Running Horse?

"Little Running Horse," J.J. answered.

As the shaman leaned forward, the talons of the Great Horned Owl tattooed on his arm seemed to flex. J.J. felt himself drawn into that place where magic could be worked, the place where Kiontawakon's consciousness went on his shamanic journeys. It was there that the shaman would call on the owl, his power animal, for guidance and help.

The sound of Kiontawakon's voice drew J.J. out of that other place. "Tell me your name, the name of the spirit who talks to you. I will not harm you."

Except tell people he was a witch, and then he really didn't want to think about what might happen to him.

"We must talk, for the good of the tribe, for the good of all the peoples of this land." Kiontawakon's voice deepened as he continued. "The Stone Person has spoken to me through this stone."

That was some stone, big as a man's fist, and made of what looked like the kind of quartz crystals that his mom collected. She had told him that some crystals were "teacher stones" that held the knowledge of the earth and its history and that some people could communicate with them.

"He has told me of your coming."

There was no point in playing dumb anymore. "My name is Jason Kramer."

Kiontawakon nodded with satisfaction. "Before the coming of the white man, we freely roamed these territories, hunting the deer, the beaver, and the bear. The Three Sisters—corn, bean, and squash—yielded up their bounty so that none went hungry. There was much merriment in our longhouses.

"In my vision I saw how the white men will trick us into signing over our ancestral lands to them, keeping the best for themselves. We will die, not the glorious death of great warriors, but as little children struck down by sickness for which our medicine has no cure, diseases brought by those who trouble our land. This is already happening."

He was really laying on a guilt trip. With a great effort, J.J. pulled his gaze away and wriggled uncomfortably on the pile of deerskin rugs in the domed bark enclosure they were sitting in. A thin spiral of smoke was drifting from a small fire burning in front of them. He could smell sweetgrass, familiar to him from the time when he'd gone with Davis to a display of his tribe's native crafts.

J.J. felt sorry for what was going to happen to the Indians— they'd gotten a raw deal, all right—but nothing he said to Kiontawakon was going to make any difference.

"I have had visions," Kiontawakon continued, "of a future time when men run about like ants on the earth, going this way and that, in machines that climb into the heavens. They have fouled the very waters.

"The breath of our mother, the earth, has been filled with noxious smells. It does not have to be so. There must be a way to let my people live in dignity."

Kiontawakon's hand dug into J.J.'s shoulder as he ordered, "You must tell the Tribal Council about your world. Because I have been training you as a shaman, they will listen to you."

Or else be branded a witch. He got the picture now.

Kiontawakon stood up. Beckoning to J.J. to follow him, he went outside. Men wearing moccasins and deerskin loincloths decorated with dyed porcupine quills were talking quietly among themselves.

The women, who wore fringed deerskin dresses as well as moccasins, were all busy. One young woman was vigorously pounding corn into flour with her mortar and pestle, while a tiny, wrinkled old woman was making a beautiful bowl out of wood. Giggling young girls threw teasing comments at him as they ran past him. Little kids played happily by themselves.

Kiontawakon didn't pause for any of this. He kept right on going in his ground-swallowing strides that made it hard for J.J. to keep up with him.

At the entrance to a building looking like a big longhouse, Kiontawakon stopped so suddenly that J.J. almost bumped into him.

"Do what I tell you," he said.

In that moment, Kiontawakon sounded a lot like Jeremy.

Walking behind Kiontawakon into the council house, J.J. saw that it was crowded with at least 100 men. This had to be the Tribal Council, made up of all the chiefs of the village councils, who met to debate big issues of war and peace. They all belonged to different tribes: Mohawks, Oneidas, Onondagas, Cayugas, and Senecas. They called themselves the Iroquois League.

The chiefs stopped talking and stared at the newcomers. Then an older man got up and welcomed them. "We would ask the shaman of the Senecas, Kiontawakon, to speak to us now."

With great dignity, the shaman rose and faced the others. "My heart is heavy, my brothers," he began. "There are many things that the Stone Person has told me, things that are troubling me.

You know that Metacom is fighting the English settlers, who have dealt severely with him and the tribes following him, even though Metacom's father, Chief Massasoit, in former times saved them from starvation by giving the settlers food and teaching them to plant corn. The great chief Massasoit also protected them from those who sought to destroy them. After he died, Alexander, his son, succeeded him as chief and was poisoned—or so his brother Metacom believes—by the English. Later, the English humiliated Metacom by requiring him to give up his guns and sign a new peace treaty, even though his father had already signed one.

"In many other ways the English treat the Wampanoags with contempt and do not respect their customs. They see this great land as something to be divided up among them, not as a sacred trust to be used by all.

"Even though the Wampanoags do not belong to our League, the whites will also bring destruction to us. I have seen into a future where the white men will plant their corn and longhouses where ours used to be. They will herd us into areas where they will command us to stay. Instead of merriment among our people, we will know sorrow and great pain.

"For these reasons, we must ally ourselves with Metacom's forces and drive the English from this land."

Kiontawakon sat down. During the heavy silence, J.J. wanted to fidget but didn't dare. It looked like he had landed right in the middle of King Philip's War. He remembered his history teacher telling the class that King Philip was really an Indian chief called Metacom, who led his Wampanoag tribe and other Indians into a war against the Puritan colonists of New England in 1675.

The English called him "king" because they thought Metacom was as arrogant as the Catholic King Philip of Spain, who had tried to conquer England in 1588. Later, James I had actually sent a crown to Chief Powhatan, father of Pocahontas, for the chief's coronation. So it wasn't uncommon for other chiefs to have coronations and be called kings.

Then an older man began to speak. "The clan matrons who chose us are against war with the English. Even if we should put a thousand of our warriors into battle and kill all the settlers, King Charles of England would send more men—an inexhaustible number like the sands of the sea—to punish us. Then where would our people be?"

"Are we to hide like the badger in his hole from these English?" cried Kiontawakon. "They do not regard us as men like them, but as inferior beings."

"They treat us well, give us weapons and other things of goodly manufacture," objected another.

"Like the firewater that turns sensible men into demons," said Kiontawakon bitterly.

The other men cast significant looks at each other. Then an old man with a face like a relief map of the Rockies spoke in measured tones. "I remember the tale that my father's father told me about the fierce chief of the Stone Giants, who wanted to wipe out our people. From the North Country came these giants, singing their war song as they marched into a deep ravine. The Great Spirit heard them and asked the Spirit of the Wind to stop them because he did not wish his people, the Senecas, to be destroyed. The wind blew so hard that it toppled great boulders upon these giants so that all of them were killed.

"Even so, my brothers, will our race be preserved, even in the face of great evils like the fevers and other diseases which the English have brought with them.

"It is not cowardly, but prudent, to side with these whites who have powerful weapons. Some among them have dealt fairly with our people and respect our customs.

"Metacom is a rash young man who acts before he thinks. He cannot win." He looked around and said with finality, "We must not help him or we will endanger the League."

"If you knew," said Kiontawakon slowly, "what will happen to the League, would you change your minds?"

J.J. felt a twinge of unease as Kiontawakon continued. "Great sorrows will come to our people. Listen to Little Running Horse."

"What can *he* tell us?" asked a younger man, skepticism written all over his hard, bony face.

"As is our custom for boys, he has fasted and meditated in the woods, where a spirit told him of many terrible things that will happen, not only to our people but to many others."

There was a buzzing among the Indians as they digested this information. Then the old one asked, "It may be that this boy is possessed of a spirit that has caused him to go mad."

Kiontawakon shook his head vigorously as he said emphatically, "No! He is not mad. This Jason spirit has also spoken to me."

Now they were all looking expectantly at him.

"Tell them what will happen in the future," said Kiontawakon softly, giving J.J. a meaningful look.

It felt hot and close in the longhouse. He didn't want to talk to these men, who had to be just about the fiercest Indians going. They gave no quarter and expected none, but could he just ignore the fact that over 3,000 Indians were going to die in this war? And that included Metacom, whose wife and kid would be sold as slaves and shipped to Bermuda.

J.J. cleared his throat. What was he going to say? His mom used to tell him that when in doubt, tell the truth.

The Indians waited impassively.

"I can't tell you about the future because I don't know exactly what will happen."

That was true enough.

Now Kiontawakon was frowning. He whispered savagely, "You will speak now about the future as you know it."

"No."

Kiontawakon glared at him. The old guy who had argued with Kiontawakon stood up and was closing the meeting by saying, "Dekanawida, the Great Peacemaker, and Hiawatha brought us the Great Law of Peace so that all the nations of the League might dwell in peace and tranquility. Let us not destroy that peace by going to war."

The younger man who had spoken before added, "Wampanoags, Nipmucks, Abenakis, Tarratines, and Narragansetts are not worth fighting for. Besides, we have no quarrel with the English. If they provoke us in the future, our warriors will fall upon them with fire and steel and teach them to respect us. For the present, let us continue to trade with them."

"And let Metacom perish?" asked Kiontawakon bitterly.

"If the Great Spirit wills it," said the old Indian firmly. "After all, Metacom and his people do not belong to our League."

"After the English destroy Metacom, they will come after us!" shouted Kiontawakon.

Now they were all getting up and walking out, and Kiontawakon was prodding him to follow him. He didn't look happy.

They walked out into the same peaceful scene they'd left a short time ago. The group of men gambling in the shade of a tree were still at it, and the women carried on with their chores.

Kiontawakon hesitated as though he was unsure what to do, then jerked his head at J.J. and headed off into the woods. It was pretty easy to walk there. The undergrowth had been cleared so that it was like strolling in a big park, except that this place was no park. A wild turkey waddling by took off when it saw them.

They came to a creek, where a beaver was fixing up his lodge.

Kiontawakon suddenly halted and asked fiercely, "In your time, will the water run clear like this? Will the beaver build his dams, or will the people press so close upon the earth that there will be much hunger and sorrow and death?"

"It's not like that."

But it was close enough. Gruesome things were always going on in the world. His history teacher, Mr. McCraik, would get all worked up about pollution, overpopulation, and what had happened to the Indians.

Now he was beginning to wonder if his teacher and this Indian guy were at least partially right.

Then Kiontawakon gripped his shoulder and said, "Jason spirit, my people believe that the English will treat them fairly as men of dignity. You and I know that this will not be so. In the future many Indian tribes will be scattered to the four directions. They will forget the old ways."

The Indian's eyes were burning with a scary light, but he was right: the Indians were going to be herded onto reservations by the U.S. government, which would savagely put down any resistance.

Digging his toes into the leaf litter, J.J. said, "Even if I could help you, I don't know if I should. If I do, then maybe something bad will happen to *my* people." Like if Metacom and his confederacy of other Indians won the war, then maybe the ancestors of men like George Washington wouldn't be born, and there would be no American Revolution. That could be a disaster for America and for the world.

The Indian's fingers were sinking deep into his flesh, as he shook him and cried, "You must help! If you do not . . ."

Then the light began to dim and objects around them fade until the last thing J.J. saw were the desperate eyes of the shaman.

CHAPTER 21

Lady Mary Montague–Geraldine Morgan A palace in
Constantinople, Turkey, 1717

It was a lovely garden, thought Geraldine, with roses, carnations, and jonquils interspersed with other flowers whose names she didn't know. Jets of water arcing into the air fell into marble basins emptying into pools in whose hidden depths she could see the movement of silver-finned fish.

Everything felt slightly unreal: the fountains, the cypresses swaying in the gentle evening breeze, the sudden laughter of someone in the palace, and the marble bench on which she was seated.

The logic that had told her time travel was not possible had apparently been confounded because here she was, inhabiting the body of Lady Mary Montague, wife of the English ambassador to Turkey, sitting in this Turkish garden halfway around the world and several centuries away from the mission garden where she had ingested the herbs that Jeremy had left for them.

It was like something out of the Arabian Nights.

So were the fancy brocaded harem pants over which hung a kind of gauzy white silk smock and over that a white-and-gold damask waistcoat covered by a caftan of the same material. A wide belt spangled with diamonds cinched her tiny waist. On her head she wore a turban.

"Lady Mary?"

The servant coming toward her was holding her long skirts above the grass. Quelling the panic threatening to engulf her, Geraldine rose to her feet.

With the querulous look of someone who has soured on life, her maid, Emma, who had traveled with them to Turkey said, "Lady Mary, the old woman you were expecting has arrived."

"I'm coming." Geraldine's initial attack of anxiety abated as information began seeping into her mind. It was amazing, she thought, how by relaxing and balancing her mind with Mary's—although she was sure that Mary wasn't conscious of what was going on—the words came out with the proper accent and intonation, as well as a certain phrasing.

Emma nodded at her and turned away with a jerky movement, stepping gingerly on the grass as though it were slivers of glass. This place might be a paradise, but not for Emma, living in fear of the Turks whom she thought of as heathens.

She led her into an opulent room of intricately patterned rugs, furniture inlaid with precious woods and gems, and priceless glowing lamps. Standing in the middle of the room and clutching a wooden soldier in one hand was a small boy, Lady Mary's seven-year-old son Edward, who was staring at an elderly woman carrying a bundle.

"Mummy, is she going to hurt me?" asked Edward in a small voice.

"Darling, no!" said Geraldine as Edward threw himself at her and hugged her tightly.

"But Emma said that she would make me sick," replied her son, his eyes big with fear as he looked at the woman who was going to inoculate him.

Her arms folded over her meager chest, Emma glared at the old woman, who was bowing awkwardly to Lady Mary and asking in halting English, "This the boy I help?"

"Does Lord Montague know of this, my lady?" interrupted Emma, her face screwed up into a frown.

Memories flooded in: the journey in 1717 from England to Turkey, where her husband was supposed to negotiate a peace between the Austrians and the Turks; their renting this palace set on a hill in Constantinople; her visits to ladies in their luxurious harems; and hours spent learning the Turkish language and poetry from a learned effendi.

"You overstep yourself, Emma," said Geraldine sharply. "Do not presume that because you have worked for me for so many years you may speak your mind on all occasions. Whether my lord approves or not of this undertaking—and he does—is none of your affair." Then, ignoring her maid, Geraldine turned to the woman who would inoculate Edward and said, "Yes, this is Edward. He is ready now for you to do the ingrafting."

Ingrafting, Geraldine drew from Lady Mary's memories, was generally done by a group of old women who went around to people's houses during September when the weather had cooled off. This must be the woman that Maitland, their doctor, had found to inoculate Edward. He had also found a suitable subject from which to gather the smallpox pus that was essential to the whole process.

From her bundle, the woman drew out a small vial and a piece of cloth. She carefully unwrapped a large needle and a shell.

"Come, my little man. This only a scratch—not hurt."

Edward shrank from the beckoning woman with the gap-toothed smile and hid his face in Geraldine's skirts.

Poor little soul, he was so frightened. Stooping down, Geraldine put her hands gently on Edward's shoulders and said, "I remember how sick I felt from the smallpox. But you will never have to go through that. In days to come when you remain strong and healthy, you will bless me for this. Now hold out your arm."

He drew back from her and cautiously extended an arm. The woman expertly opened a vein with the needle so that only a few drops of blood oozed out and then dipped the head of the needle into the smallpox pus in the nutshell. With great care, she applied the needle to Edward's arm. To protect the wound and keep it clean, she put a small shell over it. Working methodically, she bound up the wound and then repeated the procedure with the other arm.

Tears that she did nothing to hide were running down Emma's face.

Edward looked as though he was ready to start blubbering, too.

Geraldine rounded on her maid and chided, "How many of your friends in England have died already of the pox, Emma? Ingrafting the boy against the disease may save his life one day. The worst that will happen will be that he will come down with a fever. When that happens, he will be put to bed for two or three days with a mild form of smallpox. He will not necessarily have any spots on his body. Within eight days after that, he will be recovered from the illness."

Information from the mind of Lady Mary told Geraldine that female Turkish children who had been ingrafted in this manner—whose skin remained clear and unscarred—would be possible candidates for the sultan's harem.

Turning to the old woman, who was gathering up her supplies, Geraldine said, "Thank you for coming."

So it wasn't the English who had been the first to inoculate people against smallpox and not even the Turks; it had been the Chinese a century earlier. Interesting as that was, there were some big questions to be answered: Why was it important that Edward not die? His was certainly not a household name, no one important that she knew of. So what was the point of her coming here?

Still puzzling over these questions, Geraldine felt her consciousness spiral out of her body, no, Lady Mary's, and . . .

CHAPTER 22

Lady Mary Montague–Geraldine Morgan London, 1719

She was in a dressing room. Ladies in full-skirted dresses, looking like a bunch of brightly colored tulips, were powdering their faces and wigs and carrying on nonstop conversations centering primarily on their lovers and admirers.

"Lady Mary, are Turkish men better lovers than Englishmen?" asked a young woman who might have been beautiful if her face had not been pitted with scars.

"I would hardly know," murmured Geraldine.

"Oh, la, we have heard that the sultan was quite overcome by your charms," said another woman, giving her a roguish look as she tapped her on the arm with a fan.

Sultan? Then the memories began flowing once again.

Tartly, Geraldine said, "Achmed the Third is too good a Mohammedan to value any woman who belongs to another man. With five hundred women in his harem he is not lacking, but must rather be suffering, from a surfeit of carnal relations."

The ladies tittered at this sally of hers.

"I should not wish to live in a harem," Geraldine added. "One of the harem women told me about the eunuchs, especially chosen for their deformed bodies and repulsive faces, to guard the sultan's women, and about the constant and bitter fighting among the women. With my own eyes, I saw the prison-harem where every three years after a review of the sultan's women they shut up the old, sick, and barren women.

"Other eunuchs enforce strict discipline among the pages, who are taught by tutors in the palace school. These pages, according to their abilities, later serve the sultan in various ways, looking after his personal needs, his valuables, and some even ascending to high office to become governors of his provinces. Of course, in all things they must obey the sultan."

A lady whose mouth was drawn into a permanent sneer by a multitude of scars said, "In your letters you wrote that Turkish ladies bathe naked together. They must be a lewd lot."

"It is true that they go to the baths together, where they drink coffee or eat sherbet and converse while slaves braid their hair, but I saw not one wanton smile or immodest gesture among them while we sat together. On the contrary, they were as moral as any of us."

"Then they must be veritable satyrs!" said one thin matron with a disagreeable laugh.

"They have more liberty than English ladies and go about the streets disguised with long, shapeless clothes over their bodies and faces so that none can tell who they are."

"I should not be able to endure a husband who took four wives, as I believe the Turks do," observed another woman.

"No man of quality would do such a thing, nor would any woman of rank suffer it. I look upon Turkish women as the only free people in the empire. Wealthy ladies keep their money in their own hands and, if they divorce, take their wealth with them."

"Now would not that turn society upside down!" exclaimed the woman with the permanent sneer. "Perhaps that is what you are trying to do, Lady Mary, with your inoculations."

"For shame, she is but endeavoring to be of service," cried another, a beauty with fine, clear skin.

The pockmarked woman turned on her and cried, "Do you think, young lady, that inoculation will save you? When it is your time, you will be struck by the pox even as we were!"

The beauty went pale and fingered the ruby-encrusted cross at her throat.

The other, gesturing to the cross, said, "And much good that will do you whilst half of London is falling prey to the disease."

"'It is said that several thousands have died of it, and 'tis certain that many other thousands have been disfigured by it," observed the thin woman with relish.

Silence fell. It was smallpox, Geraldine realized, that had scarred most of these women's faces. They tried to cover up their scars with cerule, a thick substance, which produced a masklike appearance. She had been vaguely aware that the disease had been rampant in Europe but had not realized how it had ravaged those individuals who survived.

Sighing, she turned to the mirror in front of her and received a rude shock. Staring back at her was the reflection of a woman with pitted skin and the remnants of what had once been a fine pair of eyebrows.

Reluctant to face the women anymore, she left the dressing room and entered an immense room. Geraldine headed immediately for a small alcove between two tall windows where she could enjoy a moment or two of privacy.

The light from a myriad of candles played over lavish gowns and reflected off priceless jewels worn by both men and women who stood, bewigged and powdered, holding drinks in their hands and chattering. Except for the costumes, it might have been a cocktail party in Mayfair. The information in Lady Mary's consciousness told her that this was the home of the Prince and Princess of Wales, who had set up a separate establishment after quarrelling with the king over the latter's choice of a sponsor to the princess's latest baby.

Geraldine rubbed her hands, damp with anxiety, on her gown and then regretted doing so as she looked down at the pale silk with crimson stripes.

"Good evening. Lady Mary, I believe?"

Bowing to her was a portly man with grease stains on his green velvet coat, a man who carried himself with an air of assurance.

"You have the advantage of me, sir."

"Morley Wagstaffe of St. Bartholomew's Hospital, at your service, my lady. We have heard of your efforts to introduce the practice of ingrafting against smallpox. Why, I wonder, are you endeavoring to introduce into one of the politest nations in the world a custom employed by a pagan people?"

"I think, sir, that we might learn much from other nations." Such as using stoves to heat their houses as the good burghers of Hanover did. Geraldine shivered a little from the damp chill of the room.

Dr. Wagstaffe raised his bushy eyebrows and said, "I have heard a sermon denouncing the practice as 'an impious interference with the just and inscrutable visitations of God.' What say you to that, madam?"

Why the pompous old fool! She'd like to wipe that smirk right off his face, but what would Lady Mary do? She had to stay in character, so Geraldine said only, "Would you have innocent children die rather than treat them with a method that would guarantee their survival?"

"Only an atheist would try to circumvent God's will."

It was no use arguing with a man whose mind was encased in the prejudices of his time. He had probably been upset when they'd stopped burning witches in England.

"I regret, sir, that we will never be of the same mind in this matter."

"Mary, what are you doing here, hiding in the corner?"

Richly dressed in a brocaded dress stitched with pearls, the stately woman bearing down upon her ignored Wagstaffe, who bowed low and beetled off to the other side of the room.

"Was he being a bore, my dear?"

The neck, ears, and arms of the Princess of Wales were loaded with a careless array of diamonds, emeralds, and rubies that did nothing to relieve the plainness of her features, but her smile was welcoming and her eyes kind.

Mary certainly traveled in the most elevated of social circles.

"The gentleman was no more of a bore than many others, Your Highness."

"I hope you turned some of that justly celebrated wit of yours upon the wretched fellow," said Princess Caroline. "I have no idea how he got in here. But come—Handel is going to play one of his new anthems for us. Oh, and there is your great friend, that clever little Mr. Pope. I hear he has written some new verses that are very complimentary to you."

She was pointing to a short little man, misshapen and plain featured. This dwarfish little fellow was the author of *The Rape of the Lock* and other poems and essays? Geraldine immediately felt ashamed that she expected the famous poet to look like Lord Byron. What did his appearance matter? This man had turned the lens of his wit upon the court scene and summed up the perpetual gossip with an incisive, "At every word a reputation dies."

The princess was taking her arm and saying, "After the music we shall play at cards. You shall partner Mr. Steele, who observed to me only last week that your memory will be sacred to future ages because of the great work you are doing in helping to rid England of a terrible disease."

As Geraldine recalled, Steele was another wit who had given the name *Tatler* to a newspaper—in honor of the fair sex, as he put it.

No wonder Mary, a very bright and well-educated woman, who had written poetry, too, and critiqued that of Pope's, had later fallen out with Pope. He, like Steele, praised women, but subtly put them down.

Distracted, a rush of images came then: mothers with great sores running with pus from smallpox, lying in bed and beseeching her to ingraft their children; scores of her rich friends rushing to the country where they hoped to escape the worst of the disease.

"Mary," said the princess, turning and looking her fully in the face, "I would like to protect my children from the pox, but I must be sure that I am making the right decision."

She was looking for reassurance, realized Geraldine. However, she would have to be careful with the princess, a strong-willed woman who liked to make up her own mind about things.

"I will ingraft my own little daughter—who is but a baby now—when she is older."

The princess fanned herself with a painted ivory fan. "Quite so, but I would like some more proof that the smallpox venom will protect against the disease."

What could she say to the princess? What would she accept as proof? In the 20th century, scientists did experiments for years before they came to conclusions, but here in 1719 there wasn't time for that. Inoculating the princess's pet monkey wasn't an option, either.

The princess was beginning to look around her, smiling graciously at Pope making his way with some difficulty through the dense crowd.

She was losing the princess's attention. Then she had it. "May I suggest, Your Highness, that my surgeon Maitland, who learned the process from a Turkish surgeon, be given permission to ingraft a few criminals under sentence of death at Newgate. If they recover, then you might with perfect assurance ingraft your children."

The princess brightened and turned her attention fully upon Geraldine. "My dear Mary. A wonderful idea! Instruct Maitland to carry out this procedure at once. I shall await the outcome with the greatest of interest."

The reason for her coming here walked away. If the experiment worked and the princess had her children ingrafted, then the rest of England would follow suit. People who would have died from the disease would live, including certain individuals who would play key roles in the formation of the United States of America.

CHAPTER 23

Adrienne (Madame de Lafayette)–Laney Morgan
Paris, France, September 1774

Laney was sure that she was going to puke right then and there over the sick woman lying half-conscious in a bed reeking of pus and vomit. The woman, who had been her personal maid, had to be dying. The woman's face, including her eyelids and even her lips, were covered with huge sores oozing pus. And the smell! It was totally gross.

"Madame, you should not be here!" said a scandalized maid, wringing her hands as she hung back in the doorway.

"Isn't anyone looking after this woman?"

"*Oui,* but her fate is in the hands of *le bon Dieu.*"

"Can't the doctor do something?"

Memories of cool sheets, the family doctor, with his shaggy white hair and liver-spotted hands, and the cherry-flavored medicine that was her favorite, and her dad reading about the adventures of Pooh Bear, all came pouring into Laney's mind.

"What, madame?" asked the maid, who was her mother's personal servant. "The doctor, he can do nothing for her."

Nothing. Laney shivered. What kind of world was this where people went through such incredible suffering? Oh, she knew that people in her own time were going through similar misery from diseases like AIDS and malaria and river blindness, but it wasn't real to her, not like this wreck of a woman lying on her deathbed.

This era wasn't like 20th-century North America where the sick and dying were segregated into hospitals, where they could die in an orderly fashion, not hideously like this where you could see every aspect of their suffering.

Laney shuddered and turned away. She'd never complain about a zit on her face again.

The last three weeks here in 18th-century France had been a revelation. After putting the bit of cloth with the herbs on it on her tongue, she'd found herself in the body of 15-year-old Adrienne, married to a marquis, and not just any old nobleman, but Marie Joseph Paul Yves Roch Gilbert du Motier de Lafayette, who would become a hero of the American Revolution. She had even written an essay on him for her American history class.

The information in Adrienne's consciousness revealed that her father, the duke, had bought the 16-year-old Lafayette a captaincy in the Dragoons, although Lafayette wouldn't take actual command for two years. He had to learn first from a senior officer how to drill his men and how to recruit, equip, and maintain his troops.

His duties seemed to be pretty light and left him with a lot of spare time, which he spent in going to dinners and entertainments and, if you could read between the lines of his letters to her, chasing other women. This was considered normal behavior for the aristocracy. Marriages were like business arrangements, uniting wealthy families. Once married, individuals behaved as they liked, although they were expected to be discreet about their activities.

She was getting used to living here, although she missed her parents and friends and 20th century amusements like movies, but she had to admit that there were quite a few perks to being an aristocrat. She really liked not having to do any cooking or cleaning, although she was expected to help manage the large household of the Noailles mansion.

And then there was Mignon, Adrienne's tiny lapdog. At first the dog had growled, and refused to come to her, but after offering the dog a treat, he had started accepting food from Laney's hands.

Sometimes dogs were smarter than humans. Mignon knew that Laney wasn't her owner but accepted her as her new mistress. Now the dog followed her everywhere, even sleeping on her bed.

Once Laney had even gone to a musical performance. It wasn't like you could go in your jeans. Here, the women all tried to outdo each other in clothes and hairdos. The guys were just as vain, dressing up in tights and silk shirts and satin waistcoats and jewels; they were every bit as colorful as the women and even more arrogant than the guys back home. From the talk she'd overheard, all the married women were dying to make love to them.

For the rich, it was one continual party. For the poor, it was quite a different story. Laney didn't think she could ever forget the hordes of street people, most of them barefoot even though the weather was cold, whom she'd seen begging in the streets or trying to sell their pitiful goods of half-rotten fruit or crudely made articles.

If you had to live here, it was nice to have wealthy aristocrats like the Duke and Duchess d'Ayen for your parents, even though they were pretty bossy and the duchess always seemed to be at her prayers. Maybe she was so religious because she'd survived smallpox, which had marked her pretty badly.

Anyway, in these times, you were expected to obey your parents— and your husband, of course. At the beginning of their married life, Adrienne hadn't seen much of Lafayette because he was stationed at Metz while she was living in Paris with her family.

Now, however, he was on leave. Lafayette was easy to get along with and kind of cute in his own way, even if he wasn't exactly handsome. For one thing, his nose was too pointy, but he was a decent guy with a good sense of humor.

In the future, he was going to be a great hero. However, if she'd figured it right, he wouldn't go to America for another few years.

Pulling herself out of her reverie, Laney said to the maid, "See that this poor woman has everything she needs." One of the advantages of being rich was that you could get things done.

"*Oui, madame,*" the maid said as she curtsied.

Taking her skirts in her hands as she hurried down the hall, Laney remembered that Lafayette had been eating supper with Louis XV when the king had come down with the pox. Two weeks later, after suffering horribly, the king had died. Louis XVI had been so scared of getting smallpox, too, that he had himself and the entire royal family vaccinated.

The whole smallpox thing must have made a big impression on her husband because he had insisted upon being vaccinated. That was why they were here now in this "small" house, which was bigger than her entire school building! Her mother had come along to nurse Lafayette, sick in bed from the effects of the vaccination.

"Adrienne, there you are," said the duchess, sweeping down the corridor toward her. "Have you seen where my maid packed the pomade for my hair?"

Adrienne's mother, a woman of plain, angular features, looked very imposing in an elaborate silk dress.

"No, *maman*. Could it be in your boudoir in the small inlaid box you brought with you?"

"Perhaps. I'll call my maid and tell her to look for it. If you wish, Adrienne, you may visit your husband now, but only for a short time. He is feverish today. And remember not to get too close to him. You have never had the pox."

Without waiting for a reply, the duchess swept off.

Laney found Lafayette lying very still in the big four-poster bed where he had spent most of his time since they had arrived. Even though the thick carpet muffled her footsteps, Lafayette immediately became aware of her presence and turned his head weakly to greet her.

"Ah, dear heart, how charming you look this morning," he said. "But you are upset."

That was one of the things she liked about Lafayette; he paid attention to her. And while other aristocrats routinely lavished flowery compliments on her, Lafayette really seemed to mean it. When he complimented her and looked into her eyes, it made her heart beat faster—just like in the romance novels she'd read. No one had ever treated her like this before. Could she be falling in love with him?

"I saw this woman; she had smallpox. Oh, Lafayette, you must get well!"

"We must all die in due time, *petite,* but I do not plan to depart this earth for quite some time."

"You are too important to die young."

"I am flattered that my wife holds me so dear."

"Not just me, but many others," blurted out Laney.

A gratified smile spread over his face. "You are most charming," he murmured, "but perhaps a little influenced by the fact that you are my wife."

And by what I read in a history book, Laney wanted to shout. He was very flushed, she noted, and, so far, unmarked by the pox.

"Pray, do not, if you love me, Adrienne, keep me in this oh so delicious suspense."

As Laney impulsively made a move toward him, he warned, "You must not come closer, sweet."

"You will think I am foolish," she murmured, playing with a ribbon in her hair.

"I have never known you to be foolish, Adrienne, but always eminently practical."

When she grimaced, he added hastily, "And very charming."

"Practical!" What sort of compliment was that! At least he had the good sense to add "charming."

You couldn't get mad at a guy who was sexy and charming all at the same time. Not like some of the jerks she'd dated in high school.

Changing the topic, she asked, "How are you feeling?"

"Better, now that you are here."

But he looked worse than the day before, weaker, and more feverish. "He can't die!"

Too late, she realized that she had spoken her thoughts out loud.

"Men die every day," he murmured, "but I should like to die as did my father—in battle."

"You will see battle but not die in one."

"How so, Adrienne?"

How could she have been so stupid to say that! But now the fever was snatching away his train of thought and he was rambling. She thought she caught the words, "seek glory . . . must prove myself . . ."

"You will, oh, yes, you will, but be patient."

Turning sunken eyes on her, he gave her a smile that set her heart to beating faster and asked, "When, Adrienne, when?"

She wanted very much to say something, anything that might calm him. What harm would it do if she mentioned a few things that were going to happen? After all, he was feverish and probably wouldn't remember a thing.

"You will become a great hero, my love," she said, longing to smooth his reddish hair back from his forehead.

His head jerked nervously and he frowned.

"The Americans need you," she soothed. "You're going to be good friends with their commander, General George Washington, 'your father,' as you will call him."

At the word *father*, he quieted down. His eyes held an expression of longing. Her heart constricted, and she could hardly speak for a moment.

"You will serve with honor in the American Army as a major general, but what'll make you really famous is that your position as a hero and friend of Washington will influence French public opinion enough to gain support in France for the American cause. If it hadn't been for you, France might never have given the Americans the financial and political support that they needed to win their independence from Britain." Which was practically word for word the last paragraph in the essay she'd written about Lafayette.

"Patriots," he murmured.

She knew what he was referring to, Americans fighting in defense of their right to be a free people.

"And then?" Lafayette prompted, his eyes clearer now.

"You will be a hero in France also."

His eyes silently demanded more, but how much dared she say? How did you tell a man that his king and queen and many of his friends would be beheaded in a bloody revolution while he himself would spend five years altogether in first a Prussian and then an Austrian prison for making politically embarrassing statements?

The sick man's attention was broken once more by the fever. He was becoming restless again. She could hardly bear it, the thought of this good man living in a filthy prison and suffering from stomach and nerve troubles, sleeplessness, and fever. If only he had managed to escape to England! Maybe he would have gone on to America. She remembered reading something about his writing that if there was no hope of France regaining her freedom, that he would like to be "only an American again."

Instead, after finally being let out of prison, he had retired to their chateau at Lagrange, where he had farmed. Later on, he had reentered French politics, but the moment had passed. His ideas were no longer in vogue.

"The Americans loved you," she whispered.

He brightened at that, and she continued. "President Jefferson offered you the job of governor of Louisiana, which you turned down, and Congress granted you a lot of land."

"No money?" he joked feebly.

"Later, after your tour of the United States, they voted to give you a big sum for the money you'd spent out of your own pocket on clothing and feeding the men in your command during the Revolution. They loved you, Lafayette, and they never forgot you."

Lafayette nodded weakly at her. His eyes closed, and she saw that he had fallen asleep. If she had to stay here, there was no one she'd rather be with than this man.

Now she could feel a pulling, a loosening of her consciousness from the body of Adrienne, and she was floating out into a universe of glorious sound and light. Laney tried to look back at the man she was beginning to fall in love with, but the force that was propelling her on would not let her.

CHAPTER 24

Adrienne–Laney Morgan   Metz, France, August 7, 1775

"Enchanté, madame," said the man bowing to her.

The orchestra stopped playing, and she almost fell as she was suddenly swept into another body—no, still Adrienne's body—but in 1775, a year later, it felt different: fatter, more awkward.

A look of concern on his pale face, the man she had been dancing with steadied her and asked, "Would you care to sit down, Madame?"

She nodded. She was a little faint. Lights from hundreds of candles were reflected in the diamonds and other jewels worn by the crowd of gorgeously dressed people and softened the heavy makeup of white paint, rouge, and beauty patches of the women.

Their necks must get awfully sore from wearing those huge hairstyles, soaring two or more feet high, loaded with ostrich feathers—introduced last year by the English Duchess of Devonshire and now all the rage—as well as flowers and jewels.

Some women had taken to wearing "themed" hairdos, like Queen Marie Antoinette, who had celebrated a naval victory over the British by wearing a replica of a French battleship in her pouf. Adrienne's maid had even told her about another lady who had worn in her hairdo a birdcage with a real bird in it!

Laney had never seen such dresses in satins and silks in all colors of the rainbow and heavily embroidered with silver thread and billowing out at the waist, held in place underneath by panniers like the baskets seen on donkeys. Any one dress could have made multiple dresses for most of the girls of her graduation class.

The men were no less gorgeous in their powdered wigs, white stockings, tight-fitting breeches, and coats with lace ruffles at the cuffs. They also wore foils, which were dress swords.

Now the crowd was parting and all of them were staring, not at her, but at the man she had been dancing with. Who was he? The Duke of Gloucester, who was visiting Metz with his wife and daughter, was the answer that swam into her consciousness. She was at a ball given in his honor. Even though the duke had parted on bad terms with his brother, George III of England, who was upset that the duke had married an illegitimate woman whose mother had made hats for a living, the French still honored the fact that Gloucester was royalty.

Now Lafayette was hurrying over to her. He bowed low to the duke and said, "My thanks, Your Royal Highness, for your assistance to my wife."

"My pleasure . . ."

Comte Francois de Broglie, who had appeared out of the crowd, came up to them and said smoothly, "May I present the Marquis de Lafayette. His father was a colonel under my command in several campaigns, and now his son is a captain under my command here in Metz. He will be coming tomorrow to the dinner I am giving in your honor."

"I look forward to your presence there," said Gloucester.

"I would not miss it for the world, Your Royal Highness," said Lafayette, bowing low.

Gloucester smiled and turned away to speak to de Broglie.

In a low voice Lafayette said, "You have exerted yourself too much, Adrienne. Let us go out on the terrace." Taking her arm, he led her out onto a marble terrace where the fragrance of flowers in tall urns perfumed the night.

"I am feeling better now," said Laney.

"Perhaps you should not have come."

Laney stiffened, then turned away from Lafayette. Just when she was getting really fond of him, why was he being so cold to her?

Then she noticed something, a deepening of the darkness. Must be her imagination. She was turning back to face her husband when a shadow sprang silently from behind an urn planted with a small tree. Laney hiked up the skirt of her dress with all its petticoats and tried to kick the intruder in the groin. Good thing her dad had insisted on her taking a self-defense course. But her center of gravity felt off, her kick going to the assailant's knee instead. Her kick must have been pretty pathetic, because instead of falling, the assassin appeared to only stumble briefly. As he flailed out with his hands in order to regain his balance, the knife in his hand went spinning across the marble terrace.

Lafayette spun around and drew his foil, but the intruder was too quick. He cried out, *"Vive la revolution!"* as he leaped over the low wall of the terrace to the lawn with its many fountains below.

Several footmen and officers rushed over to them.

"A revolutionary. He tried to attack me," said Lafayette. "He was like a snake, too fast for me to run him through." Pointing to the lawn, he said, "He jumped down there."

De Broglie took charge. "Alert the guards. Scour the grounds." Looking at her, he said, "You have taken no ill, madame?"

"I trust not," said Lafayette, putting an arm around her shoulders and giving her a look that made her want to stay within his embrace forever. "She is with child."

So *that* was why he was being so protective of her and had not wanted her to exert herself! Warmth coursed through her. Lucky Adrienne to have such a husband!

Shortly after, she was bundled into a coach and driven to the house Lafayette had rented for their stay in Metz.

The next day, at Lafayette's insistence, she stayed in bed. It wasn't so bad being waited on hand and foot, but it was a little boring with no one to talk to and no television. Adrienne's mother had actually suggested that she write some letters or practice her needlework. No chance of that happening! No girls her age did that any more—not in 1992.

At least Adrienne's dog, Mignon, was there to keep her company. Laney amused herself by teaching Mignon some tricks. The dog was smart and caught on fast. What would Adrienne think when Laney left?

Lafayette had gone out for the day; he was probably drilling the 80 men under him. He returned in the middle of the afternoon and came to her room.

"How are you feeling, dear heart?" he asked, stroking one of her hands.

A quiver of delight went through her. "Very well," she answered.

"Last night you were like a veritable Minerva."

Minerva who? Oh, yeah, the Roman goddess of war, among other things. She remembered seeing a picture in history class of the goddess carrying a shield and a spear. Nice of Lafayette to think that she was so brave, but she could never tell him that the reason she had reacted so fast was due to her dad, who had drilled into her the importance of being mindful, aware at all times of what was going on around her. Her Aikido instructor was always harping on the same thing.

"I must go now, *chérie,* and get ready for the dinner tonight. I am glad that you are feeling well, but you must confine yourself to bed," he added firmly.

He laid a kiss on top of her head and was about to leave when she grabbed his sleeve and pleaded, "When you return, will you visit me and tell me about the dinner?"

If he was astonished at her insistence, he was too well-bred to show it. "As you wish," he said, caressing her hair, and left.

The afternoon and evening passed agonizingly slowly, but eventually she fell asleep. She was awakened by a light knock on her bedroom door. The candle had guttered out and the room was dark. "Come in."

Lafayette opened the door and strode over to a table, where he put down the candle he was carrying. The light threw a warm glow over the gold epaulettes on his blue-and-white dress uniform.

His face was flushed with wine and excitement. He sat down next to her on the bed and, kissing her on the cheek, asked, "You are feeling better, dear heart?"

She nodded and squirmed around in the enormous four-poster bed as she tried to sit up and make herself more comfortable.

Lafayette was quick to notice and said, "Let me, *chérie*," as he adjusted the embroidered pillows on the enormous bed.

"So what did the Duke of Gloucester say that has you so excited?" asked Laney, the nearness of her husband sending unaccustomed feelings rioting through her.

Lafayette paused for a moment, then burst out, "I have found my life's purpose. The duke, he told us . . ."

He mastered his emotion, then went on. "Until today, I have followed the usual path of young men my age, but now my eyes have been opened by this prince among men, who told us about the dispatches he had just received concerning the Americans."

Too excited to stay still, Lafayette stood up and began pacing. "You must understand, Adrienne," he said, "that like many a French patriot I have grieved over our loss of New France to Britain on the Plains of Abraham, where our general, the Marquis de Montcalm, was killed.

"Some still blame Montcalm for the loss of our colonies, but I am told that like all good officers, he fought for honor and glory and followed the instructions Versailles gave him to defend Quebec, which was central to the defense of New France.

"But even today—sixteen years later—one wonders why he was not given the requisite number of troops for this defense? And how was he to know that the British under General Wolfe would prove so wily? As a result of this defeat, the Treaty of Paris decreed that France had to give her colonies to Britain."

Lafayette sat down beside her and continued. "The duke," he said, "is a most persuasive speaker. He says these Americans have a passion for liberty and freedom. They wish to run their own affairs, not be dictated to by their king. As it is, George III allows them no say in their affairs, taxing them without consent and provoking them by other harsh measures. Adrienne, the Americans need help with troops and money if they are to overcome their masters."

He paused, looking at her lovingly, and then said quietly, "But it is wrong of me to distress you with these matters. You must rest, for our child's sake, as well as for your own—and mine. Perhaps you do not know how dear to me you have become this past year, particularly when you defended me yesterday from an assassin."

"And you to me," murmured Laney, impulsively holding out her arms to her husband. Lafayette hesitated and then began stripping off his uniform.

His eager smile was the last thing she saw as her consciousness began slipping out of Adrienne's body. She knew a brief, intense regret as she gave herself up to the inevitable.

CHAPTER 25

Tom Eldridge—Jason Kramer Pease Field Fight,
Rhode Island,
July 9, 1675

A shove sent J.J. sprawling in the dirt. Grunting, he turned over and stared up into a face streaked with grime.

"Beg pardon for smacking you down, but it would be a pity if a likely lad like yourself were to furnish a scalp for Philip's belt. It were best to lie low like Church said."

J.J. swallowed the bile that his churning stomach had forced up into his throat. His skin felt prickly, the rough clothing he was wearing chafing him in the heat.

"Uh, thanks, Mr. . . ."

"Bill Southward, at your service."

J.J. sneaked a quick look around. He was lying on his stomach near a split rail fence, which enclosed a field of peas. Dense woods lay on one side of him and a river on the other side. Men holding long-barreled flintlocks lay quietly near him. Obviously he was no longer in Little Running Horse's body, but in the body of a young white boy about his own age—Tom Eldridge. Jumbled memories swarmed into his mind: shooting squirrels to give to his mother for a stew; coming out of the woods surrounding his parents' farm only to find Indians burning their farmhouse; his mother screaming as a warrior split his father's skull and then his mother falling to the ground from a blow to her head; and his two small sisters being carried off by an Indian brave on horseback.

All Tom wanted to do after that was to fight the savages who had killed his family.

Two Indians stood up and began walking out of the field. They didn't look much like some of the Indians he'd seen hanging around the grotty hotels on Main Street back in Winnipeg in 1992. These men were tall and looked extremely fit, wearing only loincloths, feathers in their hair, and streaks of paint on their faces and bodies. J.J. swallowed hard. He couldn't, just couldn't, fire on them.

Then the Indians were running, and a plump man was standing up and calling to them.

"We want only to talk to you! We will not hurt you!"

The Indians paid no attention him but just kept coming. One of them turned and fired on the man who wanted to talk to them.

"You treacherous dog!" roared Bill, firing at the Indian, who yelled, clapped a hand to his arm, and then ran into a thicket.

"Up, lad! After Church!"

J.J. leaped up, remembering to take with him the long-barreled gun lying beside him.

The forest was dim and cool under the sheltering branches of oaks and maples that must have been standing before the time of Columbus. The volley of shots directed their way made him realize that this wasn't the time to moon over the scenery. He was surprised to find himself still standing and the men around him apparently unhurt.

As they returned fire, the man whom J.J. now recognized to be Captain Church cried, "Do not fire your guns all at once, or they'll run upon us with their hatchets!"

Feeling totally useless, J.J. turned and ran back with the others to the field of peas.

"Under the fence, lad," urged Bill, running beside him.

J.J. threw himself down in the field of peas and held his breath. Men were standing up and ramming powder and shot into the barrels of their guns. Now he could see why they hadn't been shot.

The enemy only had one chance to knock you off. Then they had to recharge their guns. That gave you time to run away, unless they came at you with hatchets as Church had said they might.

The hill above was swarming with Indians, the sunlight glinting on their weapons.

"They think to gain the advantage by surrounding us," observed Bill, lying on his stomach beside him. His bulk was comforting to the boy, but his words were not.

"So what do we do?"

"Don't fret, lad. Church has a plan. He always does. A good Christian gentleman, a man of parts, he is. I should know. His sister is my wife." Looking keenly at him, Bill asked, "You new to the Indian war?"

J.J. nodded uneasily. If Bill only understood how new!

"Then 'tis best you stick with me. Now what would your name be, lad?"

"Tom," he said. "Tom Eldridge. Sir," he added belatedly. People seemed to talk awful formal in this time period.

More of Tom's memories started pouring in: joining Church and his men to fight Indians who were burning English settlements; Church making friends of Indians living near his farm before King Philip's War and even during the war and using friendly Indians as scouts and warriors. Church used tactics he'd learned from the Sakonnet warriors he trusted, tactics like slipping through the woods and surprising the enemy, often at night when they least expected it. Church didn't wait for Metacom's forces to attack but attacked first.

They had found fresh Indian tracks that very day that led to Captain Almy's field of peas.

"I'm pleased to meet you, Tom Eldridge. As to our situation here, Church confided in me earlier that there be boats ordered to attend on him. If you look over yonder, I reckon those be the ones."

J.J. looked in the direction Bill was pointing and noticed for the first time a group of men and horses standing on the other side of the river beside several boats pulled up on the shore.

"Strip to your shirts, men," bawled Church, lying a few yards away, "so the men across the river know us to be Englishmen!"

Smart idea. The Indians weren't wearing shirts, only the English. J.J. wished that on a hot summer day like this that he could take off his shirt, too.

"Aye, aye," muttered Bill, tearing off his jacket to reveal a white shirt similar to the ones the other men were wearing.

As J.J. removed his slightly gamey-smelling jacket of deerskin, he heard three distinct shots, probably signals to their would-be rescuers.

"Now you men take shelter at that wall before the Indians gain it," said Church, pointing to a low wall some yards ahead.

Feeling very exposed, J.J. reluctantly got up and ran after Bill. Bill suddenly stooped down and grabbed some peas. "Go on, lad, gather some. It's certain you must be as hungry as me. A soldier learns to take what Providence provides when he can."

J.J. stooped down. Bill raised his flintlock and fired. A yell was suddenly cut off. J.J.'s imagination could fill in the rest. A flintlock could make a pretty messy hole in a man.

"On your feet, Tom. Be quick!" Bill yelled as with one powerful hand he hauled J.J. to his feet. They both leaped the low wall with the determination and speed of Olympic hurdlers, his mind spinning crazily as they tumbled down the small bank.

"Good work, Bill. Praise be to God for delivering you and your friend," said Church a few moments later as he tumbled down near them.

"Tom Eldridge, Benjamin. It's his first campaign."

"Pleased to make your acquaintance," said Church, his large bright eyes assessing J.J. with a friendly look. "You do well, Tom, to stay close to an old campaigner like Bill."

A volley of shots whistled over their heads, seeming to come from all directions: from the ruins of a stone house, a heap of black rocks, and from behind trees and fence posts. How were they ever going to get out of this mess?

As if reading his thoughts, Church laid a hand comfortingly on J.J.'s shoulder and said, "Many a time I've been in a tight corner, but always a heavenly Providence has watched over me."

J.J. drew a shaky breath. This time was he supposed to be that Providence? Jeremy had told him that if Church didn't stop Metacom and his Indians who were attacking the English colonies, Count Frontenac would swoop down from the north, conquer the Thirteen Colonies, and claim them for France. Then there would be no American Revolution and no America to stop the Nazis in World War II.

But how was he supposed to help Church when he was having trouble staying alive? He was more a liability to the others than anything. If it hadn't been for Bill, he'd be lying dead right now with his face in some farmer's peas.

"I'm very grateful to Bill . . ." he began awkwardly.

"I couldn't let a good Englishman have his head taken off by a pack of heathens, could I?" interrupted Bill as he clapped J.J. on the back.

"Now, Bill, some of my best soldiers are Indians, and they are as good Christians as you or me," reproved Church, his glance roving around the landscape as they talked.

He broke off and shouted to a boat putting off from the other shore, "Hallo! Send your canoe ashore!"

Now Church's men began screaming, "Help, rescue us! Our ammunition is spent!"

"The fools! They'll acquaint the Indians with our plight, who'll harry us even harder!" said Church. Then, cupping his hands around his mouth, he shouted, "Captain, send your canoe ashore or else leave! Do this or I will fire upon you!"

To J.J.'s dismay, the boat turned in the water and sailed away. Little flashes of light came from all around them, and the acrid smell of powder burned in their nostrils as the Indians began firing faster than ever.

One of the men near J.J. muttered, "I'm sore tempted to flee."

"Aye, before those devils take our heads," agreed his companion.

"You'd not get far," said Church, who had overheard their conversation. "Be sparing of your ammunition, and your courage shall be rewarded. God has preserved us thus far and shall continue to keep us safe."

The men had stopped complaining and were listening intently to Church.

The sun went down in a splendor of crimson and orange, turning the river into a frothing tide of molten gold that dazzled J.J.'s eyes and made him homesick for his grandparent's cottage on Lake of the Woods, where he'd daydreamed on their dock on many an evening just like this one.

Too soon, fingers of twilight began stalking the land, making huge shadows of the Indians, whose long whooping yells tore at J.J.'s nerves.

Where was Dan? Had he made it to New England or maybe even gone back home?

If only he could go back to the 20th century, back to Winnipeg, back to his dad and mom, back to his friends. He didn't belong here with these people who had been dead for over 300 years. This wasn't even his country! What was he doing here?

"The sloop! Benjamin, the sloop!" yelled Bill.

J.J. heard Church exclaim, "Praise be! Captain Golding has come to fetch us!"

And then Bill was pounding on his back, whispering hoarsely, "Did I not tell you, Tom, that Church would find a way?"

More like the captain, whoever he was.

"Send your canoe so we can come aboard!" shouted Church.

As a canoe came bobbing over the waves, J.J. exclaimed, "But it's so small!"

"Big enough for two stout lads at a time," said Church. "Go now, Tom. You've a good chance to make it safely on deck under cover of the fire of the ship's company."

"I'd rather wait, sir."

Church nodded, pleased, J.J. saw, by his decision to wait.

How could he explain that he wasn't being a hero; he was waiting to see if the others could make it out alive. No way could he tell this man how he really felt.

Then while his nerves crawled with fear, he had to sit and watch while close to 20 men ventured out, two at a time, into the canoe. All of them managed to get safely on board the sloop. "Your turn, lad," Church was saying. "You go with him, Bill."

Bill shook his head, his expression obstinate. "I'll wait until you both have gone."

Church began pouring powder down the long barrel of the flintlock and tamping it down with a long slender rod. "I must retrieve my cutlass and hat at the well where I drank when we first came down. I'll not leave them for the Indians to gloat over."

Bill began arguing with his brother-in-law. Church was shaking his head.

J.J. wondered if he should run to the well and grab the man's things. If he did prevent Church's death by doing this—and it was possible that he could get killed trying—he would condemn thousands of Indians, now and in the future, to lifetimes of poverty, disease, and despair. On the other hand, if Church died, Jeremy said there would be no United States. What should he do?

His mom always said to follow his intuition, but supposing his intuition was wrong?

J.J. shivered. He had to make a decision right now, and it had better be the right one.

Church put a hand on his shoulder and looked encouragingly at him. Now he was turning away. J.J. felt a surge of anger. Why was Church willing to risk dying for a stupid hat and a sword just because he didn't want the Indians to gloat over getting them?

Before he could do anything, Church grabbed his gun and charged over to the well standing about 20 yards away in a small clearing. As he snatched up his hat and cutlass—a heavy sucker with a lethal-looking blade—bullets zipped harmlessly around him. J.J. could see why both whites and Indians were in awe of the man: bullets never seemed to touch him.

That could change, and fast. Church was going to get killed. That wasn't supposed to happen! And it would be all his fault, for acting like a coward and not doing what he was sent here to do.

"To the boat, Tom!" yelled Church, who was sprinting to the river.

It was an impossible distance away, through the field and down to the shore, but with adrenaline pouring through his veins, he found himself whooping and yelling like the soldiers he'd seen in countless Westerns.

The Captain and his men on board the boat were firing enthusiastically now, while the Indians returned their fire. Vines grabbed at J.J.'s ankles as he tore through the peas, the sweat pouring down his face in the still-warm July evening.

The shooting let up a little. Either the Indians were poor shots or else their guns were very inaccurate. With a semiautomatic, a U.S. Marine could have mowed them down in seconds.

Up to his ankles now in the warm water of the river, he had only a few yards more to go. Church, crouched low in the canoe, was yelling, "Good lad!" and extending a hand to help him into the canoe.

He'd made it! J.J. was just lifting up a foot to get into the canoe when something hard and fiery slammed into his back, and then he was falling into the water facedown, voices calling him and hands pulling at him, and then a great roaring darkness . . .

CHAPTER 26

Captain Roger Golding–Caleb Morgan

Captain Golding's sloop
on the Sakonnet River,
July 9, 1675

Since he'd put the piece of cloth soaked in herbs on his tongue just a few seconds ago, Caleb was experiencing the most peculiar sensations. His eyes were playing funny tricks on him, as though he were getting cataracts and couldn't see properly, everything going dim.

Seconds later, he felt himself caught up by what felt like an invisible cloak of energy that wrapped itself about him and propelled him across the singing void, through universes of darkness, into another body.

It wasn't what he'd expected, but then he hadn't really known *what* to expect. He'd been prepared for failure but not for success.

It was a neat trick, a kind of immortality. He acknowledged to himself that he'd badly wanted, just once more, to feel the juices of a young man's body running through his veins again, to feel muscles that worked smoothly and didn't falter. When he was young, he had taken all that for granted: the splendid physical health and suppleness; the ability to stay up all night with scarcely any loss of energy; and the general feeling of well-being. Oh, he still had more stamina than many men half his age, but there was a difference now. Like a miser apportioning his gold, he was careful to expend only a rationed amount of his carefully hoarded energy. So he spent the small coin of his force, knowing that his reserve of strength was gradually dwindling until one day, bankrupted of that natural life force, death would claim him.

"Captain Golding, do you wish us to send the canoe to Mr. Church and his men?"

Dazzled by the glare of sunshine on the water, Caleb put a hand to his eyes. He was standing on a 50-foot sloop. Information from the captain's mind told him that it had a shallow draft—easy to see that it had to be shallow in this river—and a hickory keel with a hull built of oak.

Indians were firing on his crew and the sloop. On the shore lay a small body of men, Englishmen, judging by their white shirts and light complexions, who looked in desperate trouble.

A shot came whistling by his ear and right through a sail. Too close by half!

A young sailor dressed in rough, stained trousers and a shirt rushed over to him. "Captain Golding, the men's chances of surviving the Indian attack be small, sir, if we do not fetch them off."

"Send the canoe," commanded Caleb gruffly.

The sailor grinned and dashed away to carry out the order. More shots were being aimed their way, but most of them fell harmlessly short. The distance was too great.

Caleb could feel his spirits rising, the adrenaline flowing through his body, a young man's body, strong and fit.

He drew in a lungful of air, fresh, and full of the woodsy scents of a forest that had stood untouched for centuries. The river was clear and looked clean enough to drink. Pollution wasn't a problem here and wouldn't be for another couple of centuries.

A heavy burst of firing, this time from the men around him, snared his attention. It took some time for the canoe to make the ten trips to get off the 20 men. There wasn't much for him to do, just watch as the Englishmen took a run for the canoe while the soldiers on board kept the Indians busy by firing at them with those archaic weapons of theirs.

Only one man left. He seemed to be waiting for someone, a boy running through the water. The boy was yelling something. He'd just reached the canoe when he arched his back and fell into the water. The man—it had to be Church—was hauling his companion into the canoe and paddling like fury.

Another hail of bullets, miraculously missing Church, whistled though the air. Caleb let out an involuntary sigh of relief. The captain's memories told him how Church had settled on a farm in Little Compton, Rhode Island, and made friends of the Sakonnet Indians who lived near him and learned their techniques of warfare. His bravery and respect for Indians impressed the tribes and drew many to him, including Awashonks, the leader of the Sakonnets. When war came, he encouraged her not to join Philip in his war against the whites.

"Take up the lad first!" shouted Church.

When the boy was laid on the deck, it was obvious that he was quite dead.

"Poor Tom. He took the bullet meant for me. He is with our Lord now," said Church, turning the boy over and reverently closing the eyes that were staring sightlessly into the darkening sky.

Caleb shook his head and shouted an order to take up the anchor and set sail.

Then, looking at the still form of the dead boy, he was torn by the unfairness of it all, that someone so young had to die, someone about the same age as J.J.

What was it the boy had yelled? "Jeremy, get me out of here!"

Caleb stared again at the corpse. He knew with a terrible certainty that the boy lying on his deck had to have been his young cousin.

But, damn it all, this wasn't the way things were supposed to happen! No one had mentioned that in the course of attempting to change history you could get killed.

Caleb could feel a shrinking in his bones, as though he were becoming several sizes smaller and weaker. Face it, he told himself. I've been spoiled, gone soft, addicted to luxury. But I agreed to this adventure. Now I have to do whatever it takes!

Caleb straightened up and took deep breaths of the intoxicatingly fresh air. A recollection stirred in him of the time when his mother had taken him to visit an elderly aunt of hers. Lost in a labyrinth of dreams, the frail old lady sitting in her wheelchair had looked at him with faded blue eyes and patted his hand. She began whispering, so low that he had to bend to catch her words, "Caleb, bold one."

He'd often thought of that encounter. Once again, he felt that fate had placed him in difficult circumstances where he had to live up to the expectation inherent in the meaning of his name. He hoped that he had carried out his part of the mission, which was to save Church's life.

CHAPTER 27

Kiontawakon   Seneca village, July 19, 1675

In preparation for this day, Kiontawakon had fasted and meditated. Now, sitting cross-legged with only the moon and a small fire for light, he closed his eyes, relaxed his muscles, and began taking slow, regular breaths. Years of practice allowed him to quickly enter a trance, which ushered him into that magical place that was his alone, a place of comfort and safety, where he could begin his scrying.

He opened his eyes, took a deep breath, and looked into the bowl of water in front of him. A mist began forming over the surface, then condensed into an image, the face of the hated Englishman, Benjamin Church. The wily Church, who converted Indians to his religion and his cause and accepted them into his loyal band of followers, this man was by far the most dangerous of the white men, because he had that gift for making men, even the proudest of Indian warriors, love and follow him.

Why couldn't the tribal chiefs see that this white man with his honeyed words would be the instrument to destroy the New England Indians? Once they were reduced to living in a few miserable villages, they would disappear. Once they were gone, how long would it take before the Iroquois League itself would be in deadly peril?

It should be clear, even to an idiot, that Church must be destroyed, and soon.

After the festival of the ripening of strawberries had come news of the Wampanoag attack on Church and his men. Twenty white men had evaded a force of 300 warriors. Truly, Church must be a man favored by the spirits!

The chiefs in power over Church were not so wise. Metacom had slipped out of their grasp and put to the torch many of their towns. If Church could be stopped, the unwary English could be dispatched.

That meant that the Morgans who were helping Church had to be thwarted. Kiontawakon knew that words of reason would not be enough to persuade the Morgans to stop their meddling. Other means would be necessary. The Stone Person had told him that another Morgan beside the Jason spirit was about to interfere.

Ignoring the cool wind that blew off the lake, Kiontawakon began drumming softly, slipping as in a dream from the Middle World of ordinary reality into the Lower World, where he would ask—as he had many times before—the Great Horned Owl, his power animal, for help.

But as the fire burned down, no answers came. Never had the shaman dared to impose his will on the spirits but tonight, as he felt the power of those dark, primitive forces he had consulted earlier flooding through him, he sent his consciousness in search of his power animal. Finding it, the shaman thrust his will into the bird, directing its path into a great, swooping rush toward his enemy.

CHAPTER 28

Captain Prentice–Dan Morgan   The Great Swamp Fight,
December 19, 1675

. . . .

Dan squinted at the ground covered by a powdering of fresh snow sparkling with a jewel-like brilliance in the sunshine. Letting his horse pick his own way over the rugged terrain, he shivered and hunched down farther into his inadequate coat. And he'd thought Minneapolis a deep freeze in the winter. Oh, for a down-filled parka and warm boots!

He'd spent the last week being alternately terrified and outraged, although there were times when he acknowledged to himself that it was better than the life he'd been leading for the past six months. However, any romantic illusions he might have had about serving in a colonial army had been quickly dispelled when he'd landed in the body of Captain Prentice. For a 55-year-old man, the guy was in great shape, lean and hard-muscled.

The Captain's memories kept welling up like some damn stream of consciousness thing: memories of fighting under Cromwell in the English Civil War, then coming to Massachusetts Colony with his wife and daughter (the Two Graces he called them for they were both named Grace) and trying to build a life in this new country where everything was unfamiliar.

Later, at the start of King Philip's War, Prentice had been appointed Captain of the Horse after a plea from the colonists for protection from Metacom's forces, who were burning their homes and killing settlers. This came in June of 1675 after one of the colonists in Swansea had shot and wounded an Indian who had been shooting his cattle and trying to burgle his house. When Prentice and his men had hurried to Swansea, they'd been ambushed. After a brief shoot-out, the Indians had disappeared.

Since then, Captain Prentice had been chasing the Indians without much luck. The enemy knew how to slip away over trails that led to their hiding places in forests and swamps. With the guns that they had bought from the English, they were deadly and experienced fighters.

How ironic was it that he should find himself in December of 1675 in charge of a troop of cavalry! For starters, he'd hated horseback riding ever since a horse had thrown him when he was a kid. His latest experiences hadn't changed his mind. His mount, a rangy coal-black mare, seemed to know that he wasn't really her master and was becoming a damn nuisance, even trying to buck him off. His men were starting to make sniggering comments about the situation. Still, it was probably better than walking like most of the other poor guys. Each foot soldier lugged a heavy musket and carried a snapsack, which consisted of six feet of fuse, a leather belt holding a dozen or more boxes of powder, a bag of bullets, and a horn of priming powder.

He'd have felt a lot better, too, about going into hostile Indian territory if he had a decent gun, like his .30-30 Winchester that he used to take out hunting, not this poor excuse for a weapon, which misfired occasionally and took forever to load.

However, nothing seemed to bother their leader Church, who was a strange mixture of piousness and toughness and a natural at guerrilla warfare.

Dan remembered how, only a day after arriving in the captain's body, he'd found himself agreeing to go with Church. Their leader hadn't any trouble finding men to go with him. They seemed to think he led a charmed life and were willing to follow him anywhere. So Dan had moved out quietly that night with the rest of the troops marching at wide intervals while scouts looking for Indians fanned out on both sides and in front.

They'd been about an hour marching with only a crescent moon to light the way over narrow frozen trails, through woods blanketed with snow, when they'd come to a steep embankment. His mare pulled up of her own accord and whinnied as she stamped her feet. He watched as the other riders, slipping and sliding as they went, carefully edged their mounts down the slope. Then it was his turn; only his mount didn't want to move. There was one way to fix that.

Amazing what a taste of his spurs could do. His mare began moving smartly down the incline, avoiding the small bushes looking stark and bare of leaves.

Some instinct made him look up. Silhouetted against the moon, a Great Horned Owl was diving straight for him. His mare must have sensed something, too, because she neighed in panic and tried to turn sideways. Then Dan was falling, and tufted talons like steel spikes were slashing at his coat. For an instant of time, in the owl's huge black eyes rimmed in gold, Dan thought he detected a human presence. Throwing up his arms, he lashed out at the bird. Suddenly, as if released from a spell, the owl flapped its enormous wings and sailed off soundlessly into the night.

"Stupid bird! Did you see how it spooked my horse and tried to peck out my eyes?"

"Yes, 'twas passing strange, Captain Prentice. Are you hurt?" Bending over him was Church himself, wearing a concerned expression on his face.

Swallowing his anger—you had to be careful about cussing around Puritans—Dan said, "I guess I'll live." He scrambled awkwardly to his feet and dusted the snow off his pants and jacket.

"Your mittens," said Church, handing him a pair of red mittens that had fallen on the ground.

"You keep them. I've got another pair."

"I give you thanks," said Church, stuffing them into the pocket of his pants.

"I wonder what got into that damn bird. I've never seen anything like it, an owl diving at a man like that."

An Indian listening to their conversation—one of the praying Indians converted to Christianity—shook his head and said, "Bird was sent by spirit to kill you."

As if things weren't bad enough already!

Half an hour later they surprised an Indian encampment. After a brisk but short fight, they killed some and took another 18 of them prisoner.

The general had been pleased with Church's success and sent two young Native American boys as a present to Boston.

Sanctimonious hypocrites. They could quote Scripture by the hour, but didn't mind cheating the natives out of their lands and making slaves of them. He could appreciate how the Indians must have felt being turfed out of their homes. He remembered how he'd felt when a judge had awarded his ex-wife their house.

He had to admire these early Americans who had worked so hard to make homes in the wilderness. No wonder they were plenty upset when Metacom's forces burned their homes and their crops.

General Sherman would similarly slash and burn his way through the South in the Civil War. Of course, if he and the other Morgans didn't stabilize the *window* that Jeremy had talked about, there would be no Civil War.

This brought him to the point: what was he supposed to be doing here? Jeremy had said that they had to stop the Indians from wiping out the colonies, but his chief concern had been to keep his butt from getting shot off and that same butt firmly in the saddle. It seemed a crazy way to run things, not to tell him what he was supposed to do.

Dan wondered anxiously where the kids were. Laney and J.J. were normal teenagers, competent in their own surroundings, with parents to watch out for them, but would they be able to handle other times and places where they'd be on their own and expected to act like adults? He'd kept his eyes open for both of them, but it was going to be next to impossible to find any of the Morgans because they were probably in different time frames. *Elsewhen,* Jeremy had called it.

Now, December of 1675 as near as he could figure and a few days after he'd been attacked by the owl, they were on the move again, two companies from Plymouth, six from Massachusetts, five from Connecticut, and some men from Rhode Island. All in all, about 1,000 men.

They'd captured a friendly Indian named Peter, who had told the militia where the Narragansetts, who had allied themselves with Metacom and his Wampanoags, had been hiding—in a swamp, inside a bloody big fort.

Dan had hardly slept that night, sleeping on the ground on a thin blanket. In the morning when they got up at dawn, they had only a little water and hardly any food to eat.

It was about to get worse: the wind picked up, becoming a blizzard. For eight hours his horse struggled through three feet of snow in the frozen hell. The one good thing about the day was that the cold had frozen the swamp solid so that they didn't have to worry about becoming bogged down in the quagmire.

They knew they were close to the fort when Narragansett sentries began firing on them.

Finally they saw the fort, built on about five acres on an island in the middle of the swamp. The fort was built out of logs surrounded by a hedge close to 16 feet thick. As if this wasn't enough protection, a moat surrounded the fort. Indians in the four watch towers at the corners of the fort began firing as soon as they saw the militia. There seemed to be only one way into the fort, over a large log that crossed the moat. That would give the Indians a fine opportunity to pick them off one by one.

Now the general was designating certain captains to take their men and try to gain entrance to the fort.

Lucky for him that he and his men weren't in the first wave to assault the fort. Dan was no coward—he had proved that in Vietnam—but he didn't want to find out what would happen to the English if they lost. There weren't any Geneva rules of conduct of war here. They had to win. Many of the men had lost relatives and friends and knew of someone who had been killed or taken captive in the Indian raids on English settlements. In the grim lines of their faces you could see that it was payback time.

Led by their captains, the men swarmed over to the fort. A deadly rain of fire wilted the advance. The English pulled back.

A burly man in an officer's uniform called him over. "Captain Prentice, take some of your men and look for another way in. We'll cover you."

Dan nodded, got off his horse, and beckoned to his men, who eagerly volunteered. Most of them were only kids. They ducked and ran to the far side of the fort. Then he saw it: an unfinished section of one wall, about four feet high and wide enough for a few men at a time to climb over it.

They might be able after all, to get into this place. But could they do it without the Indians finding out?

Quietly, they ran back to their comrades. "Sir, we found a way in," said Dan to the commander who had sent him out to scout out the defenses of the fort.

"Good," said the Major. "Take your men and attack that section. At the same time, the rest of us will spread out around the fort and fire all at once."

Dan and his men stole back to the section they wanted to breach. But no sooner had they run over the frozen moat and climbed over the low walls, than the Narragansetts began firing at them. Now it was every man for himself. In the desperate melee, Dan saw men falling under the withering fire. But the Indians were falling, too, as a few of the militia managed to run inside and fire some deadly shots.

At the same time under covering fire, nearly 400 of the men at the entrance finally broke into the fort. Dan noticed some Indian warriors slipping over the walls of the fort into the swamp.

Inside the fort, bodies littered the ground. A figure staggered out of one of the hundreds of wigwams inside the fort. It was Captain Gardner. He must have gone after an Indian who had tried to take refuge there after the main assault force of the English had broken into the fort.

"Captain Gardner. Are you hurt?" cried Church, who had just run up.

The captain slumped to the ground, looked at Church but couldn't speak. Church took off the man's cap. The captain had been shot in the head.

"See," he muttered just loud enough for Dan to hear, "where the ball has entered his head from the direction of the upland where we entered the swamp."

Dan nodded.

"Aye. This is something General Winslow should know," said Church. Turning to a rangy-looking man with a handlebar mustache, he said, "You, Matthew, take this information to the general and have the good captain taken care of—God rest his soul. And now, Captain Prentice, we have more work to do."

Church turned and sprinted out of the fort. Through the swamp ran a broad, bloody track where the Indians had escaped with their wounded. After firing his musket at one of the escapees, he saw the warrior throw up his hands and fall down.

Stopping to reload, he caught glimpses of Church's men running past him, firing. Then a sound behind him made him turn around.

Indians, between him and the fort!

Church had seen them, too, and was cautioning his men to hold their fire and creep up on the enemy.

"For heaven's sake, don't fire! Those are friendly Indians!" yelled a sergeant in the fort.

There was a pause, like a frame of a movie suddenly frozen, then pandemonium. The sergeant had made a mistake, his last one. His body jerked from the impact of at least a dozen shots from the Indians clustered now in front of the fort.

It was like stirring up an ant heap, thought Dan as he crouched down and finished tamping down his powder. Many of the Indians fell, while others were so startled by the unexpected volley coming from behind them that they ran off in all directions, some into the swamp and some back into the fort into a ramshackle hovel.

The way he charged right back into the fort, Church had to be crazy. This time his luck seemed to have run out. Three shots rang out. Church stumbled and fell.

"Run! You can take them now. Their powder is spent," shouted Church clapping a hand to his thigh.

The men cheered and charged the hut, out of which flew a volley of arrows.

Dan put an arm around Church to support him. "We've got to get you to safety."

Holding up a tattered wad of red yarn blackened with powder burns, Church said, "Providence has saved me again, Captain Prentice, this time in the guise of your mittens."

Good thing those bullets didn't have the range or stopping power of 20th-century ones and that the yarn in those mittens had been so thick.

"If I had not stuffed them into my pocket, I should be grievously injured and unable to ride my horse," continued Church. "Ah, well, God works in mysterious ways."

"You have no idea how mysterious," was Dan's last coherent thought before what felt like a bolt of lightning surged through him, plucking him out of his host body.

CHAPTER 29

Priscilla Matthews–Marjory Morgan Bennett

Near Salem, Massachusetts, September 2, 1692

Although the man couldn't be more than 50 years old, his posture was erect as that of a much younger man. That he was also Indian made no difference to Marjory.

His dark eyes, clouding over with what she recognized as the beginnings of cataracts, held a powerful force and vigor, and in them was a kind of knowing that sent a tremor of fear through her, although the information coming to Marjory from the mind of Priscilla Matthews was that the Indian was a shaman who had once given her some herbs that had cured her husband's bilious fever. "Englishwoman," he said, "we must talk."

"Come in and sit down."

She waved him to a stool on which he seated himself gingerly like a man who wasn't used to such household furnishings.

Marjory watched as Nicholas came over and rested a hand on top of a chair to stand beside her. Nicholas Stevens had been sent to the same time and place as she, and was now living as Priscilla Matthews's husband, Josiah. After a week of living in this 17th-century New England town in a plain little house without even a bathroom, she still wasn't used to seeing him dressed in breeches and stockings and a short, close-fitting russet jacket. If ever, no *when* they left this appalling place and returned to their time period, she would never say a word about his bow ties.

Dressed in a long skirt billowing out from the several petticoats underneath it and a bodice to which was tied a pair of
sleeves covered by shoulder pieces, Marjory supposed she must
look just as odd to him.

Whatever they had to do here, she hoped they could get it over
with soon, so they could return to the comforts of 20th-century
civilization. Life here was very difficult. Simply making a meal
was a time-consuming task when you had to raise or shoot your
dinner. Knowledge gained from his host's memories had enabled
Nicholas to use the flintlock he had found in the house. With
quiet pride, he had brought her a wild turkey he had managed to
shoot.

They were fortunate to have produce from the garden to eat,
but the rest of the ripe peas, corn, cucumbers, beans, and other
vegetables would have to be picked soon and preserved for the
winter. They would need these crops to live on if they stayed
much longer.

She would also have to pick and dry the herbs used to keep
both Nicholas and her healthy. Beets, Priscilla's mind told her,
were good for getting rid of lice and dandruff. Marjory shuddered.
How had the early colonists ever survived? There was so much to
learn here!

She had been disturbed to find that one of her front teeth and
several molars were missing. Judging by the rotten state of some of
the others, she wouldn't be surprised if more were on the way out.
Part of the trouble had to be what the New Englanders ate. Even if
they didn't have any processed junk food, they ate a lot of sugar,
called a loaf here and shaped like a cone, which came from Brazil.
She had discovered the sugar in what Nicholas had informed her
was the keeping room where food supplies were stored.

Thinking of food reminded her that the Indian looked hungry. "I'll fix you something to eat," she said. "Then we can talk."

He looked at her with a wary expression and then slowly nodded.

Even though it was autumn, it was still warm. There was no
way to keep things cold. When they'd first come a week ago, she
had noticed a simmering pot of stew hanging from an iron hook

over the small fire burning in the massive fireplace. Each day she threw in more vegetables. It might not be particularly nutritious to overcook food that way, but it did fill you up and saved a lot of time.

Ladling out a generous portion onto a pewter plate, Marjory carried it, together with a spoon and two biscuits, a little burned but then she was used to baking in her Aga, her reliable stove almost as elderly as herself, to the Indian. He took it with a grunt of thanks and ate the whole thing with dispatch.

"What is your name and where are you from?" asked Nicholas.

Wiping his lips on his sleeve, the Indian answered shortly, "Kiontawakon. I live one moon's walk from here."

"You're far from home. Who are your people?"

"The Senecas. They have been overrun by the whites who are beginning to cover the land like a plague of grasshoppers and hunt my people like animals and force them to live . . . "

He began to cough, a hacking, dry sound that seemed to go on and on.

"My people cry out to me," Kiontawakon finished in a hoarse whisper.

Nicholas cleared his throat and said, "I can appreciate your distress, but why do you tell us this?"

There was a short pregnant silence. Then Kiontawakon began to speak in a slow, deliberate fashion. "There was a boy whose spirit name was Jason."

Through a roaring in her ears, Marjory heard Nicholas's quick intake of breath. Putting a hand on the table to steady herself, she sat down on a chair. Her distress had not gone unnoticed by the Indian. His gaze was fixed unwaveringly on her now.

"When did you see Jason?" she asked, her voice thin and high.

"Many, many seasons ago, before Metacom went to the spirit world and his squaw and son were sold into slavery."

"What happened to Jason?"

Kiontawakon allowed a smile to touch the corners of his lips—not a friendly smile, noted Marjory—but rather that of a predator. Ignoring her question, he said, "The Stone Person has told me that you are spirits come from the future. You can help my people so they do not have to live in shame."

"Even assuming we could do this, that's asking rather a lot."

"The Stone Person says that you two have the power."

Nicholas shook his head.

"The white woman, Susanna Morgan. Stay away from her."

"The boy, what happened to him?" demanded Nicholas.

"Died in battle," the Indian replied curtly. Then, getting up, he carefully adjusted his blanket around himself and walked out of the house.

CHAPTER 30

Kiontawakon

Near Salem, Massachusetts,
September 2, 1692

Late that night, a gibbous moon floating high above him and several miles from the nearest settlement, Kiontawakon sat by a small fire and began to meditate as he stared into the bowl of water. As the water began to swirl, the image of a sleeping white man emerged.

Kiontawakon felt his breathing and his heart rate slowing as his presence glided close to the man. Ever since the League's council had rejected his advice to help Metacom fight against the settlers, matters had gone badly for the Indians. He had seen with his own eyes the heads of Metacom and his brother-in-law, Tuspaquin, and other fierce warriors on the palisades of Fort Hill in Plymouth.

As the colonists had retaliated fiercely against the burning of their towns, the Indians had been driven farther back into the forests. Some whites, but many more of his people, had died, not only in battle but from a strange disease the whites called smallpox.

Kiontawakon's own tribe, the Senecas, had grumbled about the fact that none of his rituals had seemed to appease the spirits. Victory in warfare now belonged to the white man. It didn't matter that he had accurately foretold what would happen. Everything was his fault. He must be a witch. Even his guardian spirit had deserted him. And so, finally, in great anguish of spirit, one night he had left the dwellings of his people to roam by himself.

His one burning aim was to rid the world of Morgans and end their lineage forever.

He had learned of this one, Peter, who would continue the Morgan line. If he could be stopped, then all might be well.

The white man was dreaming now, small drops of spittle collecting at the sides of his mouth and his eyelids jerking. Give him something to dream about, something that would ensure that Peter would bring a world of trouble down upon his mother and himself!

Kiontawakon threw the last of his sacred tobacco into the fire, brought out his drum, and settled back on his haunches, ready to begin his shamanic journey to the Lower World, where he would work his magic through the spirits that lived there.

CHAPTER 31

Peter Morgan

Near Salem, Massachusetts,
September 3, 1692

The next morning when Peter Morgan awoke, he had a violent headache. This was so unusual that he immediately attributed it to the dream he'd had that night, a dream that had been frighteningly real. He had watched his mother step up to a kind of altar where the Black Man waited. Leering, he handed her a pen, which she took and signed her name with a flourish in his book. Then, to Peter's absolute horror, she pulled the demon's head down to hers and kissed him.

His heart was pounding so violently that he feared for his life. Was his mother a witch? Surely he couldn't have just imagined it. His relations with his mother had been strained for some time. The old woman kept her money close, while he—her only heir—was forced to make shift on a scant pittance.

She was always railing at him, finding fault with the way he dealt with the merchants. Just last week he'd returned from Boston, his pockets filled with coin. He'd made a good profit on her timber and produce that he and Jack had taken into town. She'd ignored that and inquired with venom in her voice as to why he had paid so much for the household goods he had bought from Captain Hartaker, goods that she would sell for a pretty penny to the colonists.

Then she'd gone on to berate him for his incompetence and wound up with her usual whining complaint that if she weren't housebound by stiffened joints, she'd go by herself and deal with the merchants as she'd done before for years.

Racked by chills that were not alleviated by the warmth of the air around him, Peter wanted nothing better than to go to his minister and ask his advice. He knew, though, that until he made up his mind as to whether or not the dream was real, that this was a thing best left undone. Already in this year of our Lord 1692, in Salem, 13-year-old Ann Putnam had accused people of witchcraft, and he knew the fever would spread.

Another spasm seized him. The penalty for witchcraft was death. Much as he disliked and even hated his mother upon occasion, he had no wish to see her die—not unless she was truly a witch. In that case, perhaps, it was only proper that he should tell Judge Hathorne so that this evil could be rooted out.

An unaccustomed excitement beginning to warm him, Peter licked his dry lips. Often while his mother was ranting at him, she would threaten to disinherit him and give her money to the poor. If she carried out her threat, he would be left penniless and unable to marry and support a family. Already some 40 years of age, he longed for the comfort of a wife and children who would rise up, as the scriptures said, and call him blessed.

The thought of going through life with nothing filled him with dread. Peter realized that he was not like his mother, who had always seemed to him a heroic and awe-inspiring figure out of Greek myth, a veritable Medusa or one of the Furies meting out terrible punishments to the unfortunate.

Peter sighed, but his spirits revived as he realized that now his mother's fate was in his hands. The time had come to take action. Exactly what action he wasn't sure, but something. He would do something. Soon.

CHAPTER 32

Priscilla Matthews–Marjory Morgan Bennett

Susanna Morgan's farm near
Salem, Massachusetts,
September 4, 1692

For the last two days since Kiontawakon had brought news of Jason's death, Nicholas had been brooding. When Marjory arose early to fix their breakfast, she found Nicholas slumped in a chair and staring fixedly at his gun on the table.

"I don't see what good we're doing," burst out Nicholas, "dumped into 1692 in New England with not a clue as to why we've come."

"Jeremy must know what he's doing."

"That may be, but is there something he's not telling us, maybe *quite a lot of somethings?*"

"I think we have to trust him."

"Why? Maybe an alternate future wouldn't be as bad as he said."

"Would you rather we had stayed home and did nothing, just let the Morgan line disappear?"

Nicholas drew back a little at this and said, "No, of course not. I just worry that J.J.'s death was a prelude to all of us being wiped out. And I'm not even a Morgan," he said with an attempt at humor.

Marjory put her hand over his. "Nicholas, I know it's frustrating not to know what's going on—not to mention having none of the amenities of modern life—but we will have to use our intuition to discover our purpose here."

"And if that's not enough?"

"I don't believe that for a minute."

"There's something I haven't told you." Nicholas ran a hand through his thinning gray hair. "We may have a problem. While going over the household goods and furniture here, I learned something."

"What did you find out?"

"I picked up that flintlock. Fourteen years ago in 1678 Josiah Matthews used it to kill a man."

Nicholas's face was white. Poor man. He was such a gentle person. It must be quite a shock to find that in the past you had killed someone and that all the emotions surrounding the past were lodged firmly in your mind.

"How did it happen?"

"I, or rather Josiah, had heard that a few cases of smallpox had been found in Boston. He was desperate to find his sister and take her away from there. When he got to her house . . ."

Nicholas stopped, overcome by emotion. Then he pulled himself together and continued. "He was too late. He found his sister and her husband in bed—dead. Ghastly sores covered their bodies. Their little boy had died the same way. But three-year-old Becky was unmarked and lying on her parents' bedroom floor. She had died from starvation."

Nicholas moistened his lips. "Then Josiah heard a noise downstairs. When he went into the parlor, he found a man there putting a locket, which Josiah had given his sister on her birthday, into his pocket. He shot him."

"Oh, Nicholas, how dreadful!"

He looked up at her and said, "It's beginning again."

"What is?"

"Smallpox. One of the things I picked up from Josiah's mind was that there have been rumors of the disease in Boston. Last

214

time it killed one-fifth of the population of that town. What will it do this time? And Salem isn't that far from Boston.

"You see what this could mean? We could die here before we ever find out what we're supposed to do."

"Why don't we delve some more into our hosts' memories? At the very least, we might learn something useful, perhaps find out why Kiontawakon doesn't want us to visit Susanna Morgan."

"We have nothing to lose," said Nicholas gloomily.

They sat back in the uncomfortable chairs and closed their eyes.

"Here's something," said Nicholas. "Two Morgans live around here, not only Susanna but also her son, Peter."

"I wonder if she's the Susanna Geraldine's been dreaming about. According to Priscilla's memories, Susanna keeps her son, her business agent, on a short leash, giving him hardly any money to live on."

"At least not enough for a family to survive on," observed Nicholas. "And if he doesn't have a family . . ."

"There won't be any Morgans," said Marjory, letting out a deep breath. "So our job must be to persuade Susanna to pay Peter a decent wage so he can have a family."

"But is it likely that a stubborn old woman like her would listen to us? From what I gather from Josiah's memories, the Matthews weren't particular friends of hers. In fact, Susanna has a history of not listening to anyone."

"Still, we have to try," argued Marjory. "And I have an idea that might work."

Susanna Morgan, her hair tucked neatly underneath a ruffled white cap and her figure encased within a full-skirted gown made of some dark, heavy stuff, could have sat for a portrait of a typical Puritan woman. Age had been cruel to her. Her skin was muddy and wrinkled, her body stooped. But her eyes were bright and filled with a wary intelligence.

Marjory was surprised that Susanna had received them at all. When she and Nicholas had arrived on the doorstep of the large house, the maid answering the door had been doubtful about letting them come in and had kept them waiting in the hallway for some minutes before returning with the message that Susanna would receive them.

They had found Susanna sitting in front of an ornate fireplace where a well-stoked fire made the room very warm. Unsmiling, she asked them to sit down.

Her voice was a surprise, resonant and vital. "So what brings you two to my house, Goody Matthews and Goodman Matthews?" she asked.

Marjory said, "Ever since childhood I have had the Sight. Lately, I have had some rather disturbing revelations."

"I have known you for years, Goody Matthews, as a God-fearing Christian woman, but if our pastor should hear of these *revelations*, he might well think you were in league with the devil. What say you to this?"

"I will tell you only the truth, Mistress Morgan, and trust to your good sense to discern whether this be from God or no."

"You may or may not have the Sight, but it puzzles me why you see fit to make me your confidant."

"Because it touches you, Goody Morgan, and your son."

Susanna's voice was harsh as she exclaimed, "Peter! What has this to do with him?"

Nicholas had that closed look on his face that told Marjory she was on her own.

"Sometimes the fate of nations depends on small things, upon whether, for instance, a man's or woman's line dies out so that those who might have performed certain works affecting the course of that nation's history never come to birth."

Dead silence. Susanna's face was impassive. Only a tic at the side of her jaw showed that she was in the grip of some strong emotion.

When her words came, they were slow but full of intensity. "Last night I dreamed of my son. I saw him going to our pastor, telling him of his suspicion that I was a witch." Susanna spat out the word *witch* with a virulence that startled Marjory.

"In my dream, they took me and condemned me to hang, and, of course, if that happened, Peter would inherit my property. It has happened to others. I will tell you this—I am ready to disown Peter. He has always hated me."

"Not hated but loved you, but he thought that you never returned that love."

Susanna laughed, a harsh, bitter sound. "You speak of things you know nothing about. He is weak."

Following an intuitive feeling that had been building in her ever since Susanna had mentioned her son, Marjory asked, "Like Jeremy?"

"What do you know of my brother?" demanded Susanna.

"He never contacted you after he went to Amsterdam. You were left to fend for yourself in London, where, if it had not been through the good offices of a certain gentleman who ensured your survival by making you his heir, you would have starved and worse."

"No one knows this," said Susanna, giving a violent start. "Do you come by this information through your gift, or have you been spying on me? What do you want from me?" she shouted.

"Only that you listen to us," said Marjory, striving to keep her voice low and soothing. "We ask nothing for ourselves, only that you follow your heart, for, you see, if the Morgan line ends with Peter, then great destruction will come upon these colonies, for his descendants have a great work to perform."

Susanna went back to her seat before the fire and sat down heavily. Most of her ill temper appeared to have left and a tiredness to have set in. "What do you suggest?" she asked with a touch of sarcasm.

Marjory tried not to let her sudden joy show. "Let Peter have enough to live on to support a wife. He is of an age when most men have married."

As though afraid of saying anything impulsive, Susanna pursed her lips together. "I will think on this matter. Good morning to you both."

I have done my best, thought Marjory, but was it good enough?

Walking back to their house, she glanced at Nicholas, who was kicking offending clods of dirt out of his way. The certainty came to her that he would be as glad as she to part. This lifetime has shown her that they had little in common.

However, it was fortunate that he had come with her. She might not have found out their incompatibility until too late. Certainly, he must know that, too.

Also, it would have been terribly awkward for her to live in that small house with Josiah Matthews, a complete stranger. And, most importantly, it was Nicholas who had hit upon the salient fact that Peter Morgan couldn't marry because he didn't have enough money to support a family.

Nicholas said little until they reached their little house. He flung himself into a chair and asked, "So what's to eat? More damn slop?"

"Yes, that's all there is," replied Marjory quietly.

Nicholas looked at her with contrition in his eyes. "I'm sorry, but this place is becoming more than I can take. Not a cup of coffee in the whole place or anything to read except a Bible, and I'm not about to start reading *that* now. When I was a boy, my parents shoved enough religion at me to last lifetimes."

Muttering something about "religious fanatics," he'd gone outside, and that was the last she'd seen of him until it became dark. When he returned, he went straight to bed. Then, when Marjory was quite sure that he was asleep, she'd slipped into bed beside him. She had no choice: it was the only bed in the whole house. As she listened to his snoring, she wondered what kind of future she or the other Morgans had, or if they even had one.

CHAPTER 33

Priscilla Matthews–Marjory Morgan Bennett

Susanna Morgan's farm near
Salem, Massachusetts,
September 4, 1692

A thumping at the door woke Marjory. Was it Indians ready to burn the house down around their heads? Stupid idea. One would never hear them until it was too late. This had to be a neighbor.

As she pulled on a robe, she reflected that it was good, for once, to feel no aches in her joints. She'd miss that part of their adventure, the body that was 20 years younger than her own, but she wouldn't miss being stuck here in this repressive society.

Nicholas was still asleep, his arm flung over his eyes, his jaw slack, and his mouth half-open. He hadn't taken too well to this time frame, either.

The man at their door had a hard, insolent look to him. "Goody Matthews?"

"Yes, and who might you be?"

"Abel Granger, Mrs. Morgan's man. She bade me tell you that she would receive you at ten o'clock sharp. It is now past eight," he said pointedly, his gaze flickering over her with barely concealed distaste.

No doubt to him she seemed like a layabout.

Ignoring his rudeness, she said, "I will be there at the appointed hour. Good day, sir."

She closed the door and went back into the bedroom.

"Who was that?" asked Nicholas sleepily.

"Abel Granger, Susanna's servant. He came to tell me that she wants to see me at ten this morning."

Nicholas opened his eyes at that. He didn't seem the least bit concerned that Susanna didn't want to see him. In a much better mood than the night before, he said, "I think I'll go out and find something to put in the pot."

While he was gone, Marjory swept the ashes out of the hearth and picked a few more vegetables to put in the pot simmering on the hearth.

When it was almost time to leave, Nicholas still had not returned. She hoped he was enjoying himself. Tramping around outside was the only time he seemed happy. Marjory went to the wardrobe that held their few clothes and chose a bonnet and cloak. She put them on and went outside.

The day was clear and cool. The sky was a bright blue with huge flocks of passenger pigeons flying overhead. By the 20th century, they had been hunted to extinction. She took a deep lungful of the bracing air filled with the scents of growing things in the fields and the forest that surrounded the small village. A faint smell of wood smoke hung in the air. In the distance, she could see the fiery red bursts of maples and men cutting down trees for wood to burn in the long winter ahead.

The mile-long walk to Susanna's was invigorating. Along the way she met a few folk, who nodded to her as they passed. She was surprised to see that some of the women were dressed very elegantly with extravagantly decorated hats and lace at their throats, their coats fastened with ornamental buttons and fancy braided trims. No doubt the pastors would thunder from their pulpits against this luxurious display.

Susanna's maid answered the door and this time immediately took her in to see Susanna, who was seated in front of a fire.

"I wished to talk with you privately," said Susanna without preamble, pointing to a chair opposite her.

She looked strained, but her voice was as firm as ever. "You have set me thinking about what will happen to my son at my demise. I am in good health, but it is not given to any of us to know the hour of our passing."

She paused and gave Marjory a keen look as she asked, "Have you more information pertaining to me or my son?"

Marjory shook her head. "Only what I told you yesterday," she said.

"Are you still persuaded of the opinion that I am too hard on Peter?"

"It is not for me to say, but surely you do not wish your property to go to strangers?"

"Not to these folk with their pious cant," muttered Susanna. "I have had a deal of trouble to bite my tongue all these years, but hard necessity has taught me the virtue of keeping my true opinions to myself. At least these Puritans respect my hard work and the fact that I have built up a thriving business of my own, where I owe nothing to anyone.

"Now as to the situation at hand; I have been acquainted with you for over twenty years, Goody Matthews. You are reported to be an honest, hardworking woman, but this is the first time I have heard of this Sight of yours."

"It is a gift, one which I have seldom shared with others for fear it might be misunderstood." That was true, at least.

"Wise, very wise, but what made you decide to share your, ah, insights with me?"

"A great compulsion was laid upon me to speak to you of this," said Marjory carefully. "And," she said, looking straight at Susanna, "I am very glad I did."

Susanna's mouth worked, and for a few moments she was unable to speak. Mastering her emotion, she said, "No one has ever spoken so truthfully to me."

"Because they fear you."

"But you do not."

"True, I respect you. You have succeeded in making a good life for yourself and your son. It must have been very difficult."

"Indeed it was."

"Sometimes it is difficult to allow one's self to love," said Marjory, half to herself.

"Love is something one hears little of around here," said Susanna. "More like judgment and damnation. But I digress. You advise me to help my son so he may marry?"

"It would seem advisable."

"For the good of the nation to come, you say." She leaned back in her chair. "I shall think on what you have told me."

And with that she would have to be satisfied. Marjory wouldn't know what Susanna had decided until the Morgan family returned to the 20th century or, if Susanna decided not to help Peter, the Morgans would not return, would never be born.

She felt sorry for Peter. With luck, he might get to choose his own bride, although Susanna, no doubt, would have a great deal to say about it, as she had a great deal to say about everything.

Marjory stood up.

"You are leaving? Will you not stay for some tea?"

Marjory shook her head. She felt a sudden urgency to go home. "Thank you, but I must leave. I'm glad we talked." Hesitating, she added, "I would appreciate it if our conversation went no further than your ears."

Using her cane to balance herself, Susanna stood up and said, "To whom would I mention it? Godspeed, Goody Matthews."

Marjory rose. With what she knew to be a certainty, she said, "I doubt we will talk again."

CHAPTER 34

Susanna Morgan

Susanna Morgan's farm,
near Salem, Massachusetts,
September 6, 1692

"You did what?"

"Mother, the mare broke her leg. I had to shoot her."

Susanna thumped her cane on the floor. "The mare was only eleven years old, good for another few years at least. I will need to buy another animal to replace her. Do you suppose that money can be plucked from trees?"

Peter hung his head, just as he used to do when he was a child. Susanna wanted to hurl her cane at him. Then he looked at her calmly and said, "Not at all, Mother."

Well, well, what was this? Was Peter finally standing up to her?

"Go on," she urged. "I can see you want to say more."

He was chewing his bottom lip, another signal that he wanted to say something. Would he do it or lapse into his usual subservient attitude? Part of her wanted him to do so, and another part wanted him to stand up for himself.

"Well, son, do have the kindness not to keep me waiting. I am old and could die at any minute."

She looked for an expression, no matter how fleeting, of joy at her words, but there was none, only a newfound firmness. "As you wish, Mother. I have worked faithfully for you for many a year.

Now it seems time that you provide me with an income that will enable me to marry and provide for a family."

"And if I don't? Then what?"

Would he threaten her? Accuse her of witchcraft? That was the scene in her dream.

Peter's mouth opened and then closed. Then he looked her full in the face—something he never did—and said firmly, "I will continue to work for you. After all, you are my mother and are all I have in this world."

Susanna turned away so that he would not see the tears that had sprung to her eyes. A painful silence ensued.

"Mother?"

Her throat closed up as a surge of love for Peter threatened to overcome her. Her son, her only kin now. Her dream of Peter accusing her of witchcraft must have been false, maybe inspired by the mayhem wreaked in Salem. What had Tituba, the minister's slave, wrought, telling stories of witchcraft to impressionable young girls like Ann Putnam? Ann and others had accused hundreds of men and woman and even a child of five years of being Satan's servants. Nineteen of these poor wretches had been hanged.

She cleared her throat. "I think we may come to some arrangement. You have been a faithful son."

She could hardly bear the sudden look of joy on Peter's face. "But there must be no slacking in your work, Peter," she warned.

"Of course not, Mother. And I thank you."

She waved away his thanks. "I will give you money to buy another mare. I hear that Goodman Johnson has one for sale. You might visit him tomorrow. Oh, and I will pay you a monthly wage—nothing exorbitant—but enough to keep you and a wife and any children you may have."

Peter could hardly contain his joy. "Again I give you thanks, Mother. There is a girl in Salem . . ."

"That hotbed of witches! Not that I believe in all the nonsense that's been going on there."

"There is a rumor that the governor's wife has been accused of being a servant of Satan," said Peter.

"Humph! A fine order of things when people of quality are subjected to that sort of thing! Mark my words, this nonsense will be coming to an end soon. The governor's wife, indeed!"

"You are right, Mother. The accusations must cease soon."

Peter actually smiled at her then. It had been many a year since he had done that. She found that she was actually enjoying that and the way he was squaring his shoulders. Why had it taken her so long to see how like his father, Paul, he was, the only man— beside her father and once Jeremy—who had ever loved her.

But she had pushed away the few men who had ventured to court her. She had assumed that they all wanted her money more than they had desired her and would take away her freedom to act as she pleased. And now Peter was all she had. But at least he had proved himself to be someone she could trust and, she admitted to herself, even someone she could love.

If what Goody Matthews had told her was correct, there would be grandchildren, some of whom would become instrumental in building a great nation. What more could an old woman ask for?

With a feeling of satisfaction, Susanna sat down in her favorite chair (the only stick of furniture belonging to Paul that she had originally brought with her) and began to daydream of a life encompassing her descendants, who would go on to become great men and women.

CHAPTER 35

Bryanna   Vernemeton, a Druid sanctuary, a little over
100 miles north of London,
April 13, A.D. 61

Bryanna looked at the body of her son lying on the pallet and tried to brush aside the sense of guilt disturbing her. While Bran had consented to allowing his body to be used temporarily by another, he had not known of her ultimate purpose. But there was no help for it. She had consulted her oracles that all said the same thing: negative forces would try to wipe out her line. If she could not stop them, Bran would die and history would take quite a different path from what had to be.

The boy moaned; his eyelids fluttered, then opened.

"Bryanna?" he asked uncertainly as he looked at her with those blue eyes that had always produced in her an aching tenderness for her son.

"You are safe here now with me," she replied to the spirit in Bran's body.

The boy, a man now of 16 years, sat up. She repressed the urge to take him in her arms and hold him close the way she used to when Bran was very young, before she had sent him away to be fostered. To be reared so in another family led to lasting friendships. The bonds of kinship in these children became as strong as that of birth parents. They learned to trust and respect their foster family and later became more apt to exchange information and even form political alliances with them. Now Bran—or rather his future self—had returned.

"I thought I died," he said, putting a hand wonderingly to the small of his back.

"You did die, or at least the host body you were in, died. Do not distress yourself. Only the body dies; the spirit is immortal and incarnates over and over again. Now there is much to discuss but before we do, have you need of food or drink?"

The boy nodded. "I feel a little weak."

"You will find wine and food over there."

He stood up and walked a little unsteadily over to the table where he began wolfing down the meat and little barley cakes she had prepared earlier.

"Where am I? *When* am I this time?" the young man asked, his mouth full of food.

"You are in the body of my son, Bran. We live here in Vernemeton, a Druid sanctuary in Alban."

The boy still looked a little dazed. Then his face cleared. He must be receiving Bran's memories.

The boy stopped eating. "Oh, yeah. Now I remember where I am this time. You're my mother—and a Druid, too."

"Yes, and you, my son, are a Druid in training."

Her foster father, the Archdruid, had spent years preparing her for her holy calling, imparting to her the ancient wisdom that few—even Druids—were given to know. She had learned that one could connect directly with the One God without the intervention of priests. Some of the gods worshipped by the Keltoi were merely aspects of the One God, while others represented very human aspects of humanity. An example of such was Teutalis, the god of war. The One God, she had learned, desired humanity to live in peace and harmony with each other.

But the Keltoi still clung to their old ways. It would take a giant upheaval to pry them loose from their old beliefs. That time was fast approaching.

She nodded. It was important to tell him enough, but not too much. Choosing her words with care, she said, "Here in our sanctuary, the chieftains of many of the tribes will be attending a very important ceremony."

Now that the spirit from the future was here, her son would not be part of that ceremony at the feast of Beltane honoring Bel, the god of fire and light, on the first of May—not if she could help it.

She went on, "Many of the chieftains believe that the tribes must unite now in order to expel the Romans."

"What will happen if they don't?"

"The sacred groves will be cut down and the sanctuaries defiled, Druid influence will be broken, and Alban will become just another outpost of the Roman Empire."

"Why would they bother the Druids? I thought they were holy people, not warriors."

She smiled sadly. This young one was so naive. He knew nothing about the all-pervasive influence that the Druids exercised on their people, an influence that extended from legal to spiritual matters.

"You must understand that a Druid is not just a priest; he also acts as a judge, a teacher, a healer, and a counselor to the king, who must obey his edicts. If one is to destroy the will and heart of the people, one must destroy the Druid priesthood.

"The Romans also fear that Druids are fomenting resistance to them. It is true that some rebels have found sanctuary on Mona, a trading depot and a most holy Druid center.

"But they have another reason for wanting to destroy us. The Romans know that we Druids control the flow of gold from the Wicklow Hills of the sacra insula, Ireland, all through this realm and across the channel dividing us from the tribes of Gaul and others.

"The Romans have a madness for gold. They do not think of it as we do, a metal out of which can be fashioned things of beauty, the most beautiful of which we use in rituals and offerings to the gods. They would seize this gold for themselves, but first they must smash the power of the Druids."

She paused. Here was the delicate part. "Would you be willing to follow my counsel?"

Under her intense scrutiny, the boy flushed. She could see the conflict going on within him. In the end, as she had known he would, he nodded cautiously.

Smiling at him she said, "Rest now. We will speak again tomorrow."

It was a journey that her oracles had told her would have fateful consequences, she reflected as she walked out of the dwelling where she had resided for so many years.

CHAPTER 36

Bran—Jason Kramer   Vernemeton, April 13, A.D. 61

Watching Bryanna's retreating back, J.J. wanted to shake information out of her the way you'd shake apples off a tree, but he suspected it wouldn't work that way. She knew far more than Bran did. J.J. sensed that her plans ran deep and that she was keeping them to herself, sharing only what she thought he should know.

The Keltoi must be the Celts. A book he'd read in grade six showed pictures of fierce long-haired men holding shields in front of their naked bodies, swinging away with long swords at the shorter, darker Romans dressed in body armor and helmets.

The Romans had taken more than 100 years to conquer Britain, he remembered, and, at that, Scotland had never been subdued. The Romans had finally built a wall to keep out the marauding Picts and Scots. Ireland had managed to stay free, too.

He must be somewhere in the time period around A.D. 61 in what would later be called England. Even if this body died, the real him would probably survive—at least according to Bryanna. Nobody had really spelled everything out; both she and Jeremy had been short on details.

He looked down at his body: his limbs were long and muscular. He'd try to look after this body better than Tom's. He shivered as he remembered running through the field of peas, trying to get to the canoe that would take him to the boat. Would Church have died if he, Jason, hadn't taken a bullet for him?

But it *did* happen, or would happen. Keeping track of time while you hopped back and forth through history got a little confusing. Restless, he stepped to the door, fastened by wooden pegs to the door frame, opened it, and went outside.

He stood on the slope of a hill on which clustered a dozen or more round, thatched buildings measuring about 50 feet across, similar to the one out of which he had just come. Dwarfing the houses was a thick grove of trees at the top of the hill. A herd of cows lowed in the distance, while a flock of geese hissed at him. Horses roamed around in an enclosure.

A thundering in his ears made him turn. A man with long fair hair stiffened into a flying mane was pounding toward him on his horse from which swung a head, the eyes still glaring and the mouth twisted into a hideous grimace. Scowling fiercely at him, at the last minute the man swerved, letting out a loud guffaw.

"Kunagnos rides like Epona herself," said a feminine voice admiringly behind him.

He knew that voice! Or Bran did, and very well, too. Emotions pouring into him along with the memories were making him blush. Swinging around, he almost knocked into a young woman. Devonna was only a few inches shorter than he was, a real Amazon with dark red hair tumbling down between two enameled combs to her slim waist. Her lightly freckled skin was tanned, her cheeks and mouth red. Two amber-colored eyes peered anxiously at him.

"You look pale, Bran. Have you been fasting over much? I know Beltane will be soon upon us, but you still have some time to prepare."

J.J. was spared from replying by the appearance of a middle-aged man whose hair had been shaved from his hairline at his forehead to the middle of the top of his head. The rest of his hair, blond mixed with gray, hung down past his shoulders. Over breeches and a linen tunic, he had flung a cloak; the blue-and-green design on it reminded J.J. of a Scottish tartan.

Coming closer the man said, "My son."

Mabon wasn't Bran's real father, who had died shortly after coming to Britain from Ireland, but his foster father.

"Mabon. Greetings. May the gods look with favor on you."

Mabon nodded and said, "Let us go find out what Kunagnos has to report."

J.J. followed Mabon and the girl into a house already crowded by dozens of other people. The lucky ones who'd arrived there first were already seated on animal skins. The rest were standing around chattering to each other. The noise level was fierce, just like between classes at his high school.

Bryanna was there, too. He waved to her. She seemed startled to see him and frowned slightly, then waved back.

Was she mad at him because he went out? Was he under house arrest or something? But if he was to do anything useful in this era, he had to know what was going on.

The noise suddenly stopped. The big guy, Kunagnos, was starting to speak. You could see he was enjoying being the center of attention.

The way he started out with flowery, complimentary phrases made him sound like one of the politicians back home. Finally, he got down to the important part. "Combroges, my people, I have ridden hard from the court of the Iceni, that kingdom, bordering on the east of the North Sea. You remember how after the death of King Prasutagus the Roman procurator, Catus Decianus, confiscated the entire wealth of the king for his emperor, even though Prasutagus had willed half his estate to the emperor Claudius.

"Not content with robbing the king's wife, Queen Boudica, and her two daughters of their inheritance, Decianus had the queen flogged and her daughters raped."

Kunagnos paused as a roar went up. Several men, their long mustaches bristling, brandished their swords.

After a few moments when the crowd fell silent, Kunagnos went on. "It is not the royal women only who suffer. Many chieftains, given gifts of money by the emperor, have now been told that these were loans to be paid back with interest. As well, their lands are forfeit to the new emperor, Nero.

"You know, too, that other tribes suffer. The Trinovantes, neighbors of the Iceni, were forced to flee their homes and lands, which were given to retired Roman army veterans who now idle away their time in theatres and baths. Not content to worship in sacred groves as we do, the former emperor Claudius had the arrogance to rear a temple to himself, built by the sweat and money of our countrymen!"

Men muttered and beat their swords against their shields. Kunagnos held up both hands. The people fell silent. "Boudica and her people arise even now to avenge their wrongs. They offer a glorious cause to fight for: the freedom of all the Keltoi. Who will join them?"

This time men and women jumped up, shouting and stomping their feet.

A man with a livid scar running down the left side of his face, stood up. After the noise had died down, he said, "I am Gruff-udd, of the tribe of the Silures in Cymru, which borders the Irish Sea. I was but a boy when I began fighting the Romans, hitting their outposts and convoys with great success. Under our leader, Caratacus, king of the Catuvellauni, who dominate the lands in the southeast, we fought well, but we were defeated more than once by the Romans under Aulus Plautius. By the time Plautius left for Rome, most of the southeast of this great island had submitted to Roman rule.

"Then Caratacus and I took refuge in Cymru in the Cambrian mountains, where he inspired the Silures and Ordovices to do battle against the Romans. We fought bravely," he said proudly, "but evil finally overtook us. Caratacus fled north and appealed to the Brigantian queen, Cartimandua, to shelter him. She played him false and handed him over in chains to the Romans for judgment."

"But the Silures and Ordovices fight on in the mountains of Cymru, do they not?" asked Kunagnos.

"Yes, for they are men of valor, but how long can they last? I have come to this sanctuary to offer up a sacrifice to Teutalis, in the hopes that this god may grant my prayers for success in battle against the Romans. And yet . . ."

He shrugged uneasily and stared off into space for a long moment before continuing, "The Roman Paulinus Seutonius is a cunning and determined leader. It is known that he was appointed specifically to wipe out resistance among my people.

"It is also rumored that the new emperor, Nero, looks for new ways to fill his treasury. He casts greedy eyes on the rich mineral deposits in our mountains, caring not if they rip out the bowels of Mother Earth to satisfy his avarice.

"As for me, I will join with you in any enterprise to break the Roman yoke and will fight until the sky falls and the sea breaks its bounds."

J.J. shivered. Gruff-udd sounded so bleak.

A hawk-faced woman with bold eyes asked, "What other tribes will help the Iceni, whose queen, Boudica, and her daughters were humiliated by the Romans?"

"The Trinovantes, Coritani, and Cornovii have pledged their aid."

"It does not seem enough," the woman muttered.

"What choice do we have? This may be the last opportunity for the tribes to unite and drive the Romans into the sea. Besides, there are favorable auguries," went on Kunagnos. "In Camulodunum, where the stench of Roman perfume must inflame the gods, there are rumors of the sea turning the color of blood. The ebb tide throws up corpses with shapes akin to those of humans. Some swear to having heard shrieks in the senate house and the theatre and have witnessed the statue of Victory topple from its lofty perch. Shall we fear when the gods favor us?"

A mighty howl split the air. The sheer animal fury of that sound made the hairs on the back of J.J.'s neck stand on end.

Then Bryanna stood up. Instantly, the assemblage stilled. "If you go to war against the Romans," she said bluntly, "those shrieks will be yours, not those of the legionaries, as you fall in battle; the corpses will be yours also that litter the seashore.

"Have you not heard from the mouth of Gruff-udd himself the result of warring with the Romans? They took Caratacus to Rome in chains. His men, who still battle on in the mountains of Cymru, are being steadily exterminated by Seutonius. Do you wish to share their end? Dire consequences await those who meddle with fate."

Her words were greeted with an uneasy muttering. Mabon turned and stared hard at J.J. Even at a distance of five or six yards, he could feel the malice in that look.

What had Bran done to deserve Mabon's dislike? Carefully, J.J. searched Bran's memory. All that came were flashes of the endless conversations the two of them had carried on.

Unlike Kunagnos and most of the others here, Mabon was a Druid, a big man in the priestly hierarchy and well respected. He had spent many years teaching initiates in the special school for aspiring Druids. Bran, who had been one of Mabon's students, would be a Druid himself one day.

More flashes of memory came, of carefully repeating the chants with their mnemonic devices that helped him remember the occult wisdom. The initiates were not allowed to write down anything; writing was only for the recording of accounts and other mundane things. They had to practice hour after hour, for years, until they had perfected their memories. They were human vessels entrusted with the sacred wisdom and must be prepared to sacrifice . . .

J.J.'s head was spinning. He got that Cymru was Wales (he had learned that back home in Winnipeg in history class), but it was a little hard to follow all the other stuff. The Welsh guy, Gruffudd, had worked up the crowd by reminding them how nasty the Romans had been to Queen Boudica and her daughters and asked for their help in defeating the Romans. Good luck with that! The Roman army was unstoppable. Bryanna was right when she said there would be "dire consequences" if they tried to oppose the Romans.

Devonna was pulling on his arm. "Come with me," she whispered.

Wrapping his long cloak tightly around himself, he followed her outside. They walked rapidly toward the grove of trees spearing the sun, which was beginning its descent in the west.

Devonna stopped under the branches of a massive oak. "You are not yourself," she said, looking hard at him. "Have you changed your mind?"

"About what?" J.J. blurted out before he could root around in Bran's memory.

She opened her mouth in surprise, then closed it and looked thoughtfully at him. "I know there are those who can change their shapes into those of the beasts or birds. The dead, too, can come back and possess the living. Has this happened to you, Bran?"

She asked it so simply that he was taken off guard. Not knowing what to say, he said nothing.

"I have loved Bran since first we met," she went on in a low voice. "It is this love I bear him that gives me the right to speak to you in this fashion. I must know if you are Bran or . . ." Her voice caught for a moment, then steadied as she went on. "Not Bran."

He could feel her pain as she gave him the kind of look he had hoped that one day a woman might give him. He couldn't lie to her. "Devonna, you're right. I'm not Bran."

She gasped a little at that, her body tensing up.

"You've got to understand, I didn't have anything to do with this." Did that sound too whiny? But it was true, except that he *had* volunteered for this time travel thing. Of course, at the time, he didn't have a clue what it would mean.

"Look, I'm only here for a little while. Then Bran will come back."

She seemed to cheer up at that. Her body, standing so stiffly, loosened up a bit.

Encouraged, he went on. "Bryanna pulled me here, but it's only temporary, and then Bran will come back and I can go home."

"I don't understand. If you go through with the ceremony, Bran can't come back. He will journey to the Other World."

"What do you mean?"

"Has Bryanna not told you? You are to be sacrificed at Beltane."

Memories surged in him: the Wicker Man, where people and animals were thrust into a giant figure made of straw and wood, which was then set on fire as a sacrifice to Bel. Burned alive! Were they going to do this to him?

The world reeled around him. Blindly, he backed up until the rough bark of an oak gouged his shoulders. "I don't . . . sacrificed? Why?"

"You heard Kunagnos. The Keltoi of this island suffer much under Roman rule. In the olden days before the Romans came, human sacrifices were offered to placate the gods. Now there are only animal offerings. I have heard some say that in this time of great trouble, we need to go back to the old ways."

"Whose idea was this?"

"I think Mabon's," said Devonna slowly, "but many agree with him in this matter."

"What about you? Do you think I should go along with this?"

The girl shuddered involuntarily, then said faintly, "If it helps the Keltoi."

"It's a waste and it won't do any good! The Romans are going to keep coming and coming. It won't make a bit of difference— except to me, and I'll be dead!"

"You are not prepared to die, then?"

He was ready to shout, "Not on your life!" but the strange look in her eyes stopped him. Would she rat on him, tell Mabon he'd chickened out? Would they grab him anyway?

He'd better watch what he said.

"I'll think about it."

She wasn't stupid. Looking skeptically at him, she stepped back. He had to stop her somehow from telling Mabon. No telling what the Druid would do if he thought his prize sacrifice was going AWOL.

"Uh, would you please not tell anyone yet about what I said, not until I've had time to think? All this is kind of a shock."

"You fear death?" Devonna asked, a hint of contempt in her voice.

"Uh, no more than anyone else I know. It's not something I think about a lot."

Devonna's voice softened. "We are told that when we die we go into another beautiful world. Then when we are ready, we are born again into another body. So we never really die."

He could listen to Devonna tell stories all night, but there was something more important that had grabbed his attention. "What's the ceremony like? How do they, you know, kill you?"

"You will receive three blows to the crown of your head, three because that is a sacred number signifying that in everything the gods are three times as powerful as men. Then you will be placed upright on a stool and strangled with a cord by the Vates."

And they were? J.J. began searching Bran's memory. The Vates were a type of priest whose job was to interpret sacrifices, which probably meant they decided who or what was to be sacrificed. They also were astrologers who had to know some mathematics.

"And then," Devonna continued, "to do homage to the god Esus, who demands human sacrifice, you will be stabbed in the throat, releasing your blood into a cauldron. Your body will be lifted onto a white horse, which will convey you to the sacred pool, where Teutates, the god of war, waits to claim you."

J.J. let out a long breath, which he hadn't realized he'd been holding. From what Bran's memories were telling him, the gods only did what you asked if you were really serious about what you were asking, and what could be more serious than sacrificing something really precious—like a human life? He wasn't going to hang around for that, not this guy. But where could he go? He couldn't expect help from Bryanna. She was probably in on it, too.

The Romans wouldn't be interested in sheltering a Druid novice. They were more likely to wipe him out with their own version of an execution, maybe crucifixion, although he'd never heard of their doing that to the Britons. More likely some soldier, figuring one Briton more or less wouldn't matter, would take a casual swipe at him with his sword. The U.S. cavalry had taken a similar attitude toward the Indians.

Oh, oh. Here was Mabon coming toward him. Wonder what he wanted. Devonna was going over to talk to him.

His foster father acknowledged her greeting without breaking stride. Even without the weird hair and the flowing cloak, he would have looked impressive. He had that air of commanding authority that expected instant obedience.

Mabon brushed aside J.J.'s formal greeting with a dismissive gesture and asked, "Do you agree with Kunagnos that we should make war on the Romans?"

It was like being suddenly called on to answer a question in class, when your mind just froze and you couldn't think of a thing. What would Bran have said? Nothing came. He'd have to make this call all on his own. Licking dry lips, he replied carefully, "It depends on your point of view."

Mabon threw back his head and laughed. Then he said drily, "Spoken like a true oracle, whose words can often be taken to mean one thing or another. I had not hoped to see such diplomacy yet in you, Bran. Does this mean that my instruction is bearing fruit?"

The knot in his gut eased. If Mabon were looking for flattery, he'd give it to him in spades.

Before he had time to say a word, Mabon said sharply, "Do not play at words with me, Bran. You have heard the voice of the Keltoi in there." He pointed back to the conical building where the meeting had been held.

"They still argue the merits of going to war with the Romans. Whatever happens, the ceremony must take place. Failure to perform it will mean famine and misery such as we have never seen. The gods must have their divine victim upon which the Keltoi may heap their sins. It is a great honor for you to be so chosen, Bran."

His protest froze on his lips. Mabon wasn't going to take no for an answer. The savage look on the Druid's face told him that. All he could do was nod.

Evidently this satisfied Mabon, for he smiled slightly and said, "I will leave you now to your contemplation. We will talk again soon." With that he left, taking great swinging strides out of the grove.

More than ever, he wanted to run away. His head hurt, and his gut was knotting up so hard he felt sick, but there was nowhere to run. He was stuck here among barbarians.

Maybe talking to a priest, a Christian one, would help. Only there wouldn't be one around here anytime soon. He'd have to tough it out himself.

CHAPTER 37

Mabon Vernemeton, Mabon's private quarters,
April 13, A.D. 61

Mabon settled himself more comfortably on a wolf skin and signaled the girl to serve him. She timidly began pouring out wine, taking care not to spill a drop. Having come all the way from Italy, the wine was expensive, but it was worth every bit of what it had cost. The locally brewed mead was sour and thin in comparison to this heavenly ambrosia.

"I will bring you the pork now, lord." Wearing a green gown fastened with a cord around her waist, she was obviously much impressed with his position. Her face, though plain, had a look of lively intelligence.

It would be important to keep her in her place but not intimidate her to the point that she would be rendered useless, so he smiled at her and said graciously, "You are doing well in my household, Aselma. You will find that I can be generous to those who diligently follow my orders."

Aselma bowed her head humbly. Her father, a landless man in the local village, had jumped at the chance for his daughter to serve the mighty Druid.

Mabon sighed. Sometimes his responsibilities weighed him down. He was expected to guide the Keltoi in all things, whether it was to arbitrate their petty quarrels, find the right herb to effect a cure for some woman's dying child, or to invoke the protection of the gods on the warriors' forays into battle.

Now the most important responsibility of his life had descended upon his shoulders. Although she never spoke of it, he knew that Bryanna kept close many arcane secrets that her foster father had passed on to her, secrets concerning the path that the human race must tread.

He had come upon some of this information almost by accident. A wandering Gaul, who had traveled to many foreign lands, had briefly sought shelter with him. They had stayed up all night talking of the many wondrous things that the traveler had seen.

In the course of their conversation, the stranger had mentioned meeting a Babylonian priest whose life he had saved. In gratitude, the priest had revealed many secret things.

One thing in particular had impressed the traveler. The Babylonians had records going back to the early days of the human race when fleets of vessels came out of the skies and the gods descended and walked with men and married their daughters. Later, these gods had left in their sky chariots, but not before they had taught humans many things. Some few on earth, like Bryanna, still carried that early knowledge.

The most important information that the Gaul had passed on to him was that there were crucial times in the affairs of men when the flow of events could be altered, by what means he had not said, only that occasionally it was done.

Change was inevitable—the Romans were seeing to that! But perhaps a man such as himself could influence that change. The Druids must continue to be in charge of the affairs of the Keltoi. It was only right that ignorant folk be guided by those who knew better, men like him—Mabon. It would be necessary to get rid of those who thought differently, even Druids like Bryanna.

One day Bran had let slip that Bryanna had told him that there was really only One God. When pressed to explain, the boy had mumbled something about the "old wisdom." It was impossible to get anything further out of him; he was too loyal to his mother.

Ever since, Mabon had wondered what else Bryanna knew. Perhaps there were powerful chants and rituals that might be particularly helpful in influencing events in the way that he knew they must go. The Archdruid might have passed on such information to her, but Mabon knew she would never tell him. She distrusted him. He could see it in her eyes. Then he must find that lever that would bend her to his purpose. "Give me the right lever," the wise Greek Archimedes had said, "and I could move the world."

Mabon would move worlds also. It was so written in the cries of the ravens and in the entrails of the animals he had sacrificed. He would be the highest Druid in the land after . . .

His thoughts sheered away from what he must do. He must focus now on the preparations to be made. Smiling at Aselma as she put the dish of pork down on the table in front of him, he picked up the still-warm meat with his hands and began tearing into it with his strong white teeth.

CHAPTER 38

Lucius– Roman Soldier–Dan Morgan

Menai Strait, opposite Mona,
Druid center of learning,
April 13, A.D. 61

The droning in his ears was louder now. *A helicopter?* Dan awoke with a start into the darkness, his heart slamming against his ribs and his mouth sour with the taste of his fear. Any minute mortar fire might be raining down upon them. Night and day he was haunted by the dread that it was his turn next to have his flesh sliced into bloody ribbons by a swarm of bullets or a land mine.

He'd led his squad of three fire teams with four men each out on patrol that day in the stinking jungle. His nerves had been on edge. Like a needle stuck in a scratch on a record, his mind had been playing the one and only theme, "We're caught in a trap, in a trap, in a trap," and it wouldn't quit, kept going round and round in an insane jingle, driving him crazy.

Mike had been boasting about the good time he'd given this sexy babe he'd laid in Saigon, repeating all the lurid details about her tits and ass and what he'd done to her and what she'd done to him, until between the jingle in his head and Mike's boasting, he was sure he was going to go nuts.

In the middle of all this jabbering, Mike had stumbled onto a land mine. He wouldn't lay anyone again. Not ever. Dan had helped the medics pick up all that was left of Mr. Wonderful.

How he'd hated that alien jungle of rotting vegetation where fear curdled your guts and gave you nightmares. You woke up to live even worse nightmares, which you couldn't have begun to imagine.

But this wasn't Vietnam. He was in another place and time, in the body of Lucius, whose memories told of his coming to Britain in A.D. 43 with the Roman army that was subduing the tribes in the southeast of Britain and up into Cymru, or what would later be called Wales. Before that, Lucius had served for six years in Gaul, a place of dense woods, fierce warriors, and little of the comforts of civilization except where the Pax Romana was enforced by the sword.

His youth had been spent battling barbarians; he was growing tired of it. He had served 24 years in the army and was only a year away from retirement—if he could stay alive that long.

Returning to Italy was not an option: his parents were probably long dead, and his friends had forgotten him. He would settle here in Britain. A farm in the south of this land and the pension that Rome offered to its veterans would afford him a good life. A wife to keep him warm at night and to provide him with sturdy sons would be all a man like him could ask for.

Dan pushed away the memories of Lucius, rolled over, and opened his eyes. He had been sleeping in a tent with six other guys. The eighth man in his contubernium was on sentry duty. Dan rubbed his eyes and winced. His right arm hurt like hell. In fact, he could hardly raise it.

Memories came of a battle, which in this timeline had happened only a week ago. A bunch of Celts, wearing bronze helmets, shirts, and trousers, had ambushed the Romans in a narrow pass in the mountains. Javelins came raining down, but the Roman shields deflected most of them. Then a shrieking horde of blue-painted warriors came pouring down from the rocks above. Lucius found himself hacking away at several of them, who had jumped his contubernium. He had just dispatched one of them with his short sword when another one lunged at him.

Lucius brought up his shield a moment too late. As if in slow motion, he saw the Celt grin, saw the blue dragon tattooed on his cheek writhe, and the sun strike his sword as it began its slow descent into Lucius's arm just above his elbow. The exultation on the barbarian's face turned to bewilderment as he clutched the dagger now sticking out of his chest.

The sword falling from his hand, Lucius pivoted to his left where Marcus was yelling, "Behind me! Get behind me!" as he pulled his dagger out of the Celt's chest.

Good old Marcus. He'd never complain about his snoring again. Soon after, it was all over. The Celts melted away into the rocky terrain, leaving several of the Roman supply wagons burning and a number of legionaries dead and others bleeding. Up to that time, he had been lucky not to get killed or banged up too hard.

Guess it was better than dying, but he wouldn't last long in this army if his arm didn't heal soon. When he returned to Camulodunum, he'd offer sacrifices to Mithras, god of victory, who was popular among soldiers, and ask for his help.

Dan pushed away the memories of the life of the man he used to be. He could identify all too well with Lucius, of being alone except for your buddies you depended on to help keep you alive in a place where the natives resented you and were trying to kill you.

Dan couldn't stand any more of these surging thoughts and the snoring of the other six guys. Opening the flap of the goatskin tent, he walked outside and nodded to the sentry on duty.

Living in cities where smog and streetlights obscured the stars, he'd never paid much attention to them. Out here in Roman Britain, the stars hung bright in constellations with which he was only vaguely familiar. By their light and that of the moon, he could make out the squat humps of tents laid out in precise rows.

His arm was hurting worse now. He unwrapped the crude bandage and looked at the swollen red wound. It was in the very same spot that his birthmark used to be. Could Gerry have been right about some birthmarks being the result of wounds received in past lives? An aching need to see her and talk to her again swept through him.

Would Lucius live long enough to get that farm and pension and that girl? No medics would be coming to airlift him out of here.

A meteorite streaked by low on the horizon on which faint streaks of the dawn were being painted. Romans would think it was a good omen for the battle to come. The wind, laden with scents of the sea, felt cold on his bare legs, but only barbarians wore trousers. Civilized men (and that included Roman soldiers) wore tunics.

At least the Britons weren't into wearing much body armor. In fact, they went naked into battle half the time. But he wasn't looking forward to fighting them. They were taller than the Romans and incredibly fierce fighters. The only good thing was that they were a disorganized lot.

Men were stirring now from their tents, going about the business of getting ready for the day. Dan could hear the braying of the pack mules, which carried their baggage, including tents and some simple tools.

When he'd first blitzed into this new body, he'd wondered about the calluses on his hands, which felt as tough as boards. He soon found out. Wherever the soldiers camped, latrines had to be dug and firewood gathered. Some things didn't change much. Today they would begin the job of building the flat-bottomed boats, which wouldn't win any America Cup races, but would do the job of transporting the legionaries of Seutonius Paulinus across the Menai Strait to Mona. The cavalry would swim across with their animals.

Dan sighed and took out an iron pan from among the baggage. His stomach got queasy just thinking about the greasy mess Marcus had served to them yesterday. All the guys had grumbled.

Might as well try his hand at cooking. He could fry up some corn along with fish, and then wash down the whole thing with the rough wine that would have to do in place of coffee. Just thinking about coffee made his mouth water.

He'd have to get used to doing without a lot of things, but for how long? As usual, he had no idea. If he were lucky, he'd be yanked out of here before the legion started the bloodbath at Mona. He didn't need more nightmares.

CHAPTER 39

Bryanna   Vernemeton, April 14, A.D. 61

Bryanna reminded herself to relax. If Mabon thought he was distressing her, he would only harry her more. Anger was not the way through this thicket of words he was attempting to weave about her, but she couldn't help the brief spurt of irritation that ran through her. How dared he talk so to the foster daughter of the Archdruid and one of the few to whom the ancient wisdom had been vouchsafed!

But Mabon was clever and ambitious. It would be unwise to stir his suspicion. She must conceal her real thoughts and discover his game.

"You and I should work together for the good of the Keltoi," continued Mabon. "We both believe in cooperation with the Romans."

"I would hope that we work for the same things: for peace in Britain and an end to the suffering of the Keltoi."

Mabon waved a hand impatiently as he said, "A time of great trouble is coming. Even now, I fear that this place is not safe."

"What are you suggesting?"

"After the sacrifice, come with me to Ireland. The Romans will not go there."

How could he be so sure? But she felt the truth of his words. Then why did she distrust him so?

"No, Mabon. I must stay here."

"You are still young. Do you know what the Romans do to young, beautiful women? Particularly after . . ." Mabon stopped, biting his lips.

He was concealing something. "After what, Mabon? Do you have knowledge of something which I do not?"

"My oracles," he said, "warn me of terrible things to come."

"Like corpses on the beach and a blood-red tide?"

Mabon expelled a sudden breath. "Do not jest, Bryanna. A bloody holocaust is about to fall upon us."

"You talk in riddles, Mabon. Speak plainly."

The Druid fingered his luxuriant mustache. "I only wish to have your cooperation. Of late, I have wondered whether you have somewhat against me. And Bran seems different, not himself."

"You are right, Mabon. Bran is not himself. He has been fasting rigorously. I have suggested that he conserve his strength by staying in seclusion until the ceremony." That would give her time to make her preparations.

Mabon nodded, not satisfied with her explanation, she could see, but accepting it for the moment.

"I have a question," he said, his air of humility sitting strangely upon him. "I know that your foster father, the Archdruid, entrusted you with much knowledge. I would learn this from you, Bryanna, so that it be preserved for the future."

So that was what he wanted! He did not care what happened to her personally, only that he learn what she knew. But she would never allow that knowledge to fall into the hands of such a one as he, a black Druid who sought personal power. Never! He had not the wisdom to deal with it.

"I cannot grant your request, Mabon. I made a vow never to reveal these secrets to any except one of my lineage, and then only if I thought that one worthy."

"You do not think me worthy."

"You are not of my lineage."

"And Bran is. Think again on this matter, Bryanna. You still have time to change your mind."

The name of her son hung between them like a sword. Mabon smiled, his smile the grin of a vulture. She scarcely noticed his departure. One thought was running through her head with the insistence of a drumbeat: Bran had to leave immediately. If Mabon discovered Bran's refusal to be sacrificed, he would not hesitate to denounce him and place on him the *glam dicon,* a curse that would render the boy helpless and isolated from the rest of the tribe. Many had died from the sheer terror and shame of being ostracized by their fellow tribesmen.

She drew out her bronze mirror from the bag hidden in her robes and stared at her reflection until it began to waver and re-form into murky images.

Enough! Over and over the images had said the same thing: Bran had to leave. His future and that of the world to come depended upon it. Replacing the mirror in her bag, she began walking toward the place where she knew Bran had gone.

CHAPTER 40

Bran—Jason Kramer   Vernemeton, April 14, A.D. 61

"C'mon, girl. You're going to love this nice piece of grass I picked especially for you."

The mare pricked her ears forward, refusing to come any closer. She was smaller than any horse he'd ever ridden, but she'd do just fine. If she was strong enough to carry a big guy like Kunagnos, she shouldn't have any problems carrying him. All he had to do was catch her. He'd been standing there for at least five minutes trying to persuade the dumb animal to come over to the fence.

"Try this," said a voice from behind him.

A low whistle and the mare trotted up like a pet dog and nuzzled Bryanna, who began stroking her.

Oh, no, the one person he didn't want to see—apart from Mabon, that is. That guy gave him the creeps. Now how was he going to get away from here?

"Bran, you must leave here tonight," said Bryanna, turning and looking him full in the face.

His jaw must have hung open a mile because she asked, "Have you not guessed it?"

He managed to croak, "Uh, no." More confidently he added, "I wasn't thrilled about the thought of being sacrificed."

"I think we should talk about this elsewhere," said Bryanna.

He followed her into the dim coolness of the grove. Putting a hand on his shoulder and another one on his cheek, she looked lovingly at him. Embarrassed, J.J. could feel tears coming into his eyes. It had been so long since he'd seen his own mother, and right now he missed her fiercely. He'd always been able to talk to her about most anything.

Bryanna stepped back. "You have conducted yourself well. I am proud of you. But now it is time for you to leave. You will go to Ireland, to the Druids, where you will continue your studies in the ancient wisdom."

Hold it. Back up. "Ireland?"

"You will be safe there. The Romans will not cross the sea."

"But I thought . . ."

Disappointment was so strong he could have cried.

"Soon, Bran. Soon you will go to your home in the future, but not until you do this one thing. You must escape to Ireland."

"I thought you wanted me to be sacrificed!"

Bryanna sighed and pushed back her heavy fair hair. "How can I speak to you in so short a time of everything that you must know? Understand this one thing: I have never wanted Bran's death. The Keltoi misunderstand the true nature of sacrifice, which is meant to be an offering up of the human vessel in a purely symbolic sense.

"However, this offering is very real, for it entails a refocusing of one's entire being so that the mean, the petty, and the impure are burned away. He becomes balanced and able to live in harmony with the universe. That is the true sacrifice."

"I thought all Druids believed in blood offerings."

Bryanna shook her head sadly. "Some do," she admitted.

"Like Mabon?"

"Yes, like Mabon. He has a different vision, which he would impose upon others—for their own good, he thinks. I see a world where the Keltoi are left free to make their own choices, where they may choose the left-hand path or the right-hand path. Choices that are made for men and women will only shrivel their souls. If a quickening of the human race is to occur, many and varied opportunities must be available for individuals to choose their own fates."

"Then why do you wish to hand us over to the Romans?" cried Devonna, coming out from behind a massive oak. "I make no apology for listening to your conversation," she said proudly with her head raised high. "What touches Bran, touches me for I, too, am to be sacrificed."

At his look of horror, she explained, "At Beltane a May Queen is chosen. As in the olden days, I am to be mated to the god into whose arms I will fall when my spirit leaves my body."

He could only look at her numbly. This gorgeous girl was going to be killed on the off chance that her sacrifice would stop the Roman tide. There was zero chance of that happening! Meantime, she'd be dead.

Bryanna seized upon Devonna's question and argued, "Child, at this time, we *must* cooperate with the Romans. They are too strong for us to fight. To do otherwise is to crush ourselves against their might."

"But why, why do the gods allow it? What have we done wrong?"

Bryanna took the sobbing girl into her arms. "You ask me to explain the reasons for pain and suffering. I believe we create it, all of us: Roman, Keltoi, and those who live in faraway lands. We are like greedy children who desire all that the senses can produce.

"We are meant to enjoy this world, but we must not forget that there is a higher purpose to this earthly existence. All humans, not just the tribes of Britain, are passing through stages of growth. As with children, growth is an uneven, sometimes difficult process, but it cannot be stopped—delayed, yes—but not stopped. We proceed towards the maturity of all the peoples of the world, for all are connected. Sometimes the route is painful.

"The Romans have come, all unknowingly, to jolt us out of our complacency, to show us different ways of behaving, to bring us new ideas. In turn, others will challenge them. Do not fret, Devonna. Matters proceed as they must."

Pulling away from Bryanna, the girl defiantly lifted her tearstained face and said, "And I must do what I must."

"You can't let them kill you!" J.J. blurted out.

Devonna was silent.

Bryanna asked her pointedly, "What is it that you wish to do?"

"It is an honor to be chosen the May Queen," said Devonna in a low voice, "and I would gladly die if . . ."

She faltered. Bryanna asked gently, "And if the gods are not pleased by human sacrifice?"

"Mabon . . ." said Devonna hesitantly.

"That old fart!" cried J.J. They didn't understand the word, but they sure got the message. The beginnings of a grin touched Devonna's lips. He felt an enormous relief. She wasn't totally brainwashed yet. Maybe he could persuade her not to go through with the sacrifice.

"Look, I don't know much about your customs, but it doesn't seem right to sacrifice a really nice girl like you. I mean, if the old fart"—J.J. said the word again, just to see Devonna's dimples when she smiled—"wants to sacrifice someone, why doesn't *he* get down there on the altar?"

"Devonna," said Bryanna, "you really can choose whether or not you would do this thing. After my long years of study, I am of the opinion that the One God takes no pleasure in the blood of sacrificial victims. Look around you. What do you see but life springing up everywhere in the natural world. Why would you interrupt that same life force flowing through you? That power is sacred. Cherish it."

Devonna looked at both of them, then lifted her chin and asked Bryanna challengingly, "How can I choose between your words and those of Mabon's? He tells me that the gods will be pleased with the sacrifice of my life. You tell me that this is not so, and you counsel Bran to forsake his duty also."

"I could tell you," said Bryanna in a voice that radiated power and sent a rush of energy down J.J.'s spine, "how the Archdruid taught me how to remember the old wisdom and access memories of the far past. I have been teaching Bran how to do this. Very few of us are left who can do the remembering. So you see why it is so important that you and Bran leave this place. You both have much to do in this lifetime."

"What have I to do with it?" asked Devonna in a high, strained voice.

"Your womb shall bring forth those who have chosen to remember, those who will teach others to remember also. For this you were born, Devonna."

"You mean we're getting married?" asked J.J.

It was a dazzling thought.

"Not if you linger here overlong," said Bryanna. Turning to Devonna, she asked, "What is your decision in this matter?"

Devonna came over to him and took his hand. Bran was one lucky guy!

"I have had doubts about the sacrifices to be made, but I had to be sure," she said, looking up at him. "I will go wherever you wish."

"When you reach Ireland, Bran—the real Bran—will be returned to you," said Bryanna. "I shall give you some food and coins, which you can hide in your garments. No one must know that you are setting out on a journey. When the moon is up, you must leave. Much trouble is coming to this place. Now go and rest. I shall speak to you later before you go."

J.J. turned to Bryanna and asked, "Aren't you coming with us?"

She shook her head. "I have much to do here," she said.

Feeling suddenly shy, J.J. nodded. Then looking at Devonna, his fears fell away. He'd get her safely to Ireland, but he hoped it wouldn't be too soon. She was one gutsy girl; he wanted to get to know her a lot better.

CHAPTER 41

Bran—Jason Kramer Near the Welsh border,
April 17, A.D. 61

Dusty and sore from riding without stirrups or proper saddles on the horses that Bryanna had given them, Devonna and he traveled by night and hid out during the day.

Following the trade routes controlled by the Druids, sometimes they were able to stay at one of the Druid sanctuaries that lined the route. The mention of Bryanna's name was all that was needed to ensure lavish hospitality, more lavish than he would have liked.

One night, after traveling for several hours, they came upon a sanctuary where a group of young Celts, dressed in tunics and brightly colored cloaks and wearing masses of gold jewelry, invited him and Devonna to eat with them. The men sported weird hairstyles, looking something like lions' manes, stiffened and bleached by lime.

Sitting down, he received a nasty shock when he noticed the table's centerpiece, a man's head embalmed in some sort of oil. The guy sitting opposite him gave him all the grisly details of how he had killed the man during a raid, even standing up and pulling down his trousers to show him the long jagged scar on his thigh where the warrior had wounded him during the fight.

Just when he was getting to really like these people, he'd find out something that his 20th-century mind balked at. Delving into

Bran's subconscious, he discovered that the human head held an important religious significance: it was thought to be the symbol of divinity, a place where the soul lived. To preserve the head was a mark of profound respect.

It turned out to be quite a party! He pigged out on some pork dishes and barley cakes and drank a little too much of the booze—an expensive wine from Gaul, he was told—poured out of bronze jugs decorated with animal heads. Usually, he didn't drink. A few times he had sneaked a beer or two with the guys. Back home in Canada, where the drinking age was 18 years old, he wouldn't be legally old enough to drink for another two years. But here at his age, you were a man and expected to fight and drink with the best of them.

You had to be careful about refusing the food and wine offered to you. Fights broke out over the silliest arguments. These guys were really touchy, especially about anything concerning their honor. When the fight was over, though, the guys would good-naturedly patch up their wounds and carry on with the singing or whatever. So he'd been real polite to his hosts and hostesses.

The women, he noticed, could be just as quarrelsome as the men, who treated them like equals. According to Devonna, women could divorce their husbands, hold land, and even act as war chieftains. Talk about women's liberation! J.J. got the feeling that Crystal would fit right in here. She was smart and had an air of self-confidence he'd noticed right away.

Much later, after most of the Celts were sacked out snoring on the floor, a woman led him and Devonna to a corner of the room, where obviously they were supposed to bunk in together, bed being some skins stuffed with straw.

Feeling a little silly about the whole thing, he took off his sandals and, still wearing his clothes, lay down on the skins. In a few moments he could feel Devonna snuggling in next to him and his body becoming aroused. He lay rigid. Maybe she'd go to sleep soon. In all fairness to Bran, he couldn't make a pass at his girl, not when he was borrowing the other guy's body. Sighing, he tried to

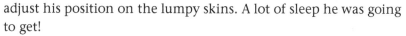

adjust his position on the lumpy skins. A lot of sleep he was going to get!

"Are you awake, Bran?" whispered Devonna.

"Yeah."

"Did you enjoy the feast?"

"I had a great time."

He jumped. She was tickling him.

Without thinking he turned and pinned her down so she couldn't move. A stray beam of moonlight showed her grinning up at him. Then she moved suggestively underneath him. That did things to him he was sure she couldn't help but notice. Good thing it was fairly dark so she couldn't see him blushing.

Conscious only of his need to touch her, he reached out tentatively and stroked her neck. His fingers came into contact with something hard.

"Where'd you get that necklace?"

"You—Bran—gave it to me before . . ."

Instinctively, he pulled away. She caressed his cheek and said softly, "Oh, Bran! Now that I am no longer to be the May Queen, it is not necessary for me to remain a virgin."

She looked at him expectantly, her lips parted slightly, and lifted toward him. Then she reached up and took out the enameled combs that held her hair in place. Her hair, smelling of herbs, fell in waves around her.

"But Bran . . ." he protested feebly.

" . . . is here."

She wound her arms around his neck and drew him down on top of her. He didn't need any more invitation than that. Maybe she wouldn't guess that it was his first time, too.

"Well, you won't need this on," he said, lifting off the necklace. "Or this, either," he continued, his hands fumbling with her robe.

Giggling, Devonna began pulling at his clothes. "Nor you," she said pertly.

Finally, there was nothing at all between them, only warm, smooth skin melding together.

"Oh, Bran," she whispered, "the gods have made me the most fortunate of women."

Plunging his hands into the springy mass of her hair, he pulled her even closer to him.

And then he stopped thinking as her wine-flavored lips met his, intoxicating him even more. He became a creature of feeling, guided by instinct, thrusting inside Devonna, surges of ecstasy coursing through him as she moaned and murmured little endearments.

As fast as it had peaked, the tide of his passion ebbed.

"Devonna?" he whispered, wondering if she had felt so . . . so blessed as he. It had not been just an act of physical passion, but a kind of sacrament, a holy union sealed with their lovemaking.

In response, she hugged him with a tenderness that made him want to cradle her in his arms forever. They lay like that for a long time until he finally fell asleep.

CHAPTER 42

Bran—Jason Kramer

Near the Menai Strait,
April 20, A.D. 61

Something was nibbling on his ear. He shook his head and looked up groggily.

Already dressed, Devonna was bending over him. "Bellenos has ridden his chariot out of the sky already," she said. "We must go now."

He must have been really tired to sleep so late. Pulling Devonna down on top of him, he kissed her soundly.

"No time for that now," she murmured. "But later . . ."

He got up then, reluctantly, and they continued making their way west.

Luckily for them, Devonna had traveled this route once before with her father, an artist working with gold and bronze, who had been famous for creating everything from jewelry to cups and other fine things. His work had brought him in close contact with Druids, who controlled the traffic in these things and bought much of his work for offerings to the gods.

It was after she had returned from her foster parents to live permanently with her own parents that she had met Mabon, who had ordered a golden cup from her father. Shortly afterward, her father had fallen sick of a wasting disease that had made him progressively weaker and thinner until he had died. A few months later, while giving birth to a stillborn son, her mother, too, had died.

Devonna's foster parents had welcomed her back. She had lived there with them until Mabon had invited her to become the May Queen. She had accepted the honor and then traveled with Kunagnos to the great sanctuary at Vernemeton, where the feast of Beltane would occur in a few weeks.

They were getting close to the coast now, staying well away from the legionary fort of Deva, which was on a river only a short march from the sea. No sense in attracting attention to themselves.

When Devonna became quieter than usual, J.J. was worried and asked her what was wrong. She said that she was homesick for her tribe, the Deceanglis, who lived around there, and for her foster parents. But visiting them could be dangerous. During the past year, the area had seen a lot of fighting between the tribe and the Romans.

They'd been relieved when they'd passed into the land of the Ordovices. It was hilly, even mountainous in places. They'd had to walk much of the way after that to spare the poor horses, which were limping by then.

They'd come across very few people: some miners, shovels and picks over their shoulders, going to work in the mines, which provided iron and copper in this region and some other travelers who looked closely at them but said little.

Devonna had said that the Ordovices had been fighting the Romans for so long that they were suspicious of all strangers.

Their food supplies had dwindled pretty fast. Along the way, Devonna managed to kill a couple of rabbits with her sling. After watching her put a stone into the strip of leather, whirl it around her head a few times, and let fly with unerring aim, he'd told her that back in his home time she'd be a natural for the Olympic rifle team. Her eyes had lit up with a warmth that made him ache with longing for her, and then she'd asked a million questions about his home. He was careful not to tell her much. All the science fiction stories he'd ever read warned against that. Even small stuff could have a big impact on future events. He was supposed to do his part to make sure that the timeline was stabilized, not change history.

Devonna was a great companion and smart, too. She knew things about living off the land that had to put her right up there with the best wilderness guide.

He had never seen anyone who could imitate birdcalls like she could. Once, she even called to her a flock of little birds, which flew down and perched in a bush.

She knew how to manage people, too—like him. Knowing that he'd have to leave her soon was producing in him an agony of feeling that he was afraid to tell her about. So he was abrupt with her sometimes when he wanted to be tender, and wound up acting very businesslike with her—or trying to. Pretending that they were only casual friends was pretty hard, especially when they were constantly together. She refused to take his moods seriously and would tease him until he laughed.

Like the time he had slipped on some wet rocks and fallen down a short muddy slope. Devonna had laughed like crazy and then gone plunging down the slope after him, falling on top of him. He was pretty sure that she had fallen on purpose because that girl was as sure-footed as a cat.

He tried to push Devonna off, but she was almost as strong as he was and just wound herself around him.

"Hey, look, someone's coming."

Devonna fell for it. As she took a quick peek, she relaxed her grip on him. Practicing a judo throw his father had taught him, he threw her off and ran up the slope. She followed him and near the top threw herself at him, catching him by the ankle. They both went tumbling down the slope, landing in a heap together at the bottom. They both laughed so hard that tears rolled down their faces.

When he could get his breath back, he said, "You're scaring the horses, Devonna."

"Those old nags. They're enjoying themselves grazing. We could enjoy ourselves, too," said Devonna, giving him one of those teasing looks that made him blush.

"Romans could be around. We'd better move it."

Devonna made a face at him and pulled his ear, but she peeled herself off him, then ran up the slope and vaulted onto her horse.

Almost too soon for both of them, they stood on the shore and looked across the strait to Mona. As they gazed at the great Druid sanctuary touched by the flames of a sinking sun, J.J. was struck by a sense of intense urgency. Devonna must have felt it, too, because they both turned at the same time and almost ran over to a fisherman mending his nets. At first the old man didn't want to take them across the strait, but his muttering about an army massing some miles away made them all the more determined to go. After paying what Devonna said was an outrageous price and further reducing their dwindling supply of coins, the fisherman finally took them across to the island.

The whole place was buzzing with activity. Rumors were flying everywhere. Their request to see the Archdruid was denied until Devonna showed Bryanna's ring to an older man, who questioned them closely about where they'd received it. When Devonna said that they preferred to talk about it to the Archdruid, the man finally granted their request.

The Archdruid received them politely in a large hall with wooden floors and low tables.

"I am Tighearnach. Please take some refreshment." He gestured to a bowl of apples that sat on a beautifully carved wooden table near them. "Now tell me, how fares Bryanna?"

J.J. took two of the apples and gave one to Devonna, who said, "She is well."

The Archdruid nodded, looking relieved. Why? Did he think Bryanna was in danger?

"Please tell me about your journey and why you found it necessary to come all this way, particularly at this time when the dangers are great."

While they explained why they had come, Tighearnach's intent gaze never left their faces. It was a little unnerving.

"I will provide you with a boat to take you across to Ireland," he said finally. "You will be safe at Tara. It is the seat of the High Kings of Ireland where Bryanna has relatives."

"You must leave soon. We have had news that Seutonius Paulinus and his two legions, as well as auxiliaries and a battle fleet, are preparing to attack this island."

"Why cannot they allow us to worship as we would?" asked Devonna bitterly.

"It is not our form of worship that Seutonius fears, but Druid influence," said Tighearnach tightly. "The Romans have had no end of trouble putting down revolts in Britain. By wiping out us Druids, they think to wipe out the power behind the rebellions."

"Will they succeed?"

The Druid looked at Devonna's face, pinched with worry. "The Keltoi will survive, child," he said, "and so will the ancient wisdom that works through us. Another time will come in which that power will work out its destiny. And now," said Tighearnach, getting up, "you must excuse me. I have preparations to make. I would suggest that you rest and gather your strength between now and the day that you depart. We will talk more on this tomorrow."

But they had not seen the Archdruid the next day or the day after that. At dawn on the third day, Tighearnach had sent for them. He looked much the same as they had first seen him, but now a kind of fatalistic calm had fallen on him.

"The Romans are encamped on the shores of the Menai Strait that separates them from us on Mona," he said. "They will be here in a short time. A boat loaded with supplies and a guide wait to take you to Ireland. My blessings upon you both."

He made a ritualistic sign and continued. "Do not fear. You are in the hands of the One who created us all, who will shelter you from the wrath to come. But now you must leave. I regret not having had more time to spend with you both. Take this with you, Bran," he said, taking from around his neck a torque made of twisted strands of gold ending in the heads of two bulls. The torque felt awkward and heavy around J.J.'s neck.

A rush of power surged through him. Images of the far past when sages brought advanced ideas to primitive peoples swam through his mind. He saw stepped pyramids in jungles where Quetzalcoatl, a bearded white man who abhorred human sacrifice, taught the Aztecs the arts of weaving, metallurgy, and other arts; then more pyramids, their white limestone coverings gleaming in the desert sunlight, where Egyptians were taught how to move huge stones and, under the influence of the pharaoh, Akhenaten, learned to worship the One God.

The images stopped. He stumbled as a feeling of dread flashed through him. He wanted to beg the Archdruid to come with them, but something in the priest's attitude dried up the words in his throat. He could only look mutely at him.

Later, in the rush of activity, things became a frantic blur. They left the house where they had been staying and had almost reached the boat when Devonna put a hand to her neck and cried, "My necklace, the one you gave me. I left it behind!"

"Don't worry about it. I—I mean Bran—will get you another one."

"I want that one, as a reminder of the first night you and I lay together."

"But the Romans are coming! We don't have time."

"It won't take me long. You can wait for me at the boat."

Their guide, a short, stocky young man with a blunt face, whose name he had said was Breandan, waved his arms around and shouted at her.

But J.J. could have told him it was no use. When Devonna made up her mind, it was next to impossible to make her change it.

"Then I'm going with you." Turning to Breandan, looking goggle-eyed with anxiety at them, he said, "You go to the boat. We'll catch up with you later."

CHAPTER 43

Bran–Jason Kramer   Mona, April 23, A.D. 61

His track coach would have been proud of the time he made running with Devonna back to the thatched house where they'd stayed as a guest of Tighearnach. But the usual Celtic boisterousness of men and women going about their chores was missing. The place was eerie, dead quiet. Everyone had gone.

"My necklace!" cried Devonna, going straight to the place where they'd shared a bed and pouncing on the beads there, shining like drops of crystallized honey.

"Great. Now let's get out of here!" A dread that he realized had been creeping up on him all morning suddenly pounced on him. His heart felt as if he'd just sprinted the 100-yard dash, and it wasn't because he'd run all the way back from the cove where Breandan was waiting with the boat. Something was going to happen very soon, something bad.

Mad shrieks from outside made the hair on his arms stand up. Devonna clutched his arm. "They're here!" she whispered.

"Out, we gotta get out of here!" he cried, pushing her ahead of him.

They burst out of the house and then stopped.

"May Andraste rot them and demons flay them alive!" cried Devonna.

It was a wonderful day, bright and sunny, with the promise of summer in the air. Back home, he'd have been lying on the beach and yakking it up with friends.

Not on this beach. Looking down the hill, he could see Roman legions lined up, shoulder to shoulder. Mounted troops waited to one side of the infantry.

Opposing them were Celtic warriors, more than half of them naked, some in wicker-sided chariots and others on foot. Next to them were women in black robes waving torches and shrieking curses. In contrast to them was a rank of Druid priests standing motionless with their arms raised and shouting curses at the Romans, calling down the wrath of heaven on their enemies.

The legions seemed hypnotized. No one moved. Maybe the Druids really had a special kind of magic . . .

A harsh command from the Roman leader astride a great black horse galvanized the massive Roman war machine into action. Holding their shields in front of them, the legionaries marched forward in tight formation, thrusting with their short swords at the Celtic warriors.

It was no contest, J.J. could see. The Celts didn't have any room to maneuver with their chariots, and their long swords were useless in hand-to-hand combat. Even when the Roman javelins didn't hit their mark, the iron heads of some of them stuck in the shields of the Celts, where they were next to impossible to get out. He saw some warriors throw down their shields and fight without them, but their courage was no match for the disciplined Romans who advanced relentlessly.

Now the legionaries were seizing the torches from the frenzied women and, to his horror, setting fire to them, their hair and clothing flaring up in long spouts of flame. On the cool ocean breeze came the stench of burning human flesh.

J.J. was sure he was going to be sick. He'd seen movies like *Predator,* which had grossed him out, but this was different. This was real.

Tears were running down Devonna's face, and she was shaking her fists.

He grabbed her arm. "C'mon, let's go. Now!"

She shrugged him off, too caught up in the scene to realize their danger.

Now the Romans had hacked their way onto open ground. Behind them sprawled dead and dying men in a welter of horses and overturned chariots. Here and there J.J. could see, fluttering in the breeze, the white robes of the fallen Druids. Even worse was the sound of the agonized groans of mortally injured men and the squeals of their stricken horses.

Two Romans were charging up the hill toward them. Fast.

"Devonna, run!" J.J. shrieked in her ear.

She threw her head back and looked dazedly at him. This time she didn't try to stop him when he took her arm and pulled at her.

From days of traveling through rough country, they were both in good shape, but so were the soldiers. He hadn't been so scared since he'd almost hit a rock and sunk his dad's boat out in Clearwater Bay. Shouts behind him spurred him on.

He didn't want to die, not again, not this way, and not Devonna, his love, his woman . . .

He looked back. A mistake. The Romans, dressed in tunics and armor familiar to him from the movies, were gaining on them. Only this was no movie! The soldiers ran with determination, their swords stained with blood.

He and Devonna didn't stand a chance against them. If only he had something to fight with! But there was nothing, only rocks littering the slope up which they were running. It was no good. They were going to die.

A yell behind him and a noise of someone falling heavily made him sneak a quick look back. One of the soldiers was lying on the ground, his hand holding on to his ankle and cursing fluently.

But the other one was almost upon them. He raised his sword and then grunted as he clapped a hand to his forehead. He fell to the ground, his armor clanking on the small stones and his sword flying out of his hands.

"Just like David and Goliath," J.J. cracked to Devonna, who was busy reloading her sling.

He smiled at her, and his heart lifted. Maybe they had a chance now.

But Devonna's face was grim as she motioned to the left of them. A small group of soldiers, four of them, were charging up the hillside toward them.

Devonna threw down her sling and stood mutely. She shook her head as he tried to get her to run. "No, Bran. It is too late," she whispered. She looked at him with those amber eyes that shone more brightly than the beads in her necklace and said, "I love you. We will go down to the Other World together. Teutates will have his sacrifice after all."

She threw her arms around him and held him tight while the soldiers ran up the hill, the sun gleaming on their weapons.

CHAPTER 44

Bryanna Vernemeton, Beltane, May 1, A.D. 61

Oblivious of the men and women who eyed her silently and respectfully, Bryanna knelt on the hard-packed earth. The only sound was the keening of the wind in the high branches of the oaks. Around them loomed the forest, a dark presence in the night where spirits walked and worked their ancient magic.

She was remembering the night she had sent Bran and Devonna away, the two young people hugging her awkwardly and then slipping away from the sanctuary. It was a difficult road they trod—Romans being only one of the dangers they faced—but she had done all she could.

A light touch on her shoulder roused her from her reverie. Kunagnos. His face was strained. He did not like what he had to do, but she could imagine how Mabon must have persuaded him: "To call down blessings on the Keltoi to ensure that the Romans never invade the sacred island . . ."

Would Bran make it to the sacra insula? He must! Ireland was one of the few places where the Keltoi lived free from Roman influence. In other lands across the sea, and soon in the length and breadth of this one, the Pax Romana held sway. And so it must be, that the new order be established.

But there must also be a place set apart where the old knowledge might be preserved. On that one thing, she and Mabon were agreed.

"Lady, are you ready?"

She smiled at Kunagnos. Her heart was peaceful. All was in the hands of the One God now. If Bran and Devonna should make it to Ireland, their children would return to the land of the Cornovii. All would take place as it must.

"I am ready."

As Kunagnos's great sword began its downward sweep, she focused on the moonlight glinting on the metal, taking the light into her heart, feeling it explode throughout her body in a myriad of crystalline drops of pure radiance . . .

CHAPTER 45

Mabon   Vernemeton, Beltane, May 1, A.D.61

With a formal, ceremonial gesture, Mabon, swathed in the skin of a white bull from which the phallus still hung, held high the head of Bryanna so that all might see. Her eyes were still open, and in them he could see . . .

He stumbled. A bad omen! A despairing gasp went up from the assembly.

Mabon pulled his attention away from the confusion of images that he had seen in her eyes: a new world where the Keltoi would incarnate, some living in longhouses and some in round homes fashioned of bark or skins in a land incredibly vast and rich, but one that other races would covet. And so the Keltoi would again be pushed aside unless there should arise one to help them.

Exulting at this glimpse into his new role in the future, Mabon hurled Bryanna's head into the sacred pool. It sank, with only a few ripples on the surface to show its passing.

"Teutates has had his due," he said in a strong voice.

The Keltoi obediently chanted the words back to him.

There. It was done. His rival had been eliminated and the gods placated. But one thing more needed attention.

When Bran and Devonna had disappeared, he had been beside himself. Then he had seen how he might turn the situation to his advantage. He had come to Bryanna and told her that if she wanted to guarantee the safety of the young people, she should offer herself in place of her son for the sacrifice. Without argument, she had agreed. Fool.

He had no intention of keeping his word. He sent a message to a Roman legate who had the ear of Seutonius to be on the watch for two young Druids who were to be killed immediately. He was sure that his request would be heeded; he had been very helpful to the Romans in the past and would continue to be.

With satisfaction, he remembered his last meeting with the Roman commander. They had met in secret in Londinium at the former home of a wealthy merchant. The house had a thatched roof and was made of clay, which had been plastered and decorated with a blue trim.

It was not his first visit to that noisy town of some 30,000 inhabitants where the streets swarmed with slaves running errands for their masters, men leading donkeys burdened down with goods, litter bearers carrying wealthy matrons, children shouting at each other, and boisterous soldiers of different nationalities, ranging from the short, swarthy Mediterranean types to tall, fair-haired Gauls.

The servant who had answered the door had taken him straight to a small but elegantly furnished room boasting a wooden floor. Seutonius sat Roman-style on a low couch and beckoned him to do likewise on another couch facing him. Several pottery lamps, with designs of birds on them, gave a dim but adequate light that flattered the grizzled visage of the Roman, whom he judged to be in his early 60s. He could be anyone's grandfather, this man with the stocky frame, his skin weathered and wrinkled like an old wineskin and hardened from too many marches through too many countries. But his eyes were cool and calculating.

"Wine, Mabon?"

Seutonius gestured toward an amphora standing next to some red-pottery tableware on a small table. The wine was a very good vintage; he could still remember its rich fruity flavor. They went through the preliminaries of inquiring after each other's family and health.

As usual, the Roman came right to the point. Running a finger around the lip of his goblet, he said, "I am troubled by reports from my spies of dissatisfaction among the Iceni. But they are only one tribe among many who plot against us. As soon as I dispatch the nest of vipers of one set of rebels, another takes its place." He paused and looked at him.

"Then you must cut off the head of the serpent."

"How?" asked Seutonius, putting down his goblet and crossing his arms across his broad chest.

"By smashing the Druid stronghold of Mona and the Archdruid with it. You will never find success in Britain otherwise, for it is the priests who control all things."

Was it contempt he saw for a moment in the Roman's eyes as Seutonius asked, "How is it that you, a Druid, can recommend destruction for your own kind?"

Mabon felt the tension in the room rise a notch. The next few minutes would be crucial to his plans. With anguish, he thought of the destruction of the sacred groves, but he resolutely focused on his goal: to offer up Britain so that Ireland might be preserved in order that the old ways might survive and he with it as the highest-ranking Druid in the land. Of course, the Archdruid would perish in the massacre, leaving the way open for him, Mabon, to direct the sacred mysteries, but from a safe place across the Irish Sea.

Calming his breathing, he said, "Perhaps we can arrive at a plan whereby we both may profit."

That night the two of them had formed a plan whereby his foes would be eliminated and, more importantly, the greater plan about which the Roman knew nothing, carried out. He had realized then how important it was to remove the boy, Bran. Like the raven, the boy's namesake, whose cries presaged doom and war most terrible, so would Bran meet a doom whereby he would be a sacrifice to ensure the continuance of a world where the common folk would be ruled by those superior to them, men like himself—Mabon.

CHAPTER 46

Lucius-Dan Morgan   Mona, April 23, A.D. 61

It could have been worse. After helping unload the horses and mules—a real pain, literally because his arm was getting so bad that he couldn't even lift it—the Decanus, who was like a sergeant or leader of his contubernium, took one look at him and ordered him to stay with the boats.

The other guys kept throwing looks of pity at him. They didn't know how relieved he was not to have to kill anyone. He had done his fair share of that in Vietnam. Hideous memories were always hovering just below the surface, ready to leap out at him.

It was bad enough listening to the shrieks of the dying horses. Hit by flying javelins, whose barbed heads must have hurt like hell, they squealed like demented souls. Watching the burning human torches was even worse.

From where he stood in one of the boats, he had a pretty good view of everything. He'd tried to keep an eye on the rest of his contubernium, who seemed to be doing okay so far. In the general melee, he'd lost track of them. Then he'd noticed Marcus, recognizable by his lumbering gait, reminding him of a particularly vicious goose that had once chased Dan on his grandfather's farm, charging up the hillside with several others of their group.

On the slope of the hill were two people trying to escape, but they didn't have a chance, not against trained soldiers. He'd seen it happen a world away: women and kids mowed down, whole villages set afire, the innocent slain with the guilty.

The pair had stopped running. Probably figured they didn't have a chance.

Damn it, run! Don't just stand there and take it!

Now the man was taking something off from around his neck and throwing it in front of the soldiers, who were running up the hill. And there was Marcus, stopping and snatching up the thing, and Gaius right behind him, putting his hand out as though arguing about it.

Must be a pretty valuable piece. Smart of the guy to delay them like that.

Now the two had taken off. Marcus and the rest couldn't have cared less, it seemed. If two people escaped for a few hours, it was nothing to them. They'd round them up eventually. After all, this was a small island. In the meantime, they were standing around arguing about who should get the piece.

You could hardly blame them. Marcus was your professional career soldier, all business, no sentiment, who had every intention of living to collect his pension and picking up enough along the way to make his retirement comfortable. Pensions for veterans were pretty small, which encouraged guys to pick up what loot they could—a kind of portable pension fund.

Meanwhile, the couple were hightailing it over to the far side of the hill, right over to where the rest of the Roman fleet was anchored. Of course, they didn't know that. A grove of trees hid the fleet from sight. A shame. After all that display of sheer guts, it seemed so unfair for them to be caught.

So what could he do? He had his orders to stay where he was. Soldiers who disobeyed orders could expect severe punishment, like being stoned to death. But he couldn't just stay here and watch them be caught and executed on the spot.

Without really thinking, Dan found himself running in the direction of the young couple. No one challenged him. The other soldiers were all too busy hacking away at their enemies to pay any attention to him.

"Hey, you over there!"

They'd seen him now and pulled up, fear apparent on their faces. Why, they were only kids! The boy put an arm protectively around the girl.

"I won't hurt you."

They were looking suspiciously at him, and why shouldn't they? They had no reason to trust him. Look at what the rest of the legion was doing to their home.

"Going that way, you'll run into the whole Roman fleet, and even if you could hide for a while in the trees, you'd eventually be caught because Seutonius has plans to set fire to all the groves."

"Then where can we go?" asked the girl, her face screwed up in an expression of despair.

"Come with me. I'll escort you over there." He pointed away from the main body of the legion and toward what would be called the Irish Sea in later times.

The boy hadn't moved. "Why should we trust you?" he asked.

"Because you haven't a hope in hell of getting out of here if you don't. Mind you, I can't guarantee anything, but at least it's a chance. You're not likely to get stopped if you're with me; if we are, I'll say you're my prisoners."

The boy stood there stubbornly. "You still haven't told me why you're helping us."

Images of Laney came into his head: Laney with her head flung back dancing to the music she loved; Laney weeping over a baby bird that their cat had killed; Laney tossing her hair over one shoulder as she twinkled at him and teased him; Laney, who couldn't bear to see suffering in any form.

"For my daughter, Laney," he said simply.

Hope dawning in his eyes, the boy asked, "Who are you? Where are you from?"

Dan opened his mouth and then closed it, not sure what to say. Then he said, "Why do you care? Let's get going before my buddies catch up to us."

He waved his sword at them, but the boy refused to move. He had guts but not much sense.

"Your name. Who are you really?"

They could go on like this all day, but there wasn't time, and what would it hurt to tell him his name?

"Dan."

The boy started violently. "Dan Morgan?"

"Yeah, why . . ."

"It's me, J.J." The boy started to shake. Shock, maybe. He had to get them out of here.

"Bran, you know this man?" asked the girl in disbelief.

"Yeah, he's someone from my time."

For the first time, the girl smiled. "The gods are truly smiling upon us."

Holding his sword in his left hand—just to make things look good in case anyone was watching—Dan explained where they were headed. He didn't have to urge them to hurry. In fact, he found it hard to keep up with them.

"Hey, not so fast! They'll think you're trying to get away from me."

They slowed down a bit after that.

As they came into sight of the fleet, a soldier hunkering down on the beach looked up and shouted, "Hail. What do you have there?"

"Slaves. They'll fetch a good price in the market."

The soldier looked bored. He nodded and said disinterestedly, "They look strong and healthy, but be sure you bind them well so they don't escape."

"Okay."

As they jogged past the soldier, Dan could feel a prickling all down his spine and a feeling that hostile eyes were observing them. They seemed so exposed out here. Not until they reached the cover of some stunted trees did he feel more comfortable.

J.J. stopped and turned around. "We can make it from here," he said. "There's someone with a boat close by who's going to take us to Ireland."

He thrust out his hand and said, "Thanks, Dan. I really appreciate your help."

No doubt about it: the kid was different, more mature.

"See you back home soon," said Dan—if they didn't get killed first. His unspoken words must have shown in his eyes because J.J.'s mouth tightened, but he said nothing, just gave his hand an extra little squeeze and then put his arm around the girl's shoulder and walked off.

Poor kids. Nice, middle-class kids like J.J. weren't used to running for their lives, although it was happening to kids in other parts of the world.

If he and J.J. got out of this alive, he'd throw one hell of a party when they got back home. After that, he'd get his life together. No kidding.

Feeling ridiculously pleased with himself, he strode back to his boat, sat down, and waited for the others.

CHAPTER 47

Bran–Jason Kramer   Mona, April 23, A.D. 61

With a tightness in his chest, J.J. watched Dan's retreating back. He wanted to yell, "Come back! Don't leave us here alone!" But he wasn't a kid any more. People were depending on him, people like Bryanna, who had charged him to take Devonna to Ireland, and Devonna, too, who was trudging along beside him, her head down as though she were thinking furiously.

They were out of the trees now, he saw. No soldiers in sight. Good thing. After the bloodbath they'd just escaped, he could see why a lot of people tended to be paranoid about the Romans.

With no cover out here, just a long line of surf breaking on a rocky beach, they were totally exposed. Where was Breandan, who was supposed to be waiting with a boat? Was that part of their escape going to get screwed up like everything else?

Devonna was checking out the scene now, too. As if guessing his thoughts she said, "Breandan should be waiting for us somewhere close by. Look, over there!"

She pointed to a pile of jumbled rocks and then broke into a run. She was so fast he could hardly keep up to her without slipping on the pebbles.

A dark head popped up from behind the rocks, then the rest of him. Breandan began jumping up and down and waving his arms. When he saw them, he jumped into a boat.

Did the water ever warm up enough to go swimming here? It was freezing, turning his feet into two icy stumps. The breeze poked fingers into every exposed part of his body and raised goose bumps all over him.

It seemed like ages before he and Devonna half fell into the boat. At least they were safe for the time being. But the boat looked so small! They were going to cross the Irish Sea in that? His dad's boat was bigger and it had a motor. This tub had a sail, true, but it didn't exactly inspire confidence in him.

"Bran!"

It was Mabon! He must have followed them here.

"Come here, Bran. I must speak with you."

The old man was being his usual arrogant self, ordering people around. No way was he going to get out of this boat and wade through that cold water just to talk it up with Mabon. He was too beat, his legs were tired, and he could hardly stand anymore. Sitting on the rough plank that served as a seat, his head drooping, he could barely keep his eyes open.

"Bran, there are matters of great import that we must discuss before you leave."

Mabon's voice was pitched low, but it carried perfectly and set up a resonant tingling in him. Maybe he *should* go see what the old guy wanted. They still had time . . .

"Bran! No!" Devonna's hand was clamped hard on his arm so that he couldn't move, not without pitching them both into the sea. Breandan, he noticed with disinterest, looked as if he was going to puke; he was that scared.

"He'll kill us!" Devonna shrieked in his ear. She was struggling with him now, and the boat was rocking from side to side. The necklace she was wearing broke suddenly, spilling the amber beads into the boat.

Something snapped in J.J. He stopped struggling and looked around as though he'd just been someone awakened from a dream. He could still feel the pull of Mabon's voice, but the pull was growing weaker.

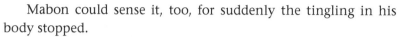

Mabon could sense it, too, for suddenly the tingling in his body stopped.

"Let's get out of here *now,* Breandan!"

Then a figure in armor darted out of the trees and began running full tilt down the beach. He was into the water before they knew what was happening. *A soldier!* Mabon hadn't been taking any chances about losing him. He would have lured him back with his hypnotic technique and then have had the Roman kill him.

Breandan was hauling away like a maniac on some ropes. The boat was slowly coming around, the wind finally catching the sail, while Devonna was screaming curses at the soldier, who had drawn his sword and was plunging through the water, up to his waist now in the surf. Then the Roman suddenly stopped, took out a dagger, and threw it straight at him. Devonna pushed J.J. down, lost her balance, and fell on top of him, while Breandan yelled gleeful obscenities about the soldier's origin.

Rough planks bruised J.J.'s back. The wind was knocked out of him. He could only lie there while Devonna fussed over him. Her hair tickled his face, and he wanted to sneeze.

His awareness began drifting out of his body. But he didn't want to leave Devonna, his girl, no, Bran's.

She seemed to sense something happening because she quieted down, shifting her weight so that he could barely feel her there. He stared into her eyes, wanting to tell her that he didn't want to leave her, but it was too late, it was all over, and he was out of there, being booted into another dimension and, oh, was he really going home?

CHAPTER 48

Lucius–Dan Morgan Mona, April 23, A.D. 61

By the time nightfall came, Dan could see huge fires burning. The sacred groves had been fired. It was a spectacular sight, thick plumes of smoke rising from the tall stands of trees as flames ran up the branches and exploded into fiery geysers of orange and red.

At least the screaming had long since stopped. Seutonius and his men must have things fairly well under control by now. Some of the men were already marching back, tired and hungry from the day's work. They were laughing and talking as though nothing had happened. But the joking and horseplay was a hyper kind of thing, a relief at having escaped death one more time.

"You missed all the action," said Catus, digging a hard elbow into Dan's ribs. Dan had never seen a guy who looked so lean: his nose and chin, even his head looked as though someone had drawn out his flesh like those characters painted by that Spanish artist. "And you should see what Marcus got."

Ignoring the sour look Catus threw at him, Marcus opened his leather pouch and drew out a tube of finely engraved gold.

"Must be worth a fortune," said Dan.

Without thinking, he stretched out his hand. After a moment's hesitation, Marcus let him hold it.

The neckpiece felt heavy and cool. Then it was as though a hidden flame inside the golden tube began to heat it up until he could hardly bear to touch it. At the same time, the faces of the men around him began to blur and recede as though he were moving away from them on a high-speed train. The shift in time was happening once again. Where was he going next? He only had a brief moment to think, I hope Lucius lives to get his farm and a pension before he was caught up in a maelstrom of energy that seemed to turn his guts inside out.

CHAPTER 49

Klaus Braun–Caleb Morgan

Near Philadelphia,
June 21, 1942

It was the first time in his life that Caleb remembered being truly afraid. It wasn't that he minded dying so much, he told himself. After all, he'd lived a long and full life. But it was *how* he was probably going to die that bothered him.

He had thought that after J.J. had saved the life of Captain Church, the timeline would have stabilized after Church had gone on to successfully defend the colonists in New England against Indian attacks. Apparently, something had gone wrong, because obviously Count Frontenac's troops from New France to the north *had* conquered New England.

That meant that in this new 20th-century timeline without the help of America, the French had been powerless to stop the rise of Germany. According to the memories of Klaus Braun, the body of the German soldier he was now in, Germany had not only swept through France in 1940 but had gone on to conquer Britain in 1941.

If that were the case, what could he, Caleb, do about anything?

Not a whole lot. What he'd seen briefly in the few hours he'd been here had appalled him.

Although they didn't know it yet, the New Englanders were a conquered race. They'd find out soon, especially after the Germans unleashed their little surprise.

The street they were driving down was the main thoroughfare in what, under other circumstances, he would have thought was a picturesque little village. Now, except for squads of marching soldiers and a few military vehicles, it was almost deserted.

The captain who had given them their orders had been brief and to the point. "Men, you've heard a lot of rumors about the ultimate weapon. Soon you will see that whatever you heard couldn't come close to what it's really like."

He was a big brute, wearing a captain's insignia on a uniform not unlike that of the Nazis, although in this timeline it was green, with a boxy cut to it. He had that same kind of arrogance that made you want to take him down a peg or two—not that he'd dare. A few days before, Caleb had seen a man being punished for insubordination. They'd stood him up against a wall in the town square and shot him. The message was plain: follow orders.

"You will leave your post here and move in close to the strike zone. After the weapon is deployed, you will commence mopping up the area. Any questions?"

The rest of the squad were staring into space. They were probably too scared to speak up. But damned if he'd go into this thing without at least getting some information.

"Sir, what kind of weapon is this?"

The captain's eyes had all the warmth of a reptile's. "You'll find out later. Dismissed."

No one moved a muscle until the captain marched off.

After they'd climbed into the trucks, which would take them to the area, a skinny soldier sitting beside him muttered, "You took a big chance, Klaus. It's not smart to get on Kreuger's bad side."

"You mean he has a good side?"

"Depends."

"What do you mean?"

"Aw, nuthin'. Except if you know what he likes, and can give it to him, he knows how to show appreciation. You know what I mean?"

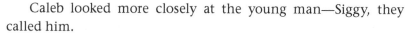

Caleb looked more closely at the young man—Siggy, they called him.

"Yeah, I know what you mean."

"Hey, somethin' bothering you? You been acting kinda funny today."

When Caleb didn't answer, Siggy went on, "Why you so worried about this mission? Like Kreuger told me yesterday, it's gonna save a lotta lives because after this the New Englanders won't have the stomach to fight any more. You'd a thought after we took Britain that they'd be sensible and give up, but not these colonials."

"What else did your good buddy tell you?" All Caleb's pent-up frustration was roiling around in him. He longed to smash the face of the little weasel beside him.

"What's got into you, Klaus?" asked Siggy, staring at him with a hurt expression on his face.

Caleb forced himself to relax. "I don't know. Maybe being away from home too long."

Siggy rubbed a downy cheek. "Yah, I know what you mean. I miss my family, too."

He didn't say anything after that, leaving Caleb to watch the scenery. It wasn't especially memorable, just mile after mile of small farms interspersed with villages.

But where were the people? Driving through the deserted countryside gave him a creepy feeling. It was as though the colonists knew that something was about to happen and had gone underground. The soldiers fell quiet and began looking around uneasily.

On the outskirts of a town the trucks came to a halt, and they were told to get out.

"Clear the building," ordered the captain, pointing to a low brick building on which hung a sign, "Gull Inn."

Grabbing his weapon, which looked like an early model rifle, Caleb jumped out of the truck with the rest of them.

Siggy was fairly bursting with excitement. Gone was his timidity. In its place was a dangerous elation that showed in the brightness of his eyes and his alert posture. "Stick by me," he whispered confidently as he began running toward the inn.

Within five minutes they'd taken the place. There had been no opposition, only the innkeeper and his family, a still-attractive middle-aged woman and their two plain-looking teenage daughters, who were told to prepare accommodations for the soldiers.

It was hot and rather humid. A breeze bearing the salty tang of the nearby ocean tickled Caleb's face. Judging from the rooms he'd glimpsed in the inn, air-conditioning hadn't been invented yet. He heard the captain nearby talking in a low voice to someone over a radio.

A commotion near the trucks made him look up. The captain was shouting something at them.

"C'mon! We gotta go!" shouted Siggy.

"Why?"

"Some trouble at the base. Damned colonials tried to sabotage our airplanes."

I don't want to go, thought Caleb in desperation, but how am I going to get out of it? If they think I'm shirking my duty, they'll shoot me! Reluctantly, he climbed back into the truck.

Sweat began trickling down his neck, right between his shoulder blades. His uniform was itchy at his groin and under his armpits, although it was too big elsewhere on his thin body.

Siggy seemed immune to all discomfort. He was unrelentingly cheerful, keeping up a steady stream of chatter that began to give Caleb a headache.

" . . . delphia a few times."

"What? What did you say?"

"I said I went there once. Lots of pretty girls."

"Where?"

"Philadelphia."

"That's the town that's going to be destroyed?"

Siggy looked at him with a sober expression. "I guess it doesn't matter now if you know. You won't tell it was me who told you?"

"No, no."

Caleb stared blindly at the narrow road. So the City of Brotherly Love was slated for extinction. For the first time in his adult life, he felt totally helpless. Here he was, in the body of the enemy, and he couldn't do a damn thing about it.

Then why was he here? There was no way he could help the Americans. All he could do was to stay alive and try not to kill any of them.

He did have some fence mending to do with Siggy. For the next 15 minutes he set himself to drawing out the man. It wasn't hard to do. Siggy was curiously innocent and trusting. Within a few minutes he had dropped his guard with Caleb and was chattering freely with him in a low voice.

"So, Siggy, what're you going to do after the war's over?"

His answer was surprising. "I'd like to get a piece of land here and set up a carpentry shop. They'll need builders, and I'm a really good carpenter. I like building things."

"Why not go back to Germany, where your family is?"

Siggy was quiet, his hands scrubbing away at each other. "They . . . they don't like people like me there," he whispered. "I'm afraid they'll take me away like they did the Jews in their resettlement program. You hear things . . ."

"What about your good buddy, Kreuger? Wouldn't he protect you?"

In a burst of strong feeling, Siggy said, "He told me not to expect anything, that we'll be together for only a little while. He'll cover his ass and leave me to cover mine."

"A real jerk."

Siggy shook his head. "He's been good to me, and he's fair with the men. Smart, too."

"Even if he is a stickler for discipline?"

Siggy shrugged. "He's not as bad as some. Now you take General Takamoto. I've heard he has men whipped to death for the slightest little thing. After the war, I'm gonna make sure I stay out of Japanese territory."

"Between them and us, I guess the world will be all carved up."

Siggy grinned. "Maybe not," he said.

"Well, who else is there? The Spanish, or maybe the French?"

Siggy guffawed. "They couldn't fight their way out of a paper bag." He leaned over and gave Caleb a conspiratorial look. "Kreuger says that soon, now that the Japanese have done a lot of the dirty work for us, we'll conquer *them*."

"Why would Germany turn on them? Isn't there enough territory for both nations?"

"That's not the point. They're Oriental. You don't want non-Aryans running the world."

"No, I guess not." Caleb felt sick to his stomach. It was the same old racist crap.

The trucks slowed and then came to a stop near what was obviously an airfield. A heavy pall of smoke lay over the twisted wreckage of what looked like burning planes. Lying crumpled on the ground were half a dozen bodies—the colonials, his countrymen.

"Attention! You men will guard the area. No one goes in or out without proper clearance. Any foul-ups . . ." Kreuger paused and glared at the men. No one needed to have it spelled out. They all knew what would happen if they screwed up.

Without talking, the men positioned themselves around the one still-serviceable airplane. Ten minutes later, five men, dressed in what he recognized (from the information contained within his host body) as air force uniforms, climbed aboard the plane. A few minutes later, the plane was climbing steadily upward, headed toward Philadelphia. An almost physical pain tore at Caleb's gut. They were going to destroy the city!

He looked wildly around. No one noticed his agitation. Everyone else was staring at the fast-disappearing plane.

The wind had dropped. A fatalistic calm settled over Caleb.

What kind of weapon were the Germans going to use—a killer virus, something in the water?

Not likely. They needed a weapon to make an immediate impact, one that could be seen and felt right away, so maybe it was something along the lines of the V-2 rockets that the Germans had developed during World War II.

Caleb waited.

Ten minutes. Fifteen.

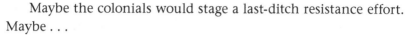

Maybe the colonials would stage a last-ditch resistance effort. Maybe . . .

And maybe there was no way out for Colonial America.

A sudden flash a few miles away made him jump. What he saw next made his flesh crawl.

Oh, no, not that horror unleashed here, too!

The mushroom cloud was rising steadily, spreading its deadly burden of radioactive gases throughout the atmosphere. Already a firestorm was beginning to sweep the area.

A cheer went up from the men around him. Caleb felt sick.

A hand slapped him on the back. "We've won!" Siggy yelled.

"You think so?" Caleb was suddenly so mad he didn't care what they thought of him. "If we stay here, we're all dead men."

Siggy looked startled.

Didn't they know anything about the effects of nuclear radiation? Maybe not. Klaus's memories included only that London had been annihilated with this weapon and that shortly afterward England had surrendered. Nothing else.

Now the captain was ordering them into the trucks again. Good idea to get out of this place. It definitely wasn't safe.

The trucks began driving at a good clip. They weren't as advanced as the vehicles that American industry turned out in his time, but they could pour on the speed when they had to.

"Hey, what's this? We're going the wrong way!"

Siggy looked at Caleb in surprise. "You really are screwed up today. This is the way to Philadelphia."

"But . . . but we should be going the other way!"

"Not according to Kreuger."

"That devil!"

"Not so loud. You want to get us into trouble?"

"You haven't seen trouble yet. We go to Philly and we die."

"What are you, some kind of psychic? We're just going to mop up there. There'll be no fight left in the colonials after what we just dropped on them—if there're any of them left alive."

"Don't you know anything, you stupid Kraut? The area's hot, radioactive. We go there and we get radiation sickness. Our hair falls out, we get sores all over us, and our red blood cells get so screwed up that we die in a few weeks or months. No cure. You get it now?"

Siggy paled. "I don't believe it. If it was that dangerous, Captain Kreuger wouldn't send us in there."

"What makes you think he wouldn't? Where is the stinking captain now? I don't see him risking his ass. Well, where is he?"

Heads twisted around and mouths opened in surprise as the other men looked at Caleb.

"Yeah, go ahead and look. We're finished, all of us, right now, unless we turn around and go back."

"How do you know? What makes you so sure?"

The objector was a tall man in his early 30s. Even the fatigue that stamped his face couldn't mask the intelligence in his eyes.

A chorus of murmured comments greeted his words.

How could he get through to these guys? He hadn't come all this way to die horribly, especially without having accomplished anything.

"Trust me on this one. Just ask yourself why they bothered to send us. The city will be devastated. There won't be any resistance. People will be too busy trying to get away. So why send us? Can you tell me that?"

His avalanche of questions seemed to have rocked the men. They began muttering among themselves.

The trucks stopped suddenly. Caleb saw why. There was no road left. It had heaved up in the same way that he had seen an earthquake in San Francisco destroy a freeway. Farther on, the road had fused into a glass-like substance. Fires were burning everywhere; not one building was standing, only blackened shells.

Where were the survivors—if any?

Then Caleb saw them. As with one voice, the men gasped. He heard Siggy beside him becoming violently sick over the side of the truck.

You couldn't tell if they were men or women, Caleb observed with a sort of detachment that he recognized as shock. They were like something out of a horror movie, those crisped, stump-like figures moaning and stumbling along like an army of zombies.

The trucks suddenly roared into reverse, bumped to a jerky stop, then turned and drove madly off, followed by the insane howling of what was left of the former inhabitants of the City of Brotherly Love.

Maybe they were the lucky ones. At least they'd die fast. Already the soldiers and himself were exposed. They'd take longer to die a slow, miserable death.

Caleb looked up at the sky, his heart contracting with misery for his country, his doomed country that had never really had a chance.

What was the point of his having seen this devastation that would live forever in his nightmares? No one—except perhaps the other Morgans—would ever believe that a rich, powerful America, the mightiest nation that had ever arisen, could ever experience such devastation. But the ancient Romans probably never thought that the day would come when barbarians would conquer them.

So was there anything he could do? He knew what he had seen, what he had felt in his gut. If there were even a slim possibility of this scenario occurring in the 20th century in his lifetime, he would work night and day to prevent this.

The light began to dim, a slow fade-out that sucked out colors, leaving a gray blight over everything. Then he felt himself being pried out of the body of his host and contracted into a single point of consciousness, enveloped by the sweetest music he'd ever experienced, a sound at once awesome and familiar, healing and soothing. Borne on the mighty waves of this music, he was swept back into his universe.

CHAPTER 50

Jason Kramer   San Juan Mission garden,
                                            June 21, 1992

J.J. straightened up cautiously. He was sitting on the bench in the mission garden, in his own body. The rest of the Morgans and Mr. S. were all there, too. He looked at his watch: June 21, 2:20 P.M., five minutes after they'd left.

Over the sudden babble he could hear Caleb saying, "I had the time of my life in Colonial America, but my jump into a future alternate timeline was pretty ghastly. Nobody had better try to tell me that nothing happened!"

By the look on everyone's faces, no one was about to.

Dan was nodding his head. The remote expression on his face made you think that he must have had a few adventures of his own, too.

Marjory had edged right over to the end of the bench that she was sitting on beside Nicholas, who didn't seem to be paying any attention to her. It was like he didn't care. Gerry had come out of her shell and was smiling at everyone. Laney was sitting erect as a little princess and looking very thoughtful. Bet she had a few things to talk about.

Only Cummings was his usual self. He was one cool guy. "Welcome back," he was saying, and then, "I have notified the sheriff's department about our assailant here."

The guy was lying on his back, out cold. Then he started groaning and trying to sit up.

"Hold still!" said Cummings, pointing the gun he held at the man.

After rubbing his arm, Dan got up and went over and checked the guy—probably for other weapons—who glared at him but stopped trying to get up.

Cummings walked over to them. Looking down at the guy on the ground, he asked, "Who are you?"

"Carlo," he muttered.

"Well, Carlo, face it—you've lost," said Dan.

"Yes," observed Cummings. "Today is the summer solstice, and the window for changing this timeline has closed."

With a bleak look on his face, Carlo looked at Cummings, then closed his eyes and murmured, "Papa."

"Your papa," said Cummings, "wanted to dominate the world."

Carlo opened his eyes and protested, "It was for their own good."

"But not their decision."

An uncertain look came into the eyes of their assailant. "But Papa said . . ."

"That you elites know better than the masses how to run their affairs? What your papa has forgotten is that the way that most people learn is by being allowed to make their own mistakes. In that sense, this world is a perfect place to learn, for by reincarnating over and over again—albeit in different scenarios, from warriors and kings to peasants—one finally learns compassion for others."

A siren wailed in the distance. Tires crunched on the gravel of the car park. Two cops hustled into the garden soon after that and took the gun from Cummings.

Carlo got up and pointed at Dan. "This man attacked me! Arrest him."

Caleb hurried over. "I'm Caleb Morgan," he said.

"The developer?" asked the younger cop, who was built like a wrestler.

Caleb puffed out his chest. "The very same," he said.

"My dad used to work for you, said you were a straight shooter. So what happened here?"

"This thug tried to kill us. If it hadn't been for Dan, he would have succeeded."

"I am Carlo Hauptman, no thug but a respectable businessman!"

"Yeah, right. So why were you trying to kill us?" asked Dan.

"We'll sort this out when we all go downtown," said the older cop in a raspy voice.

Carlo was taken into custody and held for interrogation. After the authorities were satisfied that the Morgans and Nicholas were basically just tourists, they were allowed to leave. Caleb suggested that they all go back to his place where they could order in supper and debrief.

CHAPTER 51

Jason Kramer   Caleb's mansion, June 21, 1992

They gathered in Caleb's library, where Cummings took their orders for food. After he had called a restaurant, he said, "I shouldn't be surprised if the attacks were over."

"Why is that?" asked Laney.

Giving one of his rare smiles, Cummings answered, "Since you have succeeded in stabilizing the timeline, you Morgans are no longer a threat—at least for now."

"How do we know if we really did succeed?" asked Laney.

"I'm sure there will be certain indicators."

She had her mouth open to ask some more questions when Dan cut in with, "So the reason we were attacked was that someone didn't want the timeline stabilized."

"It makes sense," broke in Nicholas. "Mind you, Marjory and I had some opposition from an Indian who tried to stop us from seeing Susanna . . ."

"Kiontawakon! He tried to make me persuade the chiefs of the Iroquois League to help Metacom against the New Englanders," cried J.J., "but I wouldn't do it."

"And quite by accident, I saved the life of Benjamin Church, who led the colonists to victory in King Phillip's War. If Church had died, there might not have been an America," said Dan. "Where did you go, Gerry?" he asked, his gaze lingering on her.

"Back into the body of Lady Mary Montague, who persuaded the Princess of Wales to inoculate her children against smallpox. That meant, you see," she explained, "that all of England eventually followed suit."

"Saved a lot of lives," said Dan, nodding his head. Then turning to his daughter he asked, "Laney, where did you go?"

"France. I was the wife of the Marquis de Lafayette."

That explained her new air of self-confidence. Living with a bunch of aristocrats must have been fun for her.

"But I'm glad to be back."

Everyone nodded in agreement. J.J. whispered to her, "Why do you think you went to that lifetime?" he asked.

"I told Lafayette he was going to be a big hero during the American Revolution, and that it was because of him France helped the Americans, who mightn't have won otherwise," she said in a rush as though it was a confession she had to make all at once.

"Sounds like that's what you were supposed to do."

At the hopeful look in her eyes, he added, "It's tough to be a hero. Maybe Lafayette needed a little encouragement to do what he was going to do, if you see what I mean."

Laney brightened and said, "Maybe it was all right, telling him about the future and all, since he was feverish anyway. He might have thought later that he'd just imagined it."

"You made him think."

"I hope so. Oh, and later I think I saved his life from an assassin. He was a great guy. I . . ." She looked down at her hands. "I found it hard to leave him." Her eyes filled with tears, and she looked away.

"I met a girl I didn't want to leave, either."

Laney brushed away her tears and looked at him compassionately. "I never thought time traveling would be like this, getting attached to people and then feeling just horrible when you had to leave them."

The food came and got cold while Dan and the others went on and on about their adventures. Marjory and Nicholas, who hardly looked at each other, told their stories, too, but were pretty reserved about the whole thing. It sounded as if they hadn't been too thrilled about living in Colonial America.

Marjory was excited when she heard that Geraldine had gone back to the 18th century. Trust the old lady to know all about Lady Mary and how she had persuaded the English to start vaccinating people against smallpox.

Then Gerry spoke up. "I have a question. Like the rest of you, I went back to another era, but how could I do that? I'm not really a Morgan. After my father died, my mother married Aunt Marjory's brother."

Dan gave a muffled exclamation and looked hard at Gerry.

"The same applies to me," said Nicholas. "I, too, am not a Morgan, yet I also went back in time."

J.J. looked at Cummings. He had that secretive, amused look on his face. When the commotion died down—everyone wanted to talk at once—Cummings said, "And yet all of you were important in some way to stabilize this timeline. Asking you to come to San Francisco was a way of getting everyone here."

"The family reunion thing," said Laney.

Cummings smiled at her and said, "Just so. Then, too, you Morgans and your friends were the ones who were willing to engage in this adventure and had lived in previous times where momentous events were happening."

After Cummings had taken away the food since most of the older people were too busy talking to eat much, except for him— it was great to eat regular food again—he got a real jolt hearing Nicholas ask, "Has it ever occurred to any of the rest of you to wonder who Jeremy really is?"

Cummings was handing around the dessert, big slices of chocolate cake, when Nicholas's question dropped into the silence.

Looking up at Cummings, J.J. was startled to see him wink. Certain things rearranged themselves. It was like when you finally figured out a really tough question in physics. You had that same "I got it!" feeling and a sense of the rightness of your answer. You just knew that you had done it the best way possible. That was the feeling he had when he connected Jeremy and the Archdruid with Cummings. In some way, they were the same person.

But how could that be? Cummings wasn't a Morgan. He was just . . . Cummings. But he knew things. Then what was he doing acting as a servant? But come to think of it, it was perfect. He was a subtle guy, didn't say much but seemed to be good at dropping little hints here and there.

Everybody got quiet then until Caleb started talking, saying that he didn't want to lose touch with the other Morgans, not after all they'd been through. Too bad they couldn't stay in San Francisco. Laney looked excited, and her father looked interested.

Glancing around at the relatives, Caleb said, "I have been wondering what to do with my fortune when I die."

That got everyone's attention.

Caleb went on. "I propose to set up a foundation that will do some good in this world. It is my belief that we need leaders— particularly in education, politics, and business—to return to the ideals that America was founded on."

"And where are you going to find those people?" asked Nicholas.

"Perhaps money could be given to certain educational institutions to offer more history and civics classes."

Laney wrinkled up her nose. "Most people my age don't care about stuff like that."

"Yeah, you're right," said J.J. "We're into movies and TV."

"And don't forget music," added Laney, smiling at him.

"Perhaps a foundation could fund scholarships to colleges that promote those sorts of values," said Marjory. "And, as Laney and J.J. pointed out, use the media to fund specials like PBS does as well as promote other television programs and movies with those themes."

"Laney mentioned the importance of music," observed Nicholas. "J.J.'s mother, Diana, invited me to a concert given by the youth orchestra that J.J. was playing in. I was struck by how well they played and the passion they had for the music. After the concert was over, their conductor explained how the kids involved in music did better in school and developed values of discipline and hard work as well as a love for music that in many of them would last their entire lives."

"Our music teacher showed us a film about the Venezuelans," said J.J. "They've set up orchestras with slum kids. Could they ever play! The other kids teach them, and they get so involved that they don't want to do drugs or get involved in crime."

Caleb nodded. "We've got to do something," he said soberly. "After what I saw in an alternate future, there's no time to waste. In the meantime, all of you are welcome to stay as long as you like."

People started drifting back to their rooms pretty fast after that, J.J. noticed.

After going to his room, he flopped onto his bed and buried his face in a pillow. A huge weight of misery settled on him. He'd never see Devonna again. She was only old bones now.

A knock at the door startled him. He didn't want to see anybody right now.

Reluctantly, he rolled off the bed and said, "C'mon in." The last person he expected to see came in and quietly shut the door behind him.

"I thought you might be in need of some refreshment, so I took the liberty of bringing you something."

"Thanks, but I don't think . . ."

Cummings put down a tray down on a small table. The aroma of hot chocolate drifted over to him. It was too much to resist.

J.J. went over to the table and sat down. He had drunk half the beverage before he noticed that Cummings was still there, sitting with his hands folded over his stomach and a faint smile on his lips. It was like he was waiting for something.

J.J. ran his tongue around the ring of chocolate around his mouth. Cummings silently handed him a napkin and waited patiently while he wiped his mouth clean.

It was beginning to get to him, how calm the guy was. What would it take to crack that, Roman soldiers running after him with their swords and a crazy Druid out to kill him or losing the first girl you ever loved?

J.J. shuddered. Then he felt the older man's hand on his shoulder.

"You have been through much, Jason, and acquitted yourself like a man."

Cummings knew, but how?

"Devonna . . ." was all he could say as a tear squeezed itself out of his eye and ran down his cheek.

"Thanks to you, she and the child you sired are safe with Bran, and the continuity of that branch of the Morgan family is thereby assured."

"But I'll never see her again!"

"No, not in that form."

Seconds, like hard pellets of granite, weighted his tongue. He wanted to yell, take out his rage on the man standing in front of him, but he didn't dare. Something knowing and wise about the man stopped him, so he said nothing until the silence got to him and he had to ask, "Who is she now?"

Cummings only cocked his head to one side and said nothing.

"Crystal? The girl I met in Kenora? Devonna kind of reminded me of her, but that means that Crystal might be the reincarnation of Devonna." So he hadn't lost her after all! Life suddenly looked wonderful, exciting even.

"So what happens now?"

"Nothing right now. Other matters may require a helping hand."

And so Cummings had gone away, and because he was so tired he had lain down and almost instantly fallen asleep and had a wonderful dream that he tried desperately to remember when he woke up, but it was no good. All he could remember was that he and Crystal, whose face kept changing into Devonna's, were together and working on something important.

CHAPTER 52

Marjory Morgan Bennett

Caleb's mansion,
June 21, 1992

"Geraldine, let's go sit on that seat in that lovely bay window for a few minutes."

Her niece looked at her in surprise and then walked over to the far side of the room.

"A magnificent view," said Marjory, seating herself on a cushion and admiring the moon silvering the tips of the waves rolling against the rocks below.

Geraldine sat down beside her aunt and said, "I think I'll go back home tomorrow, Aunt Marjory."

"You won't stay for another few days?"

"I don't think so." Geraldine gave a light laugh and continued. "I'm anxious to get back to work early."

"And Dan?"

"So that's what this is about. I like Dan," she said slowly, "but I'm not sure."

"I saw how he looked at you this evening. He's definitely interested in you."

Her niece blushed and started smoothing down her sundress.

"I understand, dear. After the affair with Charles, you may think it's too soon to become involved with another man."

"It's not that, but how do I know that Dan won't leave me in the lurch?"

Her aunt was blunt. "Did he last time?"

"You're assuming that he was Paul."

"Perhaps, but even if Dan isn't the reincarnation of Paul, sometimes you have to take a chance. And my intuition tells me that Dan is a good man who won't let you down. Just as importantly, I think you've learned some things about yourself lately, particularly from those dreams of Susanna that you've been having."

Her niece took a deep breath and said, "You might be right, but I'm still not sure . . ."

"Oh, Geraldine. Just talk to the man. If I'm not mistaken, he's waiting for you over there."

Agitated, Geraldine stood up and took a few steps toward Dan, who was sitting in the wing chair in the far corner of the library.

"I'll say good night now, dear. Just don't leave San Francisco without talking to him."

Marjory paused at the library door and saw Dan striding over to Geraldine. He reached out to her. Geraldine took a tentative step toward him.

The last thing Marjory saw before she closed the door was Dan leading Geraldine, their hands entwined, over to the window seat, where they sat and began talking, their heads close together.

Unable to sleep right away, Marjory went into the breakfast room. A slight cough from behind her made her turn around.

"I took the liberty, Mrs. Bennett, of bringing you a cup of tea."

"Thank you, Cummings. It's been a tiring time. I appreciate the tea," she said, sinking down gratefully into an armchair. Cummings put the tray with the tea things on a table and sat down opposite her.

His voice was gentle as he said, "You and the others have done humanity a great service, which is just beginning. Caleb and his new family will need your support."

An image of the future surged into her mind: Caleb and his wife, Gloria, his former secretary, were looking into a crib where their twins lay sleeping. Together, the children would grow up to influence the world in dramatic and special ways.

"Mrs. Bennett."

Marjory found herself gripping the arms of her chair and Cummings looking at her with those calm, wise eyes. "Was it enough, Cummings? Did our tampering with time really help?" she asked in a strained voice.

"More than you know, I suspect." His voice took on a resonant timbre that she hadn't noticed before. "Sages have said that this world is a school, a perfect place for individuals to learn and grow in awareness. If they do not, it is possible that they will destroy themselves. We are very near the end of a major cycle when a balance must be achieved. Many forces seek to disrupt this balance, with disastrous consequences if that happens. Your part, and that of the others, is to help preserve this equilibrium."

"Why is that so important?"

"To preserve the earth and ensure that humanity may mature into its potential."

"If we make the right choices."

"That is so. Good night, Mrs. Bennett."

Bowing slightly, he left the room with an unhurried tread, as though he had all the time in the world.

EPILOGUE

Max Hauptman   Brazil, June 22, 1992

The old man dying on his bed listened to the nurse bustling around in his room. When Carlo had phoned him yesterday about the failure to exterminate the Morgans, he'd collapsed. They had wanted to take him to a hospital, but he had forbidden it. He'd die here, in his own bed, in his own way, and in his own time.

The nurse had banished his *papagaio*. Strange how he missed it, a stupid bird that had never talked, only moped in a cage.

And Carlo. He forced himself to admit that, yes, he missed his son, even though he had failed. And with him had died the chance to change history.

Exhausted, he dozed. Images tumbled through his mind: a Celtic horde advancing on the Romans while he, Mabon, made his secret deals to betray his country, but for the greater good, always! And the Indian lifetime. "Kiontawakon," he muttered feebly. The nurse bent over him. He waved her away. She left, leaving a faintly pleasing antiseptic odor.

There had been other lifetimes, of course, but none more important than this one when he had almost succeeded in imposing his vision on the world. It would have been a glorious destiny, the Third Reich, a fitting successor to the Roman Empire, which he had admired greatly. Generations would remember him and tremble.

But in his next life, he would not make the same mistakes. The name of Hitler had become a byword, a reproach. But he had almost succeeded. Almost.

Next time . . .

The End

ACKNOWLEDGMENTS

I am very grateful to editors Laura Gray, Quressa Robinson, and Sally Mason at Hay House for their patience and helpful suggestions, which have made my book so much better than it was originally.

Thanks also to Elizabeth Diewert at Balboa Press for her encouragement and help, and to the jurists there who chose *Timewatch* as the winner of the Balboa Press Fiction contest.

Many thanks also to my stepdaughter for following her intuition and suggesting to my husband that I enter the contest. I definitely owe you, Karen!

I am also grateful to the Manitoba Arts Council who, after seeing only three chapters of a rough draft of my book, gave me a grant to assist in finishing it.

Finally, I am so grateful to my extraordinary husband, Ron Lyric, for his steadfast love and support, and for his help in editing and contributing ideas to my novel.

ABOUT THE AUTHOR

Linda Grant is the winner of the first Balboa Press fiction contest. In addition to writing, Linda has taught gifted children in public schools and developed and led courses on personal growth and self-development for adults. She worked for a brief time in film and television production, the highlight of which was her experience as the production coordinator on the IMAX film *Heartland*. The mother of two daughters and stepmother to four others, Linda lives with her husband, Ron, in Kelowna, Canada, where they have led courses on a wide range of social and metaphysical topics.

Printed in the United States
by Baker & Taylor Publisher Services